newpress CANADIAN CLASSICS

Canadian Poetry

Volume One

Edited by Jack David and Robert Lecker
Introduction by George Woodcock

A co-publication of
General Publishing Co. Limited
Toronto, Canada
and
ECW Press
Downsview, Ontario

General Paperbacks/ECW Press edition published in 1982

Fifth printing - February 1989

ISBN: 0-7736-7036-X

Printed and bound in the United States

Contents

W. WILFRED CAMPBELL 1858-1918

CHARLES G. D. ROBERTS 1860-1943

BLISS CARMAN 1861-1929

ARCHIBALD LAMPMAN 1861-1899

D. C. SCOTT 1862-1947

E. J. PRATT 1883-1964

W. W. E. ROSS 1894-1966

RAYMOND KNISTER 1899-1932

F. R. SCOTT b. 1899

ROBERT FINCH b. 1900

A. J. M. SMITH 1902-1980

EARLE BIRNEY b. 1904

LEO KENNEDY b. 1907

RALPH GUSTAFSON b. 1909

A. M. KLEIN 1909-1972

DOROTHY LIVESAY b. 1909

ANNE WILKINSON 1910-1961

IRVING LAYTON b. 1912

P. K. PAGE b. 1916

MIRIAM WADDINGTON b. 1917

MARGARET AVISON b. 1918

Canadian Poetry

An Introduction to Volume One

Anthologies have always assumed a critical role in establishing standards within a country's literature and in marking changes in the criteria of appreciation—how we read and value poetry. The archetypical collections of classical times, like Melenger's 1st-century B.C. *Garland* and the very late *Greek Anthology* (actually a Byzantine 10th-century A.D. compilation) tended to pass the verdict on traditions that were already mature or decadent, so that they have a bittersweet flavour of nostalgic afterthought. But the really historic anthologies of modern times have been somewhat different, and of two kinds.

There are those that emerge at the height of a literary tradition and pass authoritative judgments on its most significant works, as Palgrave's *Golden Treasury* did for mid-Victorian England and Quiller-Couch's *Oxford Book of English Verse* (1900) did for the high imperial world of the turn-of-the-century. Such anthologies are mandarin products that help to freeze taste over a considerable period of time, so that later attempts to revise them for modern tastes, like the 1961 expansion of *The Golden Treasury* by Oscar Williams, and Helen Gardner's 1972 *New Oxford Book of English Verse*, remain in the shadows of their predecessors, as works upholding establishment taste and merely sanctifying the modifications time has made necessary.

On the other hand, there have been the collections that emerge in young and developing literatures and take their part alongside the work of the emergent critics in discovering and defining the nature of individual creation in such a situation and of the collective trends through which tradition is modified by innovation to create works that speak for a new culture, for a realization of a national life view developing out of a growing understanding of our geography and our history, our place and time. The most historic of such collections, like *Tottel's Miscellany* (1557) and *England's Helicon* (1600) in Britain, and *Le Parnasse Contemporain* (1866-1876) in France, were more than mere selections of contemporary verse; their meaning lay in their implicit recognition that there is a collective vision which at times of literary awakening had an importance outside the visions of individual poets even when it nurtures them.

The best Canadian anthologies, it seems to me, have been of the latter kind, and I suggest this is inevitable in a literature so young that it is difficult to be authoritative because our classic writers are still living and working among us. Yet in *Canadian Poetry*, the anthology I here introduce, there are already signs of a change in approach, signs of more sharply defined choices than in earlier anthologies, of a surer sense of the direction Canadian poetry has taken in the century and a quarter since Charles Sangster, the first in time of the poets here included, published *The St. Lawrence and the Saguenay, and Other Poems* in 1856.

The earliest Canadian anthology of any importance was Edward Hartley Dewart's *Selections from Canadian Poets*, which appeared in 1864. Charles Sangster is the only one among Dewart's choices to survive into *Canadian Poetry*. And there is justice here, since most of the versifiers Dewart selected were those "dear bad poets" whom James Reaney refers to later in these pages, "Who wrote / Early in Canada / And were never of note" ("First Letter"). The only one among them, apart from Sangster, who might have found a place here on the strength of a rather cumbersome originality was Charles Heavysege, but Heavysege's memorable verse was dramatic or narrative, and such structurally massive forms have no place in a collection like *Canadian Poetry* whose contents—whether lyrical or elegiac, contemplative or satirical, traditional or experimental—are without exception poems in which brevity, if not counted as a virtue, is certainly a fact. Canada has indeed a notable tradition of longer poems, but they have already been represented in other anthologies like David Sinclair's *Nineteenth-Century Narrative Poems* (1972) and Michael Ondaatje's *The Long Poem Anthology* (1979), while fragments of such classic Canadian verse dramas as Heavysege's *Saul*, John Hunter Duvar's *De Roberval*, Charles Mair's *Tecumseh*, and Earle Birney's "Damnation of Vancouver," found a place in what has since come to be regarded as the pioneer work of critical and historical anthologizing in Canada, A. J. M. Smith's *The Book of Canadian Poetry*, which appeared first in 1943 and later, in cumulatively enlarged editions keeping up with poetic production and changes of taste, in 1948 and 1957.

Smith's anthologies are basic to any study of Canadian poetry, and all later miscellanies to a greater or lesser extent take off from them, even when the methods of selection in some way or another differ from Smith's. They begin with the seminal collection of Canadian modernist verse on which he collaborated with F. R. Scott (*New Provinces: Poems by Several Authors*, 1936) and they include, subsequent to *The Book of Canadian Poetry*, his *Oxford Book of Canadian Verse* (1960) and *Modern Canadian Verse* (1967), the last two being the first Canadian anthologies to include representative works in both English and French. But it is *The Book of Canadian Poetry* that in many ways remains Smith's most important and influential collection, because here he used the process of anthologizing not merely as a means of offering the reader an interesting and pleasing garland of verses to introduce him to the delights of Canadian poetry, but also as a means of developing historical and critical insights into the kind of poetry our environment and our history have encouraged. Smith made the act of selection a critical process, so that it was he in his various collections who first established a canon of acceptable Canadian poetry. But he also wrote a long and brilliant introduction which was a pioneer document in Canadian historical criticism; it appeared in the same year as E. K. Brown's *On Canadian Poetry*. And he introduced each poet with a concise but insightful critical and biographical note. Our view of Canadian poetry and our sense of the possibilities of Canadian criticism were both enlarged by Smith's work as an anthologist.

Canadian Poetry follows Smith's lead in many ways, and especially in its chronological arrangement by date of birth and its inclusion of critical notes, so that it is bound, like *The Book of Canadian Poetry*, to modify our view of the achievements of Canadian poets. But it differs notably in other ways.

First of all, it is not the work of a single selector-critic, but of many hands. The two general editors have been only partially involved in the task of selection; they have picked the forty-six poets to be included, but in the choice of individual poems they have mainly followed the advice of the forty-six critics who have written the comments on the individual poets. And I—the writer of this introduction—have stood apart from the whole process of selection except to the very minor extent that I picked the poems to represent Patrick Lane (Volume Two) and have written the critical note on him. In other words, more than forty critics have had a hand in this selection, and this inevitably makes it different in character from the miscellany that is the work of one anthologist, and perhaps, in detail at least, it makes it different in quality. For, while it is impossible to deny the overall importance, as a pioneer effort to define a tradition, of Smith's *Book of Canadian Poetry*, it remains true that any single critic's sympathies are uneven; he cannot possibly give equal appreciation of understanding to all the poets whose work he is considering for selection. In this way the book by many hands makes up, in the greater fairness and sensitivity of many of its individual selections, for that loosening of the central inspiring vision which takes place when an effort becomes collective.

There is another important way in which *Canadian Poetry* departs from the model Smith established in his anthologies. Smith was more historical and representative in his approach, seeking to trace the lines of Canadian poetic development from the beginning, and in the process including admittedly many fewer of the "dear bad poets" of the earlier days than Dewart but considerably more than *Cana-*

dian Poetry. The 1957 edition of *The Book of Canadian Poetry*, began before the time of known individual writers in Canada, with translations of anonymous Indian and *habitant* songs. And even the *Oxford Book of Canadian Verse* started off thirty years before Sangster, the first poet in *Canadian Poetry*, with selections from early Loyalist and immigrant works like Standish O'Grady's *The Emigrant*, and *The Rising Village* by the younger Oliver Goldsmith.

Canadian Poetry has not wholly abandoned Smith's historical approach. It still seeks to show, through a group of the most significant poets, the lines of development of Canadian verse since the 1850s. But it has largely abandoned his desire to be wholly representative in the sense of including every remotely interesting poet, and in this sense it is a more critical collection. At the same time as it retains a sense of the general development of Canadian poetry over the past century and a third, it also seeks to do justice to each of the poets it includes by devoting enough space to his or her work to give the reader a reasonable idea of its range of content and versatility of form. Ten items are included from most of the selected poets, sometimes one or two less, and often two or three more. This has automatically eliminated those many Canadian poets who wrote perhaps two or three anthologizable poems but whose work in general was not memorable. But it has also meant the adoption of an approach that is more selective than representative. The editors of *Canadian Poetry* are not saying explicitly, "These are the *best* Canadian poets," but they *are* saying, at least implicitly, "these are, for one reason or another, the most significant Canadian poets." And to this extent *Canadian Poetry,* as all anthologies do, steps beyond the rules laid down by many current academic schools of criticism, for selection is inevitably an act of evaluation, and by picking out the forty-six poets whose work appears in the following pages they are marking them with their special approval. These, they are saying, are the poets who are both interesting and valuable in their own terms and who will also tell you, if you read them well, what poetry has meant and now means in Canada.

But the selection, while not pretending to be inclusive,

does not seek in any way to be exclusive; it is an invitation to enter the realm of Canadian poetry, but not an invitation to turn back once you have read these poets. As I have said, there are long poems and dramatic poems whose size makes them impossible to include, and this even applies to many of the poets present here; Isabella Valancy Crawford, Earle Birney, E. J. Pratt, Michael Ondaatje, bpNichol, and others have all written long works that are well worth searching out. Birney's "David" and Pratt's "The Titanic" are two notable examples. And, apart from at least a dozen older lyric poets I find as good as many included here, I could immediately name a dozen younger poets who have done almost enough anthologizable work to make a third volume of *Canadian Poetry* a feasible project for the near future.

In other words, the field to which *Canadian Poetry* introduces the reader is a great deal wider than the contents of these two volumes. It deserves further exploration, not only in the sense of reading the books of the poets represented here by handfuls of their work, but also in reading the other Canadian poets who for some reason or other are absent.

No special significance should be given to the way in which the two volumes of *Canadian Poetry* have been arranged. The forty-six poets, having been placed in the order of their birthdates, have been equally divided to meet the demands of space, so that the first volume begins with Charles Sangster and ends with Margaret Avison, and the second begins with Louis Dudek and ends with bpNichol. The result is that some at least of the writers in the latter end of Volume One, which I am now introducing, like Margaret Avison and Miriam Waddington and Irving Layton, seem to have greater affinities with the poets of Volume Two than with many of those in Volume One. Yet the arrangement is not without its accidental logic. For Volume One, as it has turned out, does illustrate one theme, which is the long process by which a poetry appropriate to Canadian experience was developed out of derivative imitations of English Victorian poetry. And Volume Two shows how, once that characteristically Canadian poetry had emerged, it took on such a variegation of approach and technique that— though their births are only twenty-six years apart and they inhabit the same literary landscape—there seems an even greater difference between Louis Dudek and bpNichol than there does between Charles Sangster and Margaret Avison, who are separated by ninety-five years and the rainforest of Victorian sensibility.

Charles Sangster appropriately opens *Canadian Poetry* as the most accomplished practitioner of true colonial poetry in the Canadian tradition. His preoccupation with the Laurentian landscape precludes the later and deeper involvement of Roberts and Lampman, but he is seeing it all with expatriate eyes, using images and diction derived entirely from the England of approximately a generation earlier, so that often, reading him, one feels that here is some later Augustan tinged with romanticism—Samuel Rogers perhaps—gathering impressions of a new land. There is an extreme stylization about Sangster's evocations of the great rivers he especially loves, that reminds one of the Canadian academic painters who were his contemporaries, and indeed Sangster stays in the mind as a landscapist standing back and fitting the scene into a perspective rather than a nature poet entering it intimately in the later manner of Charles G. D. Roberts and his contemporaries.

There is a real sense of something new entering Canadian poetry with Isabella Valancy Crawford, even though in any formal sense she is far from innovatory. The diction, the imagery, the metrical shape of her poems are not greatly different from English later romantics, and if Keats and Shelley had not written, and Landseer had not painted, Crawford would not have been quite the poet she became. What is new in her is the fact that she gives herself to her poetry as none of her Canadian predecessors had done. For them poetry was part of the cultural wall that pioneer groups raised against a hostile world, and the defensiveness became an inhibition. But Crawford used poetry to liberate rather than to defend, and the prosodic clichés with which her work abounds are fired by the needs of a passionate and sometimes grotesque mind; her poems grip our imaginations because they are moved by frustrated passion and by the power of an inner vision that had little to do with the objective world in which the poet lived. When Crawford did face that world openly, she could only deal with it in terms of satire, as in such interestingly uncharacteristic poems as "A Wooing" and "The Rolling-Pin." The Crawford we value is the woman of obscure life whose bizarre hidden personality emerges so strikingly when she draws conventional imagery into the fantastic.

They hung the slaughter'd fish like swords
On saplings slender—like scimitars
Bright, and ruddied from new-dead wars,
Blaz'd in the light—the scaly hordes.

With Crawford the poetic persona first entered the Canadian scene, using the world of nature for its own obsessive purposes; she would have many successors. But with the so-called Confederation Poets who immediately follow her in this volume—Campbell and Roberts, Carman and Lampman and Scott—there was a return out of fantasy towards an apprehension of the need to recognize the actuality of the Canadian land and of the life men lived there. The pioneer age had ended, at least in the eastern colonies that originally joined in the Dominion of Canada. New generations recognized that the links with mother countries were thinning out and that love for the land of childhood experience was more real than nostalgia for a land one had never seen. In giving voice to this transference of emotional allegiances, the Confederation poets at their best not only celebrated Canadian scenes, which Sangster after all had already done, but also observed with considerable accuracy the human life they fostered and found the language and imagery to describe them. A realism entered inevitably into the process, as it always does when writers have to recognize the actual nature of the world they inhabit before they can apply to it the transfiguring processes of the imagination.

And so, in Charles G. D. Roberts and Archibald Lampman, in Duncan Campbell Scott and at times in Bliss Carman, we see not only a strange luminous factualism in evoking the landscape, but also a new use of imagery, of language, of poetic form. It emerges in lines and verses more memorable, because more original, than any used before in Canada. There is that magically unprecedented line from Roberts' sonnet, "The Mowing":

> The crying knives glide on; the green swath lies.

And there is that final verse of "Low Tide at Grand Pré" which has given Bliss Carman a lasting niche among the Canadian poets:

> The night has fallen, and the tide...
> Now and again comes drifting home
> Across these aching barrens wide,
> A sigh like driven wind or foam:
> In grief the flood is bursting home.

In Archibald Lampman the special sensibility of his group is most widely stretched. His "Heat" evokes an extraordinary impression of the physical tyranny of the central Canadian summer:

> By his cart's side the wagoner
> Is slouching slowly at his ease,
> Half-hidden in the windless blur
> Of white dust puffing to his knees.
> This wagon on the height above,
> From sky to sky on either hand,
> Is the sole thing that seems to move
> In all the heat-held land.

That is as starkly visual and as despairingly human as anything in Thomas Hardy. Yet at the same time Lampman can in "The Modern Politician" condense within a sonnet the shrewd satirical analysis of demagogic pretensions ("The little mimic of a vanished king"), and in "Midnight" can arouse a metaphysical unease as poignant as anything in Walter de la Mare.

I know not what it is I hear;
  I bend my head and hark:
I cannot drive it from mine ear,
  That crying in the dark.

Lampman never carried far into technical experimentation his desire to find ways of giving his physical and metaphysical experiences a form of expression that fitted their novelty. He found Keats and Arnold and James Thomson, possibly John Davidson and certainly his friend the younger Roberts sufficient models for his purposes. Roberts himself and Duncan Campbell Scott felt uneasily that a new approach to the Canadian land needed a new formal expression, and went beyond Lampman's metrical conservatism into what came very near to free verse, and here I feel that *Canadian Poetry* may not have adequately exemplified their audacity, for Roberts' remarkably liberated late poem, "The Iceberg," is not included, though the less interesting "Taormina" from the same 1934 volume is. Scott is indeed represented by "The Forsaken," whose broken line pattern shows how eager he was to seek in unconventional metrical patterns a way of giving expression to the strange things he had witnessed or heard of in the Canadian North. But no room has been found for that appealing and very interesting late poem, "En Route," which I think carries to its farthest degree the desire of the Confederation poets to find authentic expression for their intense involvement with the natural setting. "En Route" not merely shows the innovatory influence on Scott of the Imagist movement that he lived to witness; it even ends with a quiet statement of the validity of that encounter between the concrete and the transitory which is the essence of Imagist thinking. For once—and once only in this Introduction—I quote in its entirety a poem not included later to which the reader should have access if he is to understand completely either Scott or his contemporaries:

En Route

The train has stopped for no apparent reason
In the wilds;
A frozen lake is level and fretted over
With rippled wind lines;
The sun is burning in the South; the season
Is winter trembling at a touch of spring.
A little hill with birches and a ring
Of cedars—all so still, so pure with snow—
It seems a tiny landscape in the moon.
Long wisps of shadow from the naked birches
Lie on the white in lines of cobweb-grey;
From the cedar roots the snow had shrunk away,
One almost hears it tinkle as it thaws.
Traces there are of wild things in the snow—
Partridge at play, tracks of the foxes' paws
That broke a path to sun them in the trees.
They're going fast where all impressions go
On a frail substance—images like these,
Vagaries the unconscious mind receives
From nowhere, and lets go to nothingness
With the lost flush of last year's autumn leaves.

Roberts and Scott lived on to be the contemporaries of the modernist Canadian poets of the late 1930s and early 1940s, which helps to explain why they felt an urge to experimentation that Lampman, who died so much earlier, did not share. In other respects there is little continuity in Canadian poetry during the early twentieth century, for after the almost simultaneous emergence of Roberts, Carman, Lampman, and Scott in the 1880s and the early 1890s, no poet of any significance made an appearance until E. J. Pratt published *Newfoundland Verse* a third of a century later in 1923. And Pratt has always semed a somewhat anomalous figure in Canadian poetry, leading towards modernity by turning to the past. He chose epic and mock-epic forms, he went back to the seventeenth century for Hudibrastic metres in which to write his often heavy-handed satires, but he explored the use of the Canadian vernacular in poetry and he recognised the importance of Canadian history and geography as a basic subject matter. He was, besides, a man of idiosyncratic talent whose very use of traditional forms in an experimental way distinguished him from the self-conscious modernists who followed him.

A very different figure was W. W. E. Ross, whose importance as a Canadian modernist poet was only belatedly recognised. Ross published his first volume, *Laconics*, in 1930, and the very title was revealing; Ross brought to Canadian poetry a new simplicity of expression and a stress on imagistic clarity that had not been seen before. Though he has remained little known, his influence on poets of the 1930s and 1940s was considerable, and his "Rocky Bay" is almost a model for a certain type of Canadian landscape poem:

The iron rocks
slope sharply down
into the gleaming
of northern water,
and there is a shining
to northern water
reflecting the sky
on a keen cool morning.

To apply imagist insights to poems about the Canadian land was to give expression to the famous remark of T. E. Hulme, the English poet who is credited with inventing Imagism and who in 1906 remarked that "the first time I ever felt the necessity of the inevitableness of verse, was in the desire to reproduce the peculiar quality of feeling which is induced by the flat spaces and wide horizons of the virgin prairie of western Canada." Certainly one of the ingredients of Canadian modernism as it appeared in the 1930s was an imagist way of looking which, by stressing the visual, enabled the Canadian poets to see their environment and translate it into words with an appropriateness their predecessors never attained. Poems like F. R. Scott's "Lakeshore" and A. J. M. Smith's "The Lonely Land" are admirable examples of this process at work.

But the poets who worked together in Montreal during the late 1920s and 1930s, and in the process created a modernist movement in Canada—notably Scott and Smith and A. M. Klein—were much too polymorphous in attitude to confine themselves to Imagism in their search for alternative ways of expression to the wornout nineteenth-century examples most Canadian poets were still following. They found affinities with the English poets of the 1930s and with earlier masters like Pound and Eliot. A. J. M. Smith applied the arts of the pasticheur in the best sense as he parodically echoed seventeenth-century poets while at the same time he was writing naturalistic poems about the Canadian landscape, and A. M. Klein turned to the rich imagery of Jewish tradition and the resounding English of the Jacobeans to create his extraordinary elegiacs of modern life seen *sub specie aeternitatis*, while Leo Kennedy showed a different kind of neo-Jacobean preoccupation with corruption and madness (almost all his poems included in this volume in some way concern death and funerals), so that he seems to be returning to the past like the son of an emigrant going home.

Indeed, what strikes one now, in the 1980s, about these poets is that they were much less of a movement in the sense of sharing their visions or their voices than the literary historians with their neat patterning of the past have led us to believe. Klein's poetry, re-read, projects a vision so vibrant and at the same time so intensely personal that his tragic withdrawal from the world and from poetry becomes understandable. Neither Robert Finch's neat exercises in wit and metaphysics nor Raymond Knister's pure and natural rural lyricism now strike one as reflecting a great deal more than very private visions liberated by the mood of the period.

Yet the idea that something was going on in a collective way cannot be entirely dismissed. The modernist poets did form interlocking groups like that which centred on the *McGill Fortnightly Review* (Smith, Scott, etc.) and the later Montreal groups associated with *Preview* (P. K. Page, Patrick

Anderson, Scott, Klein) and *First Statement* (Irving Layton, Louis Dudek, John Sutherland, and the Toronto poet Raymond Souster). These groups were partly associations of convenience among poets who found it difficult to get their work published in ordinary periodicals or by ordinary publishers, but the fact that they were in this common predicament and sought a shared solution came from the circumstance that each in his or her way was rebelling against conventional poetics and seeking a way of expression that suited a personal vision. A vague cultural nationalism was endemic among these poets as it has been among their successors, but I think we are going into the matter the wrong way if we see the self-conscious desire to create a Canadian national poetry as the main factor in what happened either collectively or individually. It was the desire to find their own voices that was primary, and the movement to create a distinctive Canadian poetry that was secondary and less consciously motivated, emerging only through the poets realizing that they could be fully themselves only by living within their place and time, and giving expression to the experience they knew. But the *means* of giving that expression they often had to find elsewhere.

Thus Dorothy Livesay rightly dates her poetic awakening from her discovery of Auden and Spender, which showed that lyricism and a social conscience were compatible, and Earle Birney first found a new way of talking about Canada through his study of Old English poetry, whose density and power, and even whose diction, are strongly present in his early poems.

> Through the feckless years we have come to the time
> when to look at this quilt of lamps is a troubling delight
> Welling from Europe's bog   through Africa flowing
> and Asia drowning the lonely lumes on the oceans
> tiding up over Halifax   now to this winking
> outpost comes flooding the primal ink

Birney has been restlessly experimental throughout his long career, filling his poetry with the odour of far travels, playing with the technical developments of a younger generation, so that in late life he became one of our leading concrete poets, and on the way developing a conversational loping rhythm that serves to convey both sharp visual images and to hint at their philosophic implications.

> They are peaceful both   these spare
> men of Kashmir   and the bear
> alive is their living   too
> If   far on the Delhi way
> around him galvanic they dance
> it is merely to wear   wear
> from his shaggy body the tranced
> wish forever to stay
> only an ambling bear
> four-footed in berries.

In the end, with Dorothy Livesay, it is not her early Marxism, but her intense feminism that emerges most strongly, and that is a feminism less political than concerned with the personal intensities of the passional life, no longer dominated by the inhibitions of history and seeking

> One unit, as a tree or stone
> woman in man, and man in womb.

In some ways Dorothy Livesay has been a liberated Crawford, but she has been much more, and one of the striking aspects of her career—which she shares with Birney and P. K. Page—is the second poetic wind they all have had, returning in the 1960s and 1970s to write with even greater vigour and intensity than in their earlier careers of the 1930s and 1940s. In Page especially the moving towards an extraordinary combination of verbal economy and visionary intensity is especially striking.

For the least moving speck
I neglect God and all his angels
yet attention's funnel—
a macaw's eye—contracts,
becomes a vortex.

I have been sucked through.

In the case of other later poets of this volume, like Irving Layton, Miriam Waddington, and Margaret Avison, the careers have been more continuous, the development more steady, and in some cases the consistencies are striking, even though one sees them largely in afterthought. There can be few writers of verse in Canada who have so consciously created a poetic persona as Irving Layton, and in the end this has affected his work, which is perhaps more self-consciously poetic in its diction and its choice of imagery than anything since—say—Lampman's work. Here and there the reaction to experience is direct and compassionate, as in "The Bull Calf," but more often the poem becomes a dramatic working out of its creator's dreams and fancies, and draws its vigour from them, so that the poetic imagination becomes a way, as Layton says, "to dominate reality."

There are brightest apples in those trees
  but until I, fabulist, have spoken
they do not know their significance....

There is a world of perception dividing Layton's Dionysiac stance from Margaret Avison's austere vision which ends this volume, the vision of the seeker the condition of whose search may be not the elevation but the loss of self:

All of us, flung in one
Murky parabola,
Seek out some pivot for significance,
Leery of comet's tails, mask-merry,
Wondering at the centre
Who will gain access, search the citadel
To its last, secret door?
And what face will the violator find
When he confronts the glass?

No Canadian poet has written more movingly than Avison of the perplexities of faith and doubt, or more melded tradition—the subterranean *lingua franca* of mysticism—with a wry tenacious personal voice.

George Woodcock

Acknowledgments

We wish to thank the following authors, publishers, and copyright holders for permission to reproduce the poems in this book.

CHARLES G. D. ROBERTS: "Tantramar Revisited," "The Sower," "The Potato Harvest," "Autochthon," "The Mowing," "The Pea-Fields," "In an Old Barn," "The Solitary Woodsman," "In the Night Watches," "Taormina" from *Selected Poems of Sir Charles G. D. Roberts* by permission of Lady Joan Roberts. D. C. SCOTT: "At the Cedars" from *The Magic House and Other Poems*; "The Onondaga Madonna," "The Piper of Arll" from *Labor and the Angel*; "On the Way to the Mission," "The Forsaken," "Night Hymns on Lake Nipigon" from *New World Lyrics and Ballads*; "The Height of Land" from *Lundy's Lane and Other Poems*; "At Gull Lake: August, 1810" from *The Green Cloister: Later Poems*; "Powassan's Drum" from *The Poems of Duncan Campbell Scott* reprinted by permission John Aylen, Ottawa. E. J. PRATT: "Newfoundland," "The Shark," "The Lee-Shore," "Still Life," "Missing: Believed Dead: Returned," "Come Away, Death," "The Dying Eagle," "The Truant," selections from *Brébeuf and His Brethren* from *The Collected Works of E. J. Pratt* by permission of the Estate of E. J. Pratt. W. W. E. ROSS: "The Diver," "The Creek," "On the Supernatural," "This Form," "The Walk," "Spring Song," "Rocky Bay" from *Shapes and Sounds* by permission of the publisher. RAYMOND KNISTER: "Change," "Lake Harvest," "Stable-Talk," "The Plowman," "Feed" from *The Collected Poems of Raymond Knister* by permission of McGraw-Hill Ryerson; "The Humourist," "Sumach" [unpublished] by permission of Imogen Givens. F. R. SCOTT: "Lakeshore," "Trans Canada," "Overture," "March Field," "Trees in Ice," "Summer Camp," "Bonne Entente," "On the Terrace, Quebec," "Dancing" from *The Collected Poems of F. R. Scott* reprinted by permission of The Canadian Publishers, McClelland and Stewart Limited, Toronto. ROBERT FINCH: For permission to include the following poems of Robert Finch: "The Foreman," *Dover Beach Revisited*, 1961 and "Silverthorn Bush," *Silverthorn Bush and Other Poems*, 1966, Macmillan of Canada; "The Statue," "Train Window," and "Egg-and-Dart," *Poems*, 1946, Oxford University Press, Toronto; "When," "The Five Kine," 1948, *The Strength of the Hills*, McClelland and Stewart Ltd., "The Lovers," *Has and Is*, copyright Canada 1981, The Porcupine's Quill Inc.; thanks are due to the author and Sybil Hutchinson, literary agent. A. J. M. SMITH: "The Lonely Land," "Swift Current," "Like an Old Proud King in a Parable," "News of the Phoenix," "Noctambule," "The Archer," "Far West," "The Mermaid," "Metamorphosis," "The Wisdom of Old Jelly Roll" from *The Classic Shade* by A. J. M. Smith reprinted by permission of The Canadian Publishers, McClelland and Stewart Limited, Toronto. EARLE BIRNEY: "Hands," "Vancouver Lights," "Bushed," "El Greco: *Espolio*," "Bangkok Boy," "The Bear on the Delhi Road," "Museum of Man," "Canada Council" from *The Collected Poems of Earle Birney*, and "father grouse," "my love is young" from *Fall by Fury*, all poems reprinted by permission of The Canadian Publishers, McClelland and Stewart Limited, Toronto. LEO KENNEDY: "Words for a Resurrection," "Epithalamium," "Mad Boy's Song," "Mole Talk," "Meek Candidates for Grave Space" from *The Shrouding* by permission of the author. RALPH GUSTAFSON: "In the Yukon," "Aspects of Some Forsythia Branches" from *Selected Poems*, "Trio for Harp and Percussion" from *Corners in the Glass*, and "Landscape with Rain" from *Landscape with Rain*, all reprinted by permission of The Canadian Publishers, McClelland and Stewart Limited, Toronto; "Dedication," "Mythos," from *Flight into Darkness* by permission of Pantheon. A. M. KLEIN: "Portrait of the Poet as Landscape," "Out of the Pulver and Polished Lens," "Political Meeting," "The Rocking Chair," "Psalm xxvii: A Psalm to Teach Humility," "Heirloom," "Autobiographical," "Montreal," "Lone Bather" from *The Collected Poems of A. M. Klein* by permission of the publisher McGraw-Hill Ryerson; "Sestina on the Dialectic" [unpublished] by permission of Sandor Klein. DOROTHY LIVESAY: "Ice Age" from *Ice Age* by permission of Press Porcépic; "Day and Night," "On Looking into Henry Moore," "Bartok and the Geranium," "Fire and Reason," "Green Rain," "Lament for J. F. B. L." "Autumn: 1939," "The Three Emily's" from *Collected Poems: The Two Seasons* by permission of McGraw-Hill Ryerson. ANNE WILKINSON: "Still Life" from *Counterpoint to Sleep*; "In June and Gentle Oven" from *The Hangman Ties the Holly*; "Letter to My Children: Postscript," "Lens" from *Collected Poems*, all poems by permission of Gage Publishing. IRVING LAYTON: "The Swimmer," "The Bull Calf," "The Fertile Muck," "The Cold Green Element," "Keine Lazarovitch," "Whatever Else Poetry is Freedom," "A Tall Man Executes a Jig" from *The Collected Poems of Irving Layton*; "For My Brother Jesus" from *For My Brother Jesus*, "The Search" from *A Wild Peculiar Joy* reprinted by permission of The Canadian Publishers, McClelland and Stewart Limited, Toronto. P. K. PAGE "The Stenographers," "Adolescence," "Stories of Snow," "T-Bar," "Cross," "Another Space" from *Poems Selected and New* by permission of the author. MIRIAM WADDINGTON: "Icons," "The Season's Lovers," "The Nineteen Thirties are Over" from *Driving Home*; "Wonderful Country" from *Green World*; and "Portrait: Old Woman" from *The Price of Gold* [Oxford University Press Canada], by permission of the author. MARGARET AVISON: "The Apex Animal," "Butterfly Bones," "Easter," "Voluptuaries and Others," "The Mirrored Man" from *Winter Sun*; "The Swimmer's Moment," "Black-White Under Green," from *The Dumbfounding*; "Strong Yellow" from *Sunblue*, all poems reprinted by permission of The Canadian Publishers, McClelland and Stewart Limited, Toronto.

CHARLES SANGSTER

1822-1893

FROM *The Thousand Islands: The St. Lawrence and the Saguenay*

III

The bark leaps love-fraught from the land; the sea
Lies calm before us. Many an isle is there,
Clad with soft verdure; many a stately tree
Uplifts its leafy branches through the air;
The amorous current bathes the islets fair,
As we skip, youth-like, o'er the limpid waves;
White cloudlets speck the golden atmosphere,
Through which the passionate sun looks down, and graves
His image on the pearls that boil from the deep caves,

IV

And bathe the vessel's prow. Isle after isle
Is passed, as we glide tortuously through
The opening vistas, that uprise and smile
Upon us from the ever-changing view.
Here nature, lavish of her wealth, did strew
Her flocks of panting islets on the breast
Of the admiring River, where they grew,
Like shapes of Beauty, formed to give a zest
To the charmed mind, like waking Visions of the Blest.

V

The silver-sinewed arms of the proud Lake,
Love-wild, embrace each islet tenderly,
The zephyrs kiss the flowers when they wake
At morn, flushed with a rare simplicity;
See how they bloom around yon birchen tree,
And smile along the bank, by the sandy shore,
In lovely groups—a fair community!
The embossed rocks glitter like golden ore,
And here, the o'erarching trees form a fantastic bower.

VI

Red walls of granite rise on either hand,
Rugged and smooth; a proud young eagle soars
Above the stately evergreens, that stand
Like watchful sentinels on these God-built towers;
And near yon beds of many-colored flowers
Browse two majestic deer, and at their side
A spotted fawn all innocently cowers;
In the rank brushwood it attempts to hide,
While the strong-antlered stag steps forth with lordly stride,

VII

And slakes his thirst, undaunted, at the stream.
Isles of o'erwhelming beauty! surely here
The wild enthusiast might live, and dream
His life away. No Nymphic trains appear,
To charm the pale Ideal Worshipper
Of Beauty; nor Neriads from the deeps below;
Nor hideous Gnomes, to fill the breast with fear:
But crystal streams through endless landscapes flow,
And o'er the clustering Isles the softest breezes blow.

LYRIC TO THE ISLES.

Here the Spirit of Beauty keepeth
   Jubilee for evermore;
Here the Voice of Gladness leapeth,
   Echoing from shore to shore.
O'er the hidden watery valley,
   O'er each buried wood and glade,
Dances our delighted galley,
   Through the sunlight and the shade—
   Dances o'er the granite cells,
   Where the Soul of Beauty dwells:

Here the flowers are ever springing,
   While the summer breezes blow;
Here the Hours are ever clinging,
   Loitering before they go;
Playing round each beauteous islet,
   Loath to leave the sunny shore,
Where, upon her couch of violet,
   Beauty sits for evermore—
   Sits and smiles by day and night,
   Hand in hand with pure Delight.

Here the Spirit of Beauty dwelleth
   In each palpitating tree,
In each amber wave that welleth
   From its home, beneath the sea;
In the moss upon the granite,
   In each calm, secluded bay,
      With the zephyr trains that fan it
         With their sweet breaths all the day—
         On the waters, on the shore,
         Beauty dwelleth evermore!

VIII

Yes, here the Genius of Beauty truly dwells.
I worship Truth and Beauty in my soul.
The pure prismatic globule that upwells
From the blue deep; the psalmy waves that roll
Before the hurricane; the outspread scroll
Of heaven, with its written tomes of stars;
The dew-drop on the leaf: These I extol,
And all alike—each on a Spirit-Mars,
Guarding my Victor-Soul above Earth's prison bars.

FROM *The Happy Harvesters*

IV

Up the wide chimney rolls the social fire,
Warming the hearts of matron, youth, and sire;
Painting such grotesque shadows on the wall,
The stripling looms a giant stout and tall,
While they whose statures reach the common height
Seem spectres mocking the hilarious night.
From hand to hand the ripened fruit went round,
And rural sports a pleased acceptance found;
The youthful fiddler on his three-legged stool,
Fancied himself at least an Ole Bull;
Some easy bumpkin, seated on the floor,
Hunted the slipper till his ribs were sore;
Some chose the graceful waltz or lively reel,
While deeper heads the chess battalions wheel,
Till some old veteran, compelled to yield,
More brave than skilful, vanquished, quits the field.
As a flushed harper, when the doubtful fight
Favors the prowess of some stately knight,
In stirring numbers of triumphal song
Upholds the spirits of the victor throng,
A sturdy ploughboy, wedded to the soil,
Thus sung the praises of the partner of his toil:

FROM *Sonnets Written in the Orillia Woods*

PROEM.

ALICE, I need not tell you that the Art
That copies Nature, even at its best,
Is but the echo of a splendid tone,
Or like the answer of a little child
To the deep question of some frosted sage.
For Nature in her grand magnificence,
Compared to Art, must ever raise her head
Beyond the cognizance of human minds:
This is the spirit merely; that, the soul.
We watch her passing, like some gentle dream,
And catch sweet glimpses of her perfect face;
We see the flashing of her gorgeous robes,
And, if her mantle ever falls at all,
How few Elishas wear it sacredly,
As if it were a valued gift from heaven.
God has created; we but re-create,
According to the temper of our minds;
According to the grace He has bequeathed;
According to the uses we have made
Of His good-pleasure given unto us.
And so I love my art; chiefly, because
Through it I rev'rence Nature, and improve
The tone and tenor of the mind He gave.
God sends a Gift; we crown it with high Art,
And make it worthy the bestower, when
The talent is not hidden in the dust
Of pampered negligence and venial sin,
But put to studious use, that it may work
The end and aim for which it was bestowed.
All Good is God's; all Love and Truth are His;
We are His workers; and we dare not plead
But that He gave us largely of all these,
Demanding a discreet return, that when
The page of life is written to its close
It may receive the seal and autograph

Of His good pleasure—the right royal sign
And signet of approval, to the end
That we were worthy of the gift divine,
And through it praised the Great Artificer.

In my long rambles through Orillian woods;
Out on the ever-changing Couchiching;
By the rough margin of the Lake St. John;
Down the steep Severn, where the artist sun,
In dainty dalliance with the blushing stream,
Transcribes each tree, branch, leaf, and rock and flower,
Perfect in shape and colour, clear, distinct,
With all the panoramic change of sky—
Even as Youth's bright river, toying with
The fairy craft where Inexperience dreams,
And subtle Fancy builds its airy halls,
In blest imagination pictures most
Of bright or lovely that adorn life's banks,
With the blue vault of heaven over all;
On that serene and wizard afternoon,
As hunters chase the wild and timid deer
We chased the quiet of Medonte's shades
Through the green windings of the forest road,
Past Nature's venerable rank and file
Of primal woods—her Old Guard, sylvan-plumed—
The far-off Huron, like a silver thread,
The clue to some enchanted labyrinth,
Dimly perceived beyond the stretch of woods,
Th'approaches tinted by a purple haze,
And softened into beauty like the dream
Of some rapt seer's Apocalyptic mood;
And when at Rockridge we sat looking out
Upon the softened shadows of the night,
And the wild glory of the throbbing stars;
Where'er we bent our Eden-tinted way:
My brain was a weird wilderness of Thought:
My heart, love's sea of passion tossed and torn,
Calmed by the presence of the loving souls
By whom I was surrounded. All the while

They deemed me passing tame, and wondered when
My dreamy castle would come toppling down.
I was but driving back the aching past,
And mirroring the future. And these leaves
Of meditation are but perfumes from
The censer of my feelings; honied drops
Wrung from the busy hives of heart and brain;
Mere etchings of the artist; grains of sand
From the calm shores of that unsounded deep
Of speculation, where all thought is lost
Amid the realms of Nature and of God.

XIII

I've almost grown a portion of this place;
I seem familiar with each mossy stone;
Even the nimble chipmunk passes on,
And looks, but never scolds me. Birds have flown
And almost touched my hand; and I can trace
The wild bees to their hives. I've never known
So sweet a pause from labour. But the tone
Of a past sorrow, like a mournful rill
Threading the heart of some melodious hill,
Or the complainings of the whippoorwill,
Passes through every thought, and hope, and aim.
It has its uses; for it cools the flame
Of ardent love that burns my being up—
Love, life's celestial pearl, diffused through all its cup.

XIV

There is no sadness here. Oh, that my heart
Were calm and peaceful as these dreamy groves!
That all my hopes and passions, and deep loves,
Could sit in such an atmosphere of peace,
Where no unholy impulses would start
Responsive to the throes that never cease
To keep my spirit in such wild unrest.
'Tis only in the struggling human breast

That the true sorrow lives. Our fruitful joys
Have stony kernels hidden in their core.
Life in a myriad phases passeth here,
And death as various—an equal poise;
Yet all is but a solemn change—no more;
And not a sound save joy pervades the atmosphere.

In the Hollow

In the hollow, among the birch,
In vain through my brain for a thought I search;
I might as well seek for a crock of gold,
Buried by genii in days of old,
Down, far down in this deep ravine,
With its checkered roof of varied green.

In the hollow, among the trees,
That are rudely swung by the rising breeze,
Glintings of light are sifted down,
Like drops of gold from the forest's crown,
But never a thought in my weary brain,
Fills me with pleasure or racks with pain.

In the hollow, where light and shade
Pass to and fro as if half afraid,
Pass like ghosts of the times of old,
By none but the red man's eyes beheld,
Here in the cool of the noon of the day,
Without a thought I could live for aye.

In the hollow, with light shut out,
No care can enter or roam about;
I might seek in vain through this summer noon,
For a wood-nymph's laugh, or a witch's croon;
Here, at least, from thought's strictest search
I'm safe in the hollow among the birch.

ISABELLA VALANCY CRAWFORD

c. 1850-1887

The Roman Rose-Seller.

Not from Pæstum come my roses; Patrons, see
My flowers are Roman-blown; their nectaries
Drop honey amber, and their petals throw
Rich crimsons on the lucent marble of the shrine
Where snowy Dian lifts her pallid brow,
As crimson lips of Love may seek to warm
A sister glow in hearts as pulseless hewn.
Cæsar from Afric wars returns to-day;
Patricians, buy my royal roses; strew
His way knee-deep, as though old Tiber roll'd
A tide of musky roses from his bed to do
A wonder, wond'rous homage. Marcus Lucius, thou
To-day dost wed; buy roses, roses, roses,
To mingle with the nuptial myrtle; look,
I strip the polish'd thorns from the stems,
The nuptial rose should be a stingless flower;
Lucania, pass not by my roses. Virginia,
Here is a rose that has a canker in't, and yet
It is most glorious-dyed and sweeter smells
Than those death hath not touched. To-day they bear
The shield of Claudius with his spear upon it,
Close upon Cæsar's chariot—heap, heap it up
With roses such as these; 'tis true he's dead
And there's the canker! but, Romans, he
Died glorious, there's the perfume! and his virtues
Are these bright petals; so buy my roses, Widow.
No Greek-born roses mine. Priestess, priestess!
Thy ivory chariot stay; here's a rose and not
A white one, though thy chaste hands attend

On Vesta's flame. Love's of a colour—be it that
Which ladders Heaven and lives amongst the Gods;
Or like the Daffodil blows all about the earth;
Or, Hesperus like, is one sole star upon
The solemn sky which bridges some sad life,
So here's a crimson rose: Be thou as pure
As Dian's tears iced on her silver cheek,
And know no quality of love, thou art
A sorrow to the Gods! Oh mighty Love!
I would my roses could but chorus Thee.
No roses of Persepolis are mine. Helot, here—
I give thee this last blossom: A bee as red
As Hybla's golden toilers sucked its sweets;
A butterfly, wing'd like to Eros, nipp'd
Its new-pinked leaves; the sun, bright despot, stole
The dew night gives to all. Poor slave, methinks
A bough of cypress were as gay a gift, and yet
It hath some beauty left! a little scarlet—for
The Gods love all; a little perfume, for there is no life,
Poor slave, but hath its sweetness. Thus I make
My roses Oracles. O hark! the cymbals beat
In god-like silver bursts of sound; I go
To see great Cæsar leading Glory home,
From Campus Martius to the Capitol!

The City Tree

I stand within the stony, arid town,
  I gaze for ever on the narrow street;
I hear for ever passing up and down,
  The ceaseless tramp of feet.

I know no brotherhood with far-lock'd woods,
  Where branches bourgeon from a kindred sap:
Where o'er moss'd roots, in cool, green solitudes,
  Small silver brooklets lap.

No em'rald vines creep wistfully to me,
 And lay their tender fingers on my bark;
High may I toss my boughs, yet never see
 Dawn's first most glorious spark.

When to and fro my branches wave and sway,
 Answ'ring the feeble wind that faintly calls,
They kiss no kindred boughs but touch alway
 The stones of climbing walls.

My heart is never pierc'd with song of bird;
 My leaves know nothing of that glad unrest,
Which makes a flutter in the still woods heard,
 When wild birds build a nest.

There never glance the eyes of violets up,
 Blue into the deep splendour of my green:
Nor falls the sunlight to the primrose cup,
 My quivering leaves between.

Not mine, not mine to turn from soft delight
 Of wood-bine breathings, honey sweet, and warm;
With kin embattl'd rear my glorious height
 To greet the coming storm!

Not mine to watch across the free, broad plains
 The whirl of stormy cohorts sweeping fast;
The level, silver lances of great rains,
 Blown onward by the blast.

Not mine the clamouring tempest to defy,
 Tossing the proud crest of my dusky leaves:
Defender of small flowers that trembling lie
 Against my barky greaves.

Not mine to watch the wild swan drift above,
 Balanced on wings that could not choose between
The wooing sky, blue as the eye of love,
 And my own tender green.

And yet my branches spread, a kingly sight,
  In the close prison of the drooping air:
When sun-vex'd noons are at their fiery height,
  My shade is broad, and there

Come city toilers, who their hour of ease
  Weave out to precious seconds as they lie
Pillow'd on horny hands, to hear the breeze
  Through my great branches die.

I see no flowers, but as the children race
  With noise and clamour through the dusty street,
I see the bud of many an angel face—
  I hear their merry feet.

No violets look up, buy shy and grave,
  The children pause and lift their crystal eyes
To where my emerald branches call and wave—
  As to the mystic skies.

A Wooing

Daughter of the House of Jackson,
Maiden of the amber chignon,
Damsel of the graceful tie-back,
Virgin of the flatly ulster,
May I lay my heart before thee?
May I show my bank-book to thee?
May I, can I, dare I woo thee?
In the woodland's dim recesses,
Shine the blue eyes of the violets,
Like thine eyes of azure pensive.
In the dim and lone recesses
Of a bank, the very safest,
Lie my bonds and lurk my coupons;
Shine my dollars like to Hesper—
Like to Hesper, star of beauty,

Golden star of love and beauty!
May I woo thee? May I wed thee?
"I do not know," she answer'd sighing;
"I do not know," the parrot echoed.

Daughter of respected Jackson—
Belov'd one clad in rays of beauty,
Blended by great Woerth, the wizard;
Woerth the toiler of the satins,
Woerth the Caesar of the velvets,
Woerth the Merlin of materials.
Maiden moving as the fawn moves
In the graceful dip of Boston;
In the glide and in the lancers,
On the rollers, on the across.
Maiden, all the stars of evening,
Are the hoof-prints of the horses,
Horses which have whirl'd the red sun
All the day across the heavens.
Maiden, thro' the parks and gay streets,
I will drive two spanking trotters,
Curried, burnished like the clear pools,
And their bits shall be of silver,
Silver, not electro-plated,
And the lining of the carriage,
Shall be blue as yonder heavens.
May I woo thee? May I wed thee?
"I am not sure," she answered sighing.
"I am not sure," the parrot echoed.

Daughter of esteem'd old Jackson;
Maiden of the pencill'd eyebrow,
Damsel of the songs of Schuman;
Virgin of the notes of Thalberg;
I have just foreclos'd a mortgage,
Mortgage on a beauteous mansion,
Builded with a hot-air furnace,
Builded with a spacious ball-room,
Lighted from the city gas-works.

On the pond the water-lily
Folds her dusky leaves about her,
Floats upon the swaying current,
Dances on its undulations.
So the walls of this, my mansion,
I would close about my lily.
May I woo thee? May I wed thee?
"Let me ask my heart" she answered,
"Let me ask" the parrot echoed.

Daughter of the honour'd Jackson,
Singer of the swelling anthem,
Warbler of the opera bouffe,
Of the notes of the Creation,
And of Madam Angot's Daughter,
On thy silver thread of laughter,
I will string rare, shining di'monds,
I will hang the moonlit pearls,
And my heart shall bleed in rubies.
I will make a large insurance
On my life and on my mansion;
I will seek a larger interest
For my dollars Hesper shining,
Be more sure about my coupons,
Grub more closely in the gold dust.
Star of beauty, smile upon me,
Dear Miss Jackson, pray accept me.
"Ask Papa," she answer'd, blushing.
"They all do it," said the parrot.

The Dark Stag

A startl'd stag the blue grey night
Leaps down beyond dark pines
Behind, a length of yellow light,
    The hunter's arrow shines.

His moccasins are stain'd with red
He bends upon his knee
From cov'ring peaks his shafts are sped
The blue mists plume his mighty head!
Well may the dark stag flee!

The pale moon like a snow-white doe
Bounds by his dappl'd flank;
They beat the stars down as they go
As wood-bells growing rank.
The winds lift dew-laps from the ground
Leap from dry shaking reeds
Their hoarse bays shake the cedars round—
With keen cries on the trail they bound—
Swift, swift the dark stag speeds!

Roar the rent lakes, as through the waves
Their silver warriors plunge
As vaults from core of crystal caves
The vast, fierce Maskelonge.
Red torches of the sumach glow
Fall's council fires are lit
The bittern, squaw-like, scolds the air
The wild duck splashes loudly, where
The waving rice-spears knit.

Shaft after shaft the red sun speeds—
Rent the stag's dappl'd side.
His breast to fangs of hoarse winds bleeds
He staggers on the tide.
He feels the hungry waves of space
Rush at him high and blue
The white spray smites his dusky face
Swifter the sun's swift arrows race
And pierce his strong heart through.

Away! his white doe far behind
Lies wounded on the plain

Yells at his flank the nimblest wind—
    His large tears fall like rain
Like lily-pads shall clouds grow white
    About his darkling way
From her bald nest upon the height
The red-ey'd eagle sees his flight
He falters—turns—the antler'd night
    The black stag stands at bay!

His feet are in the waves of space
    His antlers broad and dun,
He low'rs, and turns his velvet face
    To front the hunter sun,
He stamps the lilied clouds and high,
    His branches fill the west—
The lean stork sails across the sky—
The shy loon shrieks to see him die
    The winds leap at his breast.

His antlers fall—once more he spurns
    The hoarse hounds of the day
His blood upon the crisp blue burns
    Reddens the mounting spray.
His branches smite the wave—with cries
    The shrill winds pausing, flag
He sinks in space—red glow the skies;
The brown earth crimsons as he dies,
    The stout and lusty stag!

The Canoe

My masters twain made me a bed
Of pine-boughs resinous, and cedar;
Of moss, a soft and gentle breeder
Of dreams of rest; and me they spread
With furry skins, and laughing said,
"Now she shall lay her polish'd sides,

As queens do rest, or dainty brides,
Our slender lady of the tides!"

My masters twain their camp-soul lit,
Streamed incense from the hissing cones,
Large, crimson flashes grew and whirl'd
Thin, golden nerves of sly light curl'd
Round the dun camp, and rose faint zones,
Half way about each grim bole knit,
Like a shy child that would bedeck
With its soft clasp a Brave's red neck;
Yet sees the rough shield on his breast,
The awful plumes shake on his crest,
And fearful drops his timid face,
Nor dares complete the sweet embrace.

Into the hollow hearts of brakes,
Yet warm from sides of does and stags,
Pass'd to the crisp dark river flags;
Sinuous, red as copper snakes,
Sharp-headed serpents, made of light,
Glided and hid themselves in night.

My masters twain, the slaughter'd deer
Hung on fork'd boughs—with thongs of leather.
Bound were his stiff, slim feet together—
His eyes like dead stars cold and drear;
The wand'ring firelight drew near
And laid its wide palm, red and anxious,
On the sharp splendor of his branches;
On the white foam grown hard and sere
　　On flank and shoulder.
Death—hard as breast of granite boulder,
　　And under his lashes
Peer'd thro' his eyes at his life's grey ashes.

My masters twain sang songs that wove
(As they burnish'd hunting blade and rifle)

A golden thread with a cobweb trifle—
Loud of the chase, and low of love.

"O Love, art thou a silver fish?
Shy of the line and shy of gaffing,
Which we do follow, fierce, yet laughing,
Casting at thee the light-wing'd wish,
And at the last shall we bring thee up
From the crystal darkness under the cup
　　Of lily folden,
　　On broad leaves golden?

"O Love! art thou a silver deer,
Swift thy starr'd feet as wing of swallow,
While we with rushing arrows follow;
And at the last shall we draw near,
And over thy velvet neck cast thongs—
Woven of roses, of stars, of songs?
　　New chains all moulden
　　Of rare gems olden!"

They hung the slaughter'd fish like swords
On saplings slender—like scimitars
Bright, and ruddied from new-dead wars,
Blaz'd in the light—the scaly hordes.

They pil'd up boughs beneath the trees,
Of cedar-web and green fir tassel;
Low did the pointed pine tops rustle,
The camp fire blush'd to the tender breeze.

The hounds laid dew-laps on the ground,
With needles of pine sweet, soft and rusty—
Dream'd of the dead stag stout and lusty;
A bat by the red flames wove its round.

The darkness built its wigwam walls
Close round the camp, and at its curtain
Press'd shapes, thin woven and uncertain,
As white locks of tall waterfalls.

The Lily Bed

His cedar paddle, scented red,
He thrust down through the lily-bed.

Cloak'd in a golden pause he lay
Lock'd in the arms of the bay.

Trembl'd alone his bark canoe
As shocks of bursting lilies flew—

Through the still pulses of the tide,
And smote the frail boat's silv'ry side.

Or when, beside the sedges thin
Flash'd the sharp jewel of a fin.

Or when, a wizard swift and bold
A dragon fly dash'd out in gold

And fire and flame, the wid'ning rings
Of waters whisp'ring to his wings.

Or when, like wing'd and burning soul
Dropp'd from the gloom an oriole—

On the cool wave, as to the balm
Of the Great Spirit's open palm—

The freed soul flies. Soft silence clung
To the still hours as trendrils hung,

In darkness carven, from the trees
Sedge-buried to their burly knees.

Stillness sat in her lodge of leaves,
Clung golden shadows to its eaves:

And on its spicy floor like maize
Red-ripe fell sheaves of knotted rays.

The wood, a proud and crested brave;
Bead-bright, a maiden, stood the wave.

And he had told his tale of love
With voice of eagle and of dove

Of loud, peak'd pines his tongue had made,
His lips soft blossoms of the shade

That kiss'd her silver lips—hers cool
As lilies on his inmost pool.

Till now he stood in triumph's rest
His image in her crystal breast.

One isle, 'tween blue and blue did melt
A bead of wampum from the belt,

Of Manitou—a purple rise
On the far shore slipp'd up the skies.

His cedar paddle scented red
He drew up from the lily-bed.

All lily-lock'd, all lily-lock'd
The light bark on the blossoms rock'd—

Their cool lips round the sharp prow sang,
Their soft palms to the pale sides sprang.

With breasts and lips they wove a bar—
Stole from her lodge the Ev'ning Star

With golden hand she grasp'd the mane
Of a red cloud on the azure plain—

It by the con'd red sunset flew
Cool winds from its bright nostrils blew.

They sway'd the high dark trees and low
Swept the lock'd lilies to and fro.

With cedar paddle, scented red
He push'd out from the lily-bed!

The Rolling-Pin

Beneath grave Sister Claudia's eyes,
She droops the dimple of her chin:
Drops frolic glances from far skies,
Upon her fairy rolling-pin.

Outside the convent maple stirs
Her leafy playmate, plum'd and tall:
The sweet far organ swells and birrs
And shakes the green vine on the wall.

The golden shuttle of her years
Across the loom of life has fled:
In light, gay flashes—all her tears
Have rounded for her dear dove dead.

Her laugh, a zig-zag butterfly
Of silver sound, that hardly knows
Against what joyous blossom's dye
Mirth's breath its fairy flutt'ring blows

The rose rays on her finger tips
Kiss satin rose to rip'ning mold;
She purses up her rose bright lips.
She twines the thread of glitt'ring gold.

A snowflake fair her soul might soil,
A lilycup hold all her sin
And stainless stay, O fairy toil,
The decking of the Rolling-Pin!

W. WILFRED CAMPBELL

1858-1918

Indian Summer

ALONG the line of smoky hills
The crimson forest stands,
And all the day the blue-jay calls
Throughout the autumn lands.

Now by the brook the maple leans
With all his glory spread,
And all the sumachs on the hills
Have turned their green to red.

Now by great marshes wrapt in mist,
Or past some river's mouth,
Throughout the long, still autumn day
Wild birds are flying south.

Vapor and Blue

Domed with the azure of heaven,
Floored with a pavement of pearl,
Clothed all about with a brightness
Soft as the eyes of a girl,

Girt with a magical girdle,
Rimmed with a vapor of rest—
These are the inland waters,
These are the lakes of the west.

Voices of slumberous music,
  Spirits of mist and of flame,
Moonlit memories left here
  By gods who long ago came,

And vanishing left but an echo
  In silence of moon-dim caves,
Where haze-wrapt the August night slumbers,
  Or the wild heart of October raves.

Here where the jewels of nature
  Are set in the light of God's smile;
Far from the world's wild throbbing,
  I will stay me and rest me awhile.

And store in my heart old music,
  Melodies gathered and sung
By the genies of love and of beauty
  When the heart of the world was young.

August Evening on the Beach, Lake Huron

A LURID flush of sunset sky,
  An angry sketch of gleaming lake,
I will remember till I die
The sound, of pines that sob and sigh,
  Of waves upon the beach that break.

'Twas years ago, and yet it seems,
  O love, but only yesterday
We stood in holy sunset dreams,
While all the day's diaphanous gleams
  Sobbed into silence bleak and gray.

We scarcely knew, but our two souls
  Like night and day rushed into one;
The stars came out in gleaming shoals:

While, like a far-off bell that tolls,
  Came voices from the wave-dipped sun.

We scarcely knew, but hand in hand,
  With subtle sense, was closer pressed;
As we two walked in that old land
Forever new, whose shining strand
  Goes gleaming round the world's great breast.

What was it sweet our spirits spoke?
  No outward sound of voice was heard.
But was it bird or angel broke
The silence, till a dream voice woke
  And all the night was music-stirred?

What was it, love, did mantle us,
  Such fire of incense filled our eyes?
The moon-light was not ever thus:
Such star-born music rained on us,
  We grew so glad and wonder-wise.

But this, O love, was long ago,
  Although it seems but yesterday
The moon rose in her silver glow,
As she will rise on nights of woe,
  On hands uplift, on hearts that pray.

A lurid flush of sunset sky,
  An angry sketch of gleaming lake;
I will remember till I die,
The sound of pines that sob and sigh,
  Of waves upon the beach that break.

The Dread Voyage

TRIM the sails the weird stars under—
Past the iron hail and thunder,
Past the mystery and the wonder,
    Sails our fated bark;

Past the myriad voices hailing,
Past the moaning and the wailing,
The far voices failing, failing,
    Drive we to the dark.

Past the headlands grim and sombre,
Past the shores of mist and slumber,
Leagues on leagues no man may number,
    Soundings none can mark;
While the olden voices calling,
One by one behind are falling;
Into silence dread, appalling,
    Drift we to the dark.

Far behind, the sad eyes yearning,
Hands that wring for our returning,
Lamps of love yet vainly burning:
    Past the headlands stark!
Through the wintry snows and sleeting,
On our pallid faces beating,
Through the phantom twilight fleeting,
    Drive we to the dark.

Without knowledge, without warning,
Drive we to no lands of morning;
Far ahead no signals horning
    Hail our nightward bark.
Hopeless, helpless, weird, outdriven,
Fateless, friendless, dread, unshriven,
For some race-doom unforgiven,
    Drive we to the dark.

Not one craven or unseemly;
In the flare-light gleaming dimly,
Each ghost-face is watching grimly:
    Past the headlands stark!
Hearts wherein no hope may waken,
Like the clouds of night wind-shaken,
Chartless, anchorless, forsaken,
    Drift we to the dark.

How One Winter Came in the Lake Region

FOR weeks and weeks the autumn world stood still,
Clothed in the shadow of a smoky haze;
The fields were dead, the wind had lost its will,
And all the lands were hushed by wood and hill,
In those grey, withered days.

Behind a mist the blear sun rose and set,
At night the moon would nestle in a cloud;
The fisherman, a ghost, did cast his net;
The lake its shores forgot to chafe and fret,
And hushed its caverns loud.

Far in the smoky woods the birds were mute,
Save that from blackened tree a jay would scream,
Or far in swamps the lizard's lonesome lute
Would pipe in thirst, or by some gnarlèd root
The tree-toad trilled his dream.

From day to day still hushed the season's mood,
The streams stayed in their runnels shrunk and dry;
Suns rose aghast by wave and shore and wood,
And all the world, with ominous silence, stood
In weird expectancy:

When one strange night the sun like blood went down,
Flooding the heavens in a ruddy hue;
Red grew the lake, the sere fields parched and brown,
Red grew the marshes where the creeks stole down,
But never a wind-breath blew.

That night I felt the winter in my veins,
A joyous tremor of the icy glow;
And woke to hear the north's wild vibrant strains,
While far and wide, by withered woods and plains,
Fast fell the driving snow.

Out of Pompeii

SHE lay, face downward, on her bended arm,
   In this her new, sweet dream of human bliss,
Her heart within her fearful, fluttering, warm,
   Her lips yet pained with love's first timorous kiss.
She did not note the darkening afternoon,
   She did not mark the lowering of the sky
O'er that great city. Earth had given its boon
   Unto her lips, love touched her and passed by.

In one dread moment all the sky grew dark,
   The hideous rain, the panic, the red rout,
Where love lost love, and all the world might mark
   The city overwhelmed, blotted out
Without one cry, so quick oblivion came,
   And life passed to the black where all forget;
But she,—we know not of her house or name,—
   In love's sweet musings doth lie dreaming yet.

The dread hell passed, the ruined world grew still,
   And the great city passed to nothingness:
The ages went and mankind worked its will.
   Then men stood still amid the centuries' press,
And in the ash-hid ruins opened bare,
   As she lay down in her shamed loveliness,
Sculptured and frozen, late they found her there,
   Image of love 'mid all that hideousness.

Her head, face downward, on her bended arm,
   Her single robe that showed her shapely form,
Her wondrous fate love keeps divinely warm
   Over the centuries, past the slaying storm,
The heart can read in writings time hath left,
   That linger still through death's oblivion;
And in this waste of life and light bereft,
   She brings again a beauty that had gone.

And if there be a day when all shall wake,
  As dreams the hoping, doubting human heart,
The dim forgetfulness of death will break
  For her as one who sleeps with lips apart;
And did God call her suddenly, I know
  She'd wake as morning wakened by the thrush,
Feel that red kiss across the centuries glow,
  And make all heaven rosier by her blush.

In Holyrood

1897

I stand in Edinburgh, in Holyrood,
Where Scotland's Mary flaunted; iron Knox came,
With cavernous eyes and words of prophet-flame,
And broke her soul as bonds of brittle wood:—
And all stern Scotland's evil and her good,
Her austere ghosts, her souls of fiery shame,
Her adamantine passions none could tame,
Arise anew and drip in Rizzio's blood.

Here in these walls, these guilty corridors,
Beside[1] that bed where Elizabeth's eyes look down;—
Across the centuries with their fading band
Of angry years of Presbyterian frown,—
I only know these tears[2] of weird remorse;
The woman rules. All else is shifting sand.

[1] In Queen Mary's bedroom in Holyrood, a portrait of Queen Elizabeth hangs on the wall above the bed.

[2] It is said that Knox, during this memorable interview, made the Queen weep.

Bereavement of the Fields

IN MEMORY OF ARCHIBALD LAMPMAN, WHO DIED FEBRUARY 10, 1899

Soft fall the February snows, and soft
Falls on my heart the snow of wintry pain;
For never more, by wood or field or croft,
Will he we knew walk with his loved again;
No more, with eyes adream and soul aloft,
In those high moods where love and beauty reign,
Greet his familiar fields, his skies without a stain.

Soft fall the February snows, and deep,
Like downy pinions from the moulting breast
Of all the mothering sky, round his hushed sleep,
Flutter a million loves upon his rest,
Where once his well-loved flowers were fain to peep,
With adder-tongue and waxen petals prest,
In young spring evenings reddening down the west.

Soft fall the February snows, and hushed
Seems life's loud action, all its strife removed,
Afar, remote, where grief itself seems crushed,
And even hope and sorrow are reproved;
For he whose cheek erstwhile with hope was flushed,
And by the gentle haunts of being moved,
Hath gone the way of all he dreamed and loved.

Soft fall the February snows, and lost,
This tender spirit gone with scarce a tear,
Ere, loosened from the dungeons of the frost,
Wakens with yearnings new the enfranchised year,
Late winter-wizened, gloomed, and tempest-tost;
And Hesper's gentle, delicate veils appear,
When dream anew the days of hope and fear.

And Mother Nature, she whose heart is fain,
Yea, she who grieves not, neither faints nor fails,

Building the seasons, she will bring again
March with rudening madness of wild gales,
April and her wraiths of tender rain,
And all he loved,—this soul whom memory veils,
Beyond the burden of our strife and pain.

Not his to wake the strident note of song,
Nor pierce the deep recesses of the heart,
Those tragic wells, remote, of might and wrong;
But rather, with those gentler souls apart,
He dreamed like his own summer days along,
Filled with the beauty born of his own heart,
Sufficient in the sweetness of his song.

Outside this prison-house of all our tears,
Enfranchised from our sorrow and our wrong,
Beyond the failure of our days and years,
Beyond the burden of our saddest song,
He moves with those whose music filled his ears,
And claimed his gentle spirit from the throng,—
Wordsworth, Arnold, Keats, high masters of his song.

Like some rare Pan of those old Grecian days,
Here in our hours of deeper stress reborn,
Unfortunate thrown upon life's evil ways,
His inward ear heard ever that satyr horn
From Nature's lips reverberate night and morn,
And fled from men and all their troubled maze,
Standing apart, with sad, incurious gaze.

And now, untimely cut, like some sweet flower
Plucked in the early summer of its prime,
Before it reached the fullness of its dower,
He withers in the morning of our time;
Leaving behind him, like a summer shower,
A fragrance of earth's beauty, and the chime
Of gentle and imperishable rhyme.

Songs in our ears of winds and flowers and buds
And gentle loves and tender memories
Of Nature's sweetest aspects, her pure moods,
Wrought from the inward truth of intimate eyes
And delicate ears of him who harks and broods,
And, nightly pondering, daily grows more wise,
And dreams and sees in mighty solitudes.

Soft fall the February snows, and soft
He sleeps in peace upon the breast of her
He loved the truest; where, by wood and croft,
The wintry silence folds in fleecy blur
About his silence, while in glooms aloft
The mighty forest fathers, without stir,
Guard well the rest of him, their rare sweet worshipper.

CHARLES G. D. ROBERTS

1860-1943

Tantramar Revisited

Summers and summers have come, and gone with the flight
 of the swallow;
Sunshine and thunder have been, storm, and winter, and
 frost;
Many and many a sorrow has all but died from remembrance,
Many a dream of joy fall'n in the shadow of pain.
Hands of chance and change have marred, or moulded, or
 broken,
Busy with spirit or flesh, all I most have adored;
Even the bosom of Earth is strewn with heavier shadows,—
Only in these green hills, aslant to the sea, no change!
Here where the road that has climbed from the inland valleys
 and woodlands,
Dips from the hill-tops down, straight to the base of the
 hills,—
Here, from my vantage-ground, I can see the scattering
 houses,
Stained with time, set warm in orchards, meadows, and
 wheat,
Dotting the broad bright slopes outspread to southward and
 eastward,
Wind-swept all day long, blown by the south-east wind.

Skirting the sunbright uplands stretches a riband of meadow,
Shorn of the labouring grass, bulwarked well from the sea,
Fenced on its seaward border with long clay dykes from the
 turbid
Surge and flow of the tides vexing the Westmoreland shores.

Yonder, toward the left, lie broad the Westmoreland marshes, —
Miles on miles they extend, level, and grassy, and dim,
Clear from the long red sweep of flats to the sky in the distance,
Save for the outlying heights, green-rampired Cumberland Point;
Miles on miles outrolled, and the river-channels divide them, —
Miles on miles of green, barred by the hurtling gusts.

Miles on miles beyond the tawny bay is Minudie.
There are the low blue hills; villages gleam at their feet.
Nearer a white sail shines across the water, and nearer
Still are the slim, grey masts of fishing boats dry on the flats.
Ah, how well I remember those wide red flats, above tide-mark
Pale with scurf of the salt, seamed and baked in the sun!
Well I remember the piles of blocks and ropes, and the net-reels
Wound with the beaded nets, dripping and dark from the sea!
Now at this season the nets are unwound; they hang from the rafters
Over the fresh-stowed hay in upland barns, and the wind
Blows all day through the chinks, with the streaks of sunlight, and sways them
Softly at will; or they lie heaped in the gloom of a loft.

Now at this season the reels are empty and idle; I see them
Over the lines of the dykes, over the gossiping grass.
Now at this season they swing in the long strong wind, thro' the lonesome
Golden afternoon, shunned by the foraging gulls.
Near about sunset the crane will journey homeward above them;
Round them, under the moon, all the calm night long,
Winnowing soft grey wings of marsh-owls wander and wander,
Now to the broad, lit marsh, now to the dusk of the dyke.

Soon, thro' their dew-wet frames, in the live keen freshness
    of morning,
Out of the teeth of the dawn blows back the awakening wind.
Then, as the blue day mounts, and the low-shot shafts of
    the sunlight
Glance from the tide to the shore, gossamers jewelled with
    dew
Sparkle and wave, where late sea-spoiling fathoms of
    drift-net
Myriad-meshed, uploomed sombrely over the land.

Well I remember it all. The salt, raw scent of the margin;
While, with men at the windlass, groaned each reel, and the
    net,
Surging in ponderous lengths, uprose and coiled in its station;
Then each man to his home,—well I remember it all!

Yet, as I sit and watch, this present peace of the landscape,—
Stranded boats, these reels empty and idle, the hush,
One grey hawk slow-wheeling above yon cluster of
    haystacks,—
More than the old-time stir this stillness welcomes me home.
Ah, the old-time stir, how once it stung me with rapture,—
Old-time sweetness, the winds freighted with honey and salt!
Yet will I stay my steps and not go down to the marshland,—
Muse and recall far off, rather remember than see,—
Lest on too close sight I miss the darling illusion,
Spy at their task even here the hands of chance and change.

The Sower

A brown, sad-coloured hillside, where the soil
  Fresh from the frequent harrow, deep and fine,
  Lies bare; no break in the remote sky-line,
Save where a flock of pigeons streams aloft,
Startled from feed in some low-lying croft,
  Or far-off spires with yellow of sunset shine;
  And here the Sower, unwittingly divine,
Exerts the silent forethought of his toil.

Alone he treads the glebe, his measured stride
Dumb in the yielding soil; and though small joy
Dwell in his heavy face, as spreads the blind
Pale grain from his dispensing palm aside,
This plodding churl grows great in his employ;—
God-like, he makes provision for mankind.

The Potato Harvest

A high bare field, brown from the plough, and borne
Aslant from sunset; amber wastes of sky
Washing the ridge; a clamour of crows that fly
In from the wide flats where the spent tides mourn
To yon their rocking roosts in pines wind-torn;
A line of grey snake-fence, that zigzags by
A pond and cattle; from the homestead nigh
The long deep summonings of the supper horn.

Black on the ridge, against that lonely flush,
A cart, and stoop-necked oxen; ranged beside
Some barrels; and the day-worn harvest-folk,
Here emptying their baskets, jar the hush
With hollow thunders. Down the dusk hillside
Lumbers the wain; and day fades out like smoke.

Autochthon

I

I am the spirit astir
To swell the grain
When fruitful suns confer
With labouring rain;
I am the life that thrills
In branch and bloom;
I am the patience of abiding hills,
The promise masked in doom.

II

When the sombre lands are wrung
 And storms are out,
And giant woods give tongue,
 I am the shout;
And when the earth would sleep,
 Wrapped in her snows,
I am the infinite gleam of eyes that keep
 The post of her repose.

III

I am the hush of calm,
 I am the speed,
The flood-tide's triumphing psalm,
 The marsh-pool's heed;
I work in the rocking roar
 Where cataracts fall;
I flash in the prismy fire that dances o'er
 The dew's ephemeral ball.

IV

I am the voice of wind
 And wave and tree,
Of stern desires and blind,
 Of strength to be;
I am the cry by night
 At point of dawn,
The summoning bugle from the unseen height,
 In cloud and doubt withdrawn.

V

I am the strife that shapes
 The stature of man,
The pang no hero escapes,
 The blessing, the ban;

I am the hammer that moulds
The iron of our race,
The omen of God in our blood that a people beholds,
The foreknowledge veiled in our face.

The Mowing

This is the voice of high midsummer's heat.
The rasping vibrant clamour soars and shrills
O'er all the meadowy range of shadeless hills,
As if a host of giant cicadae beat
The cymbals of their wings with tireless feet,
Or brazen grasshoppers with triumphing note
From the long swath proclaimed the fate that smote
The clover and timothy-tops and meadowsweet.

The crying knives glide on; the green swath lies.
And all noon long the sun, with chemic ray,
Seals up each cordial essence in its cell,
That in the dusky stalls, some winter's day,
The spirit of June, here prisoned by his spell,
May cheer the herds with pasture memories.

The Pea-Fields

These are the fields of light, and laughing air,
And yellow butterflies, and foraging bees,
And whitish, wayward blossoms winged as these,
And pale green tangles like a seamaid's hair.
Pale, pale the blue, but pure beyond compare,
And pale the sparkle of the far-off seas
A-shimmer like these fluttering slopes of peas,
And pale the open landscape everywhere.

From fence to fence a perfumed breath exhales
  O'er the bright pallor of the well-loved fields,—
My fields of Tantramar in summer-time;
  And, scorning the poor feed their pasture yields,
Up from the bushy lots the cattle climb
  To gaze with longing through the grey, mossed rails.

In an Old Barn

Tons upon tons the brown-green fragrant hay
  O'erbrims the mows beyond the time-warped eaves,
  Up to the rafters where the spider weaves,
Though few flies wander his secluded way.
Through a high chink one lonely golden ray,
  Wherein the dust is dancing, slants unstirred.
  In the dry hush some rustlings light are heard,
Of winter-hidden mice at furtive play.

Far down, the cattle in their shadowed stalls,
  Nose-deep in clover fodder's meadowy scent,
  Forget the snows that whelm their pasture streams,
The frost that bites the world beyond their walls.
  Warm housed, they dream of summer, well content
  In day-long contemplation of their dreams.

The Solitary Woodsman

When the grey lake-water rushes
Past the dripping alder-bushes,
  And the bodeful autumn wind
In the fir-tree weeps and hushes,—

When the air is sharply damp
Round the solitary camp,
  And the moose-bush in the thicket
Glimmers like a scarlet lamp,—

When the birches twinkle yellow,
And the cornel bunches mellow,
  And the owl across the twilight
Trumpets to his downy fellow,—

When the nut-fed chipmunks romp
Through the maples' crimson pomp,
  And the slim viburnum flushes
In the darkness of the swamp,—

When the blueberries are dead,
When the rowan clusters red,
  And the shy bear, summer-sleekened,
In the bracken makes his bed,—

On a day there comes once more
To the latched and lonely door,
  Down the wood-road striding silent,
One who has been here before.

Green spruce branches for his head,
Here he makes his simple bed,
  Couching with the sun, and rising
When the dawn is frosty red.

All day long he wanders wide
With the grey moss for his guide,
  And his lonely axe-stroke startles
The expectant forest-side.

Toward the quiet close of day
Back to camp he takes his way,
  And about his sober footsteps
Unafraid the squirrels play.

On his roof the red leaf falls,
At his door the bluejay calls,
  And he hears the wood-mice hurry
Up and down his rough log walls;

Hears the laughter of the loon
Thrill the dying afternoon;
   Hears the calling of the moose
Echo to the early moon.

And he hears the partridge drumming,
The belated hornet humming,—
   All the faint, prophetic sounds
That foretell the winter's coming.

And the wind about his eaves
Through the chilly night-wet grieves,
   And the earth's dumb patience fills him,
Fellow to the falling leaves.

In the Night Watches

When the little spent winds are at rest in the tamarack tree
In the still of the night,
And the moon in her waning is wan and misshapen,
And out on the lake
The loon floats in a glimmer of light,
And the solitude sleeps,—
Then I lie in my bunk wide awake,
And my long thoughts stab me with longing,
Alone in my shack by the marshes of lone Margaree.

Far, oh so far in the forests of silence they lie,
The lake and the marshes of lone Margaree,
And no man comes my way.
Of spruce logs my cabin is builded securely;
With slender spruce saplings its bark roof is battened down
      surely;
In its rafters the mice are at play,
With rustlings furtive and shy,
In the still of the night.

Awake, wide-eyed, I watch my window-square,
Pallid and grey.
(O Memory, pierce me not! O Longing, stab me not!
O ache of longing memory, pass me by, and spare,
And let me sleep!)
Once and again the loon cries from the lake.
Though no breath stirs
The ghostly tamaracks and the brooding firs,
Something as light as air leans on my door.

Is it an owl's wing brushes at my latch?
Are they of foxes, those light feet that creep
Outside, light as fall'n leaves
On the forest floor?
From the still lake I hear
A feeding trout rise to some small night fly.
The splash, how sharply clear!
Almost I see the wide, slow ripple circling to the shore.

The spent winds are at rest. But my heart, spent and faint,
is unresting,
Long, long a stranger to peace . . .
O so Dear, O so Far, O so Unforgotten-in-dream,
Somewhere in the world, somewhere beyond reach of my
questing.
Beyond seas, beyond years,
You will hear my heart in your sleep, and you will stir
restlessly;
You will stir at the touch of my hand on your hair;
You will wake with a start,
With my voice in your ears
And an old, old ache at your heart,
(In the still of the night)
And your pillow wet with tears.

Taormina

A little tumbled city on the height,
  Basking above the cactus and the sea!
What pale, frail ghosts of memory come to-night
  And call back the forgotten years to me!
    Taormina, Taormina,
    And the month of the almond blossom.

In an old book I find a withered flower,
  And withered dreams awake to their old fire.
How far have danced your feet since that fair hour
  That brought us to the land of heart's desire!
    Taormina, Taormina,
    Oh, the scent of the almond blossom.

The grey-white monastery-garden wall
  O'erpeers the white crag, and the flung vines upclamber
In the white sun, and cling and seem to fall,—
  Brave bougainvilleas, purple and smoky amber.
    Taormina, Taormina,
    And the month of the almond blossom.

You caught your breath, as hand in hand we stood
  To watch the luminous peak of Aetna there
Soaring above the cloudy solitude,
  Enmeshed in the opaline Sicilian air.
    Taormina, Taormina,
    Oh, the scent of the almond blossom.

We babbled of Battos and brown Corydon,—
  Of Amaryllis coiling her dark locks,—
Of the sad-hearted satyr grieving on
  The tomb of Helicè among the rocks
      O'erhung with the almond blossom,—

Of how the goat-boy wrenched apart the vines
  That veiled the slim-limbed Chloe at her bath,
And followed her fleet-foot flight among the pines
  And caught her close, and kissed away her wrath.
    Taormina, Taormina,
    And the month of the almond blossom.

And then—you turned impetuously to me!
  We saw the blue hyacinths at our feet; and came
To the battlements, and looked down upon the sea—
  And the sea was a blue flame!

* * * * *

The blue flame dies. The ghosts come back to me.
    Taormina, Taormina,
    Oh, the scent of the almond blossom.

BLISS CARMAN

1861-1929

Low Tide on Grand Pré

The sun goes down, and over all
  These barren reaches by the tide
Such unelusive glories fall,
  I almost dream they yet will bide
  Until the coming of the tide.

And yet I know that not for us,
  By any ecstasy of dream,
He lingers to keep luminous
  A little while the grievous stream,
  Which frets, uncomforted of dream—

A grievous stream, that to and fro
  Athrough the fields of Acadie
Goes wandering, as if to know
  Why one beloved face should be
  So long from home and Acadie.

Was it a year or lives ago
  We took the grasses in our hands,
And caught the summer flying low
  Over the waving meadow lands,
  And held it there between our hands?

The while the river at our feet—
  A drowsy inland meadow stream—
At set of sun the after-heat
  Made running gold, and in the gleam
  We freed our birch upon the stream.

There down along the elms at dusk
  We lifted dripping blade to drift,
Through twilight scented fine like musk,
  Where night and gloom awhile uplift,
  Nor sunder soul and soul adrift.

And that we took into our hands
  Spirit of life or subtler thing—
Breathed on us there, and loosed the bands
  Of death, and taught us, whispering,
  The secret of some wonder-thing.

Then all your face grew light, and seemed
  To hold the shadow of the sun;
The evening faltered, and I deemed
  That time was ripe, and years had done
  Their wheeling underneath the sun.

So all desire and all regret,
  And fear and memory, were naught;
One to remember or forget
  The keen delight our hands had caught;
  Morrow and yesterday were naught.

The night has fallen, and the tide . . .
  Now and again comes drifting home,
Across these aching barrens wide,
  A sigh like driven wind or foam:
  In grief the flood is bursting home.

A Northern Vigil

Here by the gray north sea,
  In the wintry heart of the wild,
Comes the old dream of thee,
  Guendolen, mistress and child.

The heart of the forest grieves
   In the drift against my door;
A voice is under the eaves,
   A footfall on the floor.

Threshold, mirror and hall,
   Vacant and strangely aware,
Wait for their soul's recall
   With the dumb expectant air.

Here when the smouldering west
   Burns down into the sea,
I take no heed of rest
   And keep the watch for thee.

I sit by the fire and hear
   The restless wind go by,
On the long dirge and drear,
   Under the low bleak sky.

When day puts out to sea
   And night makes in for land,
There is no lock for thee,
   Each door awaits thy hand!

When night goes over the hill
   And dawn comes down the dale,
It's O for the wild sweet will
   That shall no more prevail!

When the zenith moon is round,
   And snow-wraiths gather and run,
And there is set no bound
   To love beneath the sun,

O wayward will, come near
   The old mad wilful way,
The soft mouth at my ear
   With words too sweet to say!

Come, for the night is cold,
The ghostly moonlight fills
Hollow and rift and fold
Of the eerie Ardise hills!

The windows of my room
Are dark with bitter frost,
The stillness aches with doom
Of something loved and lost.

Outside, the great blue star
Burns in the ghostland pale,
Where giant Algebar
Holds on the endless trail.

Come, for the years are long,
And silence keeps the door,
Where shapes with the shadows throng
The firelit chamber floor.

Come, for thy kiss was warm,
With the red embers' glare
Across thy folding arm
And dark tumultuous hair!

And though thy coming rouse
The sleep-cry of no bird,
The keepers of the house
Shall tremble at thy word.

Come, for the soul is free!
In all the vast dreamland
There is no lock for thee,
Each door awaits thy hand.

Ah, not in dreams at all,
Fleering, perishing, dim,
But thy old self, supple and tall,
Mistress and child of whim!

The proud imperious guise,
  Impetuous and serene,
The sad mysterious eyes,
  And dignity of mien!

Yea, wilt thou not return,
  When the late hill-winds veer,
And the bright hill-flowers burn
  With the reviving year?

When April comes, and the sea
  Sparkles as if it smiled,
Will they restore to me
  My dark Love, empress and child?

The curtains seem to part;
  A sound is on the stair,
As if at the last ... I start;
  Only the wind is there.

Lo, now far on the hills
  The crimson fumes uncurled,
Where the caldron mantles and spills
  Another dawn on the world!

Vagabond Song

There is something in the autumn that is native to my
    blood—
Touch of manner, hint of mood;
And my heart is like a rhyme,
With the yellow and the purple and the crimson keeping
    time.

The scarlet of the maples can shake me like a cry
Of bugles going by.
And my lonely spirit thrills
To see the frosty asters like a smoke upon the hills.

There is something in October sets the gypsy blood astir;
We must rise and follow her,
When from every hill of flame
She calls and calls each vagabond by name.

At the Great Release

When the black horses from the house of Dis
Stop at my door and the dread charioteer
Knocks at my portal, summoning me to go
On the far solitary unknown way
Where all the race of men fare and are lost,
Fleeting and numerous as the autumnal leaves
Before the wind in Lesbos of the Isles;

Though a chill draught of fear may quell my soul
And dim my spirit like a flickering lamp
In the great gusty hall of some old king,
Only one mordant unassuaged regret,
One passionate eternal human grief,
Would wring my heart with bitterness and tears
And set the mask of sorrow on my face.

Not youth, nor early fame, nor pleasant days,
Nor flutes, nor roses, nor the taste of wine,
Nor sweet companions of the idle hour
Who brought me tender joys, nor the glad sound
Of children's voices playing in the dusk;
All these I could forget and bid good-bye
And pass to my oblivion nor repine.

Not the green woods that I so dearly love,
Nor summer hills in their serenity,
Nor the great sea mystic and musical,
Nor drone of insects, nor the call of birds,
Nor soft spring flowers, nor the wintry stars;
To all the lovely earth that was my home
Smiling and valiant I could say farewell.

But not, oh, not to one strong little hand,
To one droll mouth brimming with witty words,
Nor ever to the unevasive eyes
Where dwell the light and sweetness of the world
With all the sapphire sparkle of the sea!
Ah, Destiny, against whose knees we kneel
With prayer at evening, spare me this one woe!

And wondered, as there came the sad
Eternal whisper of the sea,
Which one of all my pale dead loves
Had spent the night with me.

The Ships of Saint John

Where are the ships I used to know,
  That came to port on the Fundy tide
Half a century ago,
  In beauty and stately pride?

In they would come past the beacon light,
  With the sun on gleaming sail and spar,
Folding their wings like birds in flight
  From countries strange and far.

Schooner and brig and barkentine,
  I watched them slow as the sails were furled,
And wondered what cities they must have seen
  On the other side of the world.

Frenchman and Britisher and Dane,
  Yankee, Spaniard and Portugee,
And many a home ship back again
  With her stories of the sea.

Calm and victorious, at rest
From the relentless, rough sea-play,
The wild duck on the river's breast
Was not more sure than they.

The creatures of a passing race,
The dark spruce forests made them strong,
The sea's lore gave them magic grace,
The great winds taught them song.

And God endowed them each with life—
His blessing on the craftsman's skill—
To meet the blind unreasoned strife
And dare the risk of ill.

Not mere insensate wood and paint
Obedient to the helm's command,
But often restive as a saint
Beneath the Heavenly hand.

All the beauty and mystery
Of life were there, adventure bold,
Youth, and the glamour of the sea
And all its sorrows old.

And many a time I saw them go
Out on the flood at morning brave,
As the little tugs had them in tow,
And the sunlight danced on the wave.

There all day long you could hear the sound
Of the caulking iron, the ship's bronze bell,
And the clank of the capstan going round
As the great tides rose and fell.

The sailors' songs, the Captain's shout,
The boatswain's whistle piping shrill,
And the roar as the anchor chain runs out,—
I often hear them still.

I can see them still, the sun on their gear,
The shining streak as the hulls careen,
And the flag at the peak unfurling,—clear
As a picture on a screen.

The fog still hangs on the long tide-rips,
The gulls go wavering to and fro,
But where are all the beautiful ships
I knew so long ago?

Windflower

Between the roadside and the wood,
Between the dawning and the dew,
A tiny flower before the sun,
Ephemeral in time, I grew.

And there upon the trail of spring,
Not death nor love nor any name
Known among men in all their lands
Could blur the wild desire with shame.

But down my dayspan of the year
The feet of straying winds came by;
And all my trembling soul was thrilled
To follow one lost mountain cry.

And then my heart beat once and broke
To hear the sweeping rain forebode
Some ruin in the April world,
Between the woodside and the road.

Tonight can bring no healing now;
The calm of yesternight is gone;
Surely the wind is but the wind,
And I a broken waif thereon.

The Grave Tree

Let me have a scarlet maple
For the grave-tree at my head,
With the quiet sun behind it,
In the years when I am dead.

Let me have it for a signal,
Where the long winds stream and stream,
Clear across the dim blue distance,
Like a horn blown in a dream;

Scarlet when the April vanguard
Bugles up the laggard Spring.
Scarlet when the bannered Autumn,
Marches by unwavering.

I would sleep, but not too soundly,
Where the sunning partridge drums,
Till the crickets hush before him
When the Scarlet Hunter comes.

When the apples burn their reddest
And the corn is in the sheaves,
I shall stir and waken lightly
At a footfall in the leaves.

It will be the Scarlet Hunter
Come to tell me time is done;
On the idle hills forever
There will stand the idle sun.

Then fear not, my friends, to leave me
In the boding autumn vast;
There are many things to think of
When the roving days are past.

Leave me by the scarlet maple,
When the journeying shadows fail,
Waiting till the Scarlet Hunter
Pass upon the endless trail.

ARCHIBALD LAMPMAN

1861-1899

Among the Timothy

Long hours ago, while yet the morn was blithe,
Nor sharp athirst had drunk the beaded dew,
A mower came, and swung his gleaming scythe
Around this stump, and, shearing slowly, drew
Far round among the clover, ripe for hay,
A circle clean and gray;
And here among the scented swathes that gleam,
Mixed with dead daisies, it is sweet to lie
And watch the grass and the few-clouded sky,
Nor think but only dream.

For when the noon was turning, and the heat
Fell down most heavily on field and wood,
I too came hither, borne on restless feet,
Seeking some comfort for an aching mood.
Ah! I was weary of the drifting hours,
The echoing city towers,
The blind gray streets, the jingle of the throng,
Weary of hope that like a shape of stone
Sat near at hand without a smile or moan,
And weary most of song.

And those high moods of mine that sometime made
My heart a heaven, opening like a flower,
A sweeter world where I in wonder strayed,
Begirt with shapes of beauty and the power
Of dreams that moved through that enchanted clime
With changing breaths of rhyme,

Were all gone lifeless now, like those white leaves
   That hang all winter, shivering dead and blind
   Among the sinewy beeches in the wind,
      That vainly calls and grieves.

Ah! I will set no more mine overtaskèd brain
   To barren search and toil that beareth nought,
For ever following with sore-footed pain
   The crossing pathways of unbournèd thought;
   But let it go, as one that hath no skill,
      To take what shape it will,
An ant slow-burrowing in the earthy gloom,
   A spider bathing in the dew at morn,
Or a brown bee in wayward fancy borne
      From hidden bloom to bloom.

Hither and thither o'er the rocking grass
   The little breezes, blithe as they are blind,
Teasing the slender blossoms pass and pass,
   Soft-footed children of the gipsy wind,
   To taste of every purple-fringèd head
      Before the bloom is dead;
And scarcely heed the daisies that, endowed
   With stems so short they cannot see, up-bear
   Their innocent sweet eyes distressed, and stare
      Like children in a crowd.

Not far to fieldward in the central heat,
   Shadowing the clover, a pale poplar stands
With glimmering leaves that, when the wind comes, beat
   Together like innumerable small hands,
   And with the calm, as in vague dreams astray,
      Hang wan and silver-gray;
Like sleepy maenads, who in pale surprise,
   Half-wakened by a prowling beast, have crept
   Out of the hidden covert, where they slept,
      At noon with languid eyes.

The crickets creak, and through the noonday glow,
  That crazy fiddler of the hot mid-year,
The dry cicada plies his wiry bow
  In long-spun cadence, thin and dusty sere;
  From the green grass the small grasshoppers' din
    Spreads soft and silvery thin;
And ever and anon a murmur steals
  Into mine ears of toil that moves alway,
  The crackling rustle of the pitch-forked hay
    And lazy jerk of wheels.

And so I lie and feel the soft hours wane,
  To wind and sun and peaceful sound laid bare,
That aching dim discomfort of the brain
  Fades off unseen, and shadowy-footed care
  Into some hidden corner creeps at last
    To slumber deep and fast;
And gliding on, quite fashioned to forget,
  From dream to dream I bid my spirit pass
  Out into the pale green ever-swaying grass
    To brood, but no more fret.

And hour by hour among all shapes that grow
  Of purple mints and daisies gemmed with gold
In sweet unrest my visions come and go;
  I feel and hear and with quiet eyes behold;
  And hour by hour, the ever-journeying sun,
    In gold and shadow spun,
Into mine eyes and blood, and through the dim
  Green glimmering forest of the grass shines down,
  Till flower and blade, and every cranny brown,
    And I are soaked with him.

Midnight

From where I sit, I see the stars,
  And down the chilly floor
The moon between the frozen bars
  Is glimmering dim and hoar.

Without in many a peakèd mound
  The glinting snowdrifts lie;
There is no voice or living sound;
  The embers slowly die.

Yet some wild thing is in mine ear;
  I hold my breath and hark;
Out of the depth I seem to hear
  A crying in the dark;

No sound of man or wife or child,
  No sound of beast that groans,
Or of the wind that whistles wild,
  Or of the tree that moans:

I know not what it is I hear;
  I bend my head and hark:
I cannot drive it from mine ear,
  That crying in the dark.

The Frogs

I

Breathers of wisdom won without a quest,
  Quaint uncouth dreamers, voices high and strange
  Flutists of lands where beauty hath no change,
And wintry grief is a forgotten guest,
Sweet murmurers of everlasting rest,
  For whom glad days have ever yet to run,
  And moments are as æons, and the sun
But ever sunken half-way toward the west.

Often to me who heard you in your day,
  With close rapt ears, it could not choose but seem

That earth, our mother, searching in what way
 Men's hearts might know her spirit's inmost dream;
  Ever at rest beneath life's change and stir,
  Made you her soul, and bade you pipe for her.

II

In those mute days when spring was in her glee,
 And hope was strong, we knew not why or how,
 And earth, the mother, dreamed with brooding brow,
Musing on life, and what the hours might be,
When love should ripen to maternity,
 Then like high flutes in silvery interchange
 Ye piped with voices still and sweet and strange,
And ever as ye piped, on every tree

The great buds swelled; among the pensive woods
 The spirits of first flowers awoke and flung
From buried faces the close-fitting hoods,
 And listened to your piping till they fell,
 The frail spring-beauty with her perfumed bell,
The wind-flower, and the spotted adder-tongue.

III

All the day long, wherever pools might be
 Among the golden meadows, where the air
 Stood in a dream, as it were moorèd there
For ever in a noon-tide reverie,
Or where the birds made riot of their glee
 In the still woods, and the hot sun shone down,
 Crossed with warm lucent shadows on the brown
Leaf-paven pools, that bubbled dreamily,

Or far away in whispering river meads
 And watery marshes where the brooding noon,
 Full with the wonder of its own sweet boon,
Nestled and slept among the noiseless reeds,
 Ye sat and murmured, motionless as they,
 With eyes that dreamed beyond the night and day.

IV

And when day passed and over heaven's height,
  Thin with the many stars and cool with dew,
  The fingers of the deep hours slowly drew
The wonder of the ever-healing night,
No grief or loneliness or rapt delight
  Or weight of silence ever brought to you
  Slumber or rest; only your voices grew
More high and solemn; slowly with hushed flight

Ye saw the echoing hours go by, long-drawn,
  Nor ever stirred, watching with fathomless eyes,
  And with your countless clear antiphonies
Filling the earth and heaven, even till dawn,
  Last-risen, found you with its first pale gleam,
  Still with soft throats unaltered in your dream.

V

And slowly as we heard you, day by day,
  The stillness of enchanted reveries
  Bound brain and spirit and half-closèd eyes,
In some divine sweet wonder-dream astray;
To us no sorrow or upreared dismay
  Nor any discord came, but evermore
  The voices of mankind, the outer roar,
Grew strange and murmurous, faint and far away.

Morning and noon and midnight exquisitely,
  Rapt with your voices, this alone we knew,
Cities might change and fall, and men might die,
  Secure were we, content to dream with you
    That change and pain are shadows faint and fleet,
    And dreams are real, and life is only sweet.

Heat

From plains that reel to southward, dim,
The road runs by me white and bare;
Up the steep hill it seems to swim
Beyond, and melt into the glare.
Upward half-way, or it may be
Nearer the summit, slowly steals
A hay-cart, moving dustily
With idly clacking wheels.

By his cart's side the wagoner
Is slouching slowly at his ease,
Half-hidden in the windless blur
Of white dust puffing to his knees.
This wagon on the height above,
From sky to sky on either hand,
Is the sole thing that seems to move
In all the heat-held land.

Beyond me in the fields the sun
Soaks in the grass and hath his will;
I count the marguerites one by one;
Even the buttercups are still.
On the brook yonder not a breath
Disturbs the spider or the midge.
The water-bugs draw close beneath
The cool gloom of the bridge.

Where the far elm-tree shadows flood
Dark patches in the burning grass,
The cows, each with her peaceful cud,
Lie waiting for the heat to pass.
From somewhere on the slope near by
Into the pale depth of the noon
A wandering thrush slides leisurely
His thin revolving tune.

In intervals of dreams I hear
  The cricket from the droughty ground;
The grasshoppers spin into mine ear
  A small innumerable sound.
I lift mine eyes sometimes to gaze:
  The burning sky-line blinds my sight:
The woods far off are blue with haze:
  The hills are drenched in light.

And yet to me not this or that
  Is always sharp or always sweet;
In the sloped shadow of my hat
  I lean at rest, and drain the heat;
Nay more, I think some blessèd power
  Hath brought me wandering idly here:
In the full furnace of this hour
  My thoughts grow keen and clear.

In November

With loitering step and quiet eye,
Beneath the low November sky,
I wandered in the woods, and found
A clearing, where the broken ground
Was scattered with black stumps and briers,
And the old wreck of forest fires.
It was a bleak and sandy spot,
And, all about, the vacant plot,
Was peopled and inhabited
By scores of mulleins long since dead.
A silent and forsaken brood
In that mute opening of the wood,
So shrivelled and so thin they were,
So gray, so haggard, and austere,
Not plants at all they seemed to me,
But rather some spare company
Of hermit folk, who long ago,

Wandering in bodies to and fro,
Had chanced upon this lonely way,
And rested thus, till death one day
Surprised them at their compline prayer,
And left them standing lifeless there.

There was no sound about the wood
Save the wind's secret stir. I stood
Among the mullein-stalks as still
As if myself had grown to be
One of their sombre company,
A body without wish or will.
And as I stood, quite suddenly,
Down from a furrow in the sky
The sun shone out a little space
Across that silent sober place,
Over the sand heaps and brown sod,
The mulleins and dead goldenrod,
And passed beyond the thickets gray,
And lit the fallen leaves that lay,
Level and deep within the wood,
A rustling yellow multitude.

And all around me the thin light,
So sere, so melancholy bright,
Fell like the half-reflected gleam
Or shadow of some former dream;
A moment's golden reverie
Poured out on every plant and tree
A semblance of weird joy, or less,
A sort of spectral happiness;
And I, too, standing idly there,
With muffled hands in the chill air,
Felt the warm glow about my feet,
And shuddering betwixt cold and heat,
Drew my thoughts closer, like a cloak,
While something in my blood awoke,
A nameless and unnatural cheer,
A pleasure secret and austere.

The Modern Politician

What manner of soul is his to whom high truth
Is but the plaything of a feverish hour,
A dangling ladder to the ghost of power!
Gone are the grandeurs of the world's iron youth,
When kings were mighty, being made by swords.
Now comes the transit age, the age of brass,
When clowns into the vacant empires pass,
Blinding the multitude with specious words.
To them faith, kinship, truth and verity,
Man's sacred rights and very holiest thing,
Are but the counters at a desperate play,
Flippant and reckless what the end may be,
So that they glitter, each his little day,
The little mimic of a vanished king.

On the Companionship with Nature

Let us be much with Nature; not as they
That labour without seeing, that employ
Her unloved forces, blindly without joy;
Nor those whose hands and crude delights obey
The old brute passion to hunt down and slay;
But rather as children of one common birth,
Discerning in each natural fruit of earth
Kinship and bond with this diviner clay.
Let us be with her wholly at all hours,
With the fond lover's zest, who is content
If his ear hears, and if his eye but sees;
So shall we grow like her in mould and bent,
Our bodies stately as her blessèd trees,
Our thoughts as sweet and sumptuous as her flowers.

The City of the End of Things

Beside the pounding cataracts
Of midnight streams unknown to us
'Tis builded in the leafless tracts
And valleys huge of Tartarus.
Lurid and lofty and vast it seems;
It hath no rounded name that rings,
But I have heard it called in dreams
The City of the End of Things.

Its roofs and iron towers have grown
None knoweth how high within the night,
But in its murky streets far down
A flaming terrible and bright
Shakes all the stalking shadows there,
Across the walls, across the floors,
And shifts upon the upper air
From out a thousand furnace doors;
And all the while an awful sound
Keeps roaring on continually,
And crashes in the ceaseless round
Of a gigantic harmony.
Through its grim depths re-echoing
And all its weary height of walls,
With measured roar and iron ring,
The inhuman music lifts and falls.
Where no thing rests and no man is,
And only fire and night hold sway;
The beat, the thunder and the hiss
Cease not, and change not, night nor day.

And moving at unheard commands,
The abysses and vast fires between,
Flit figures that with clanking hands
Obey a hideous routine;
They are not flesh, they are not bone,
They see not with the human eye,

And from their iron lips is blown
A dreadful and monotonous cry;
And whoso of our mortal race
Should find that city unaware,
Lean Death would smite him face to face,
And blanch him with its venomed air:
Or caught by the terrific spell,
Each thread of memory snapt and cut,
His soul would shrivel and its shell
Go rattling like an empty nut.

It was not always so, but once,
In days that no man thinks upon,
Fair voices echoed from its stones,
The light above it leaped and shone:
Once there were multitudes of men,
That built that city in their pride,
Until its might was made, and then
They withered age by age and died.
But now of that prodigious race,
Three only in an iron tower,
Set like carved idols face to face,
Remain the masters of its power;
And at the city gate a fourth,
Gigantic and with dreadful eyes,
Sits looking toward the lightless north,
Beyond the reach of memories;
Fast rooted to the lurid floor,
A bulk that never moves a jot,
In his pale body dwells no more,
Or mind, or soul,—an idiot!

But sometime in the end those three
Shall perish and their hands be still,
And with the master's touch shall flee
Their incommunicable skill.
A stillness absolute as death
Along the slacking wheels shall lie,
And, flagging at a single breath,

The fires shall moulder out and die.
The roar shall vanish at its height,
And over that tremendous town
The silence of eternal night
Shall gather close and settle down.
All its grim grandeur, tower and hall,
Shall be abandoned utterly,
And into rust and dust shall fall
From century to century;
Nor ever living thing shall grow,
Or trunk of tree, or blade of grass;
No drop shall fall, no wind shall blow,
Nor sound of any foot shall pass:
Alone of its accursèd state,
One thing the hand of Time shall spare,
For the grim Idiot at the gate
Is deathless and eternal there.

The Largest Life

I

I lie upon my bed and hear and see.
The moon is rising through the glistening trees;
And momently a great and sombre breeze,
With a vast voice returning fitfully,
Comes like a deep-toned grief, and stirs in me,
Somehow, by some inexplicable art,
A sense of my soul's strangeness, and its part
In the dark march of human destiny.
What am I, then, and what are they that pass
Yonder, and love and laugh, and mourn and weep?
What shall they know of me, or I, alas!
Of them? Little. At times, as if from sleep,
We waken to this yearning passionate mood,
And tremble at our spiritual solitude.

II

Nay, never once to feel we are alone,
While the great human heart around us lies:
To make the smile on other lips our own,
To live upon the light in others' eyes:
To breathe without a doubt the limpid air
Of that most perfect love that knows no pain:
To say—I love you— only, and not care
Whether the love come back to us again,
Divinest self-forgetfulness, at first
A task, and then a tonic, then a need;
To greet with open hands the best and worst,
And only for another's wound to bleed:
This is to see the beauty that God meant,
Wrapped round with life, ineffably content.

III

There is a beauty at the goal of life,
A beauty growing since the world began,
Through every age and race, through lapse and strife
Till the great human soul complete her span.
Beneath the waves of storm that lash and burn,
The currents of blind passion that appall,
To listen and keep watch till we discern
The tide of sovereign truth that guides it all;
So to address our spirits to the height,
And so attune them to the valiant whole,
That the great light be clearer for our light,
And the great soul the stronger for our soul:
To have done this is to have lived, though fame
Remember us with no familiar name.

D. C. SCOTT

1862-1947

At the Cedars

TO W. W. C.

You had two girls—Baptiste—
One is Virginie—
Hold hard—Baptiste!
Listen to me.

The whole drive was jammed
In that bend at the Cedars,
The rapids were dammed
With the logs tight rammed
And crammed; you might know
The Devil had clinched them below.

We worked three days—not a budge,
'She's as tight as a wedge, on the ledge,'
Says our foreman;
'Mon Dieu! boys, look here,
We must get this thing clear.'

He cursed at the men
And we went for it then;
With our cant-dogs arow,
We just gave he-yo-ho;
When she gave a big shove
From above.

The gang yelled and tore
For the shore,
The logs gave a grind
Like a wolf's jaws behind,
And as quick as a flash,
With a shove and a crash,
They were down in a mash,
But I and ten more,
All but Isaac Dufour,
Were ashore.

He leaped on a log in the front of the rush,
And shot out from the bind
While the jam roared behind;
As he floated along
He balanced his pole
And tossed us a song.
But just as we cheered,
Up darted a log from the bottom,
Leaped thirty feet square and fair,
And came down on his own.

He went up like a block
With the shock,
And when he was there
In the air,
Kissed his hand
To the land;
When he dropped
My heart stopped,
For the first logs had caught him
And crushed him;
When he rose in his place
There was blood on his face.

There were some girls, Baptiste,
Picking berries on the hillside,
Where the river curls, Baptiste,
You know—on the still side
One was down by the water,
She saw Isaac
Fall back.

She did not scream, Baptiste,
She launched her canoe;
It did seem, Baptiste,
That she wanted to die too,
For before you could think
The birch cracked like a shell
In that rush of hell,
And I saw them both sink—

Baptiste!—
He had two girls,
One is Virginie,
What God calls the other
Is not known to me.

The Onondaga Madonna

She stands full-throated and with careless pose,
This woman of a weird and waning race,
The tragic savage lurking in her face,
Where all her pagan passion burns and glows;
Her blood is mingled with her ancient foes,
And thrills with war and wildness in her veins;
Her rebel lips are dabbled with the stains
Of feuds and forays and her father's woes.

And closer in the shawl about her breast,
The latest promise of her nation's doom,
Paler than she her baby clings and lies,
The primal warrior gleaming from his eyes;
He sulks, and burdened with his infant gloom,
He draws his heavy brows and will not rest.

The Piper of Arll

There was in Arll a little cove
Where the salt wind came cool and free:
A foamy beach that one would love,
If he were longing for the sea.

A brook hung sparkling on the hill,
The hill swept far to ring the bay;
The bay was faithful, wild or still,
To the heart of the ocean far away.

There were three pines above the comb
That, when the sun flared and went down,
Grew like three warriors reaving home
The plunder of a burning town.

A piper lived within the grove,
Tending the pasture of his sheep;
His heart was swayed with faithful love,
From the springs of God's ocean clear and deep.

And there a ship one evening stood,
Where ship had never stood before;
A pennon bickered red as blood,
An angel glimmered at the prore.

About the coming on of dew,
The sails burned rosy, and the spars
Were gold, and all the tackle grew
Alive with ruby-hearted stars.

The piper heard an outland tongue,
With music in the cadenced fall;
And when the fairy lights were hung,
The sailors gathered one and all,

And leaning on the gunwales dark,
Crusted with shells and dashed with foam,
With all the dreaming hills to hark,
They sang their longing songs of home.

When the sweet airs had fled away,
The piper, with a gentle breath,
Moulded a tranquil melody
Of lonely love and longed-for death.

When the fair sound began to lull,
From out the fireflies and the dew,
A silence held the shadowy hull,
Until the eerie tune was through.

Then from the dark and dreamy deck
An alien song began to thrill;
It mingled with the drumming beck,
And stirred the braird upon the hill.

Beneath the stars each sent to each
A message tender, till at last
The piper slept upon the beach,
The sailors slumbered round the mast.

Still as a dream till nearly dawn,
The ship was bosomed on the tide;
The streamlet, murmuring on and on,
Bore the sweet water to her side.

Then shaking out her lawny sails,
Forth on the misty sea she crept;
She left the dawning of the dales,
Yet in his cloak the piper slept.

And when he woke he saw the ship,
Limned black against the crimson sun;
Then from the disc he saw her slip,
A wraith of shadow—she was gone.

He threw his mantle on the beach,
He went apart like one distraught,
His lips were moved—his desperate speech
Stormed his inviolable thought.

He broke his human-throated reed,
And threw it in the idle rill;
But when his passion had its mead,
He found it in the eddy still.

He mended well the patient flue,
Again he tried its varied stops;
The closures answered right and true,
And starting out in piercing drops,

A melody began to drip
That mingled with a ghostly thrill
The vision-spirit of the ship,
The secret of his broken will.

Beneath the pines he piped and swayed,
Master of passion and of power;
He was his soul and what he played,
Immortal for a happy hour.

He, singing into nature's heart,
Guiding his will by the world's will,
With deep, unconscious, childlike art
Had sung his soul out and was still.

And then at evening came the bark
That stirred his dreaming heart's desire;
It burned slow lights along the dark
That died in glooms of crimson fire.

The sailors launched a sombre boat,
And bent with music at the oars;
The rhythm throbbing every throat,
And lapsing round the liquid shores,

Was that true tune the piper sent,
Unto the wave-worn mariners,
When with the beck and ripple blent
He heard that outland song of theirs.

Silent they rowed him, dip and drip,
The oars beat out an exequy,
They laid him down within the ship,
They loosed a rocket to the sky.

It broke in many a crimson sphere
That grew to gold and floated far,
And left the sudden shore-line clear,
With one slow-changing, drifting star.

Then out they shook the magic sails,
That charmed the wind in other seas,
From where the west line pearls and pales,
They waited for a ruffling breeze.

But in the world there was no stir,
The cordage slacked with never a creak,
They heard the flame begin to purr
Within the lantern at the peak.

They could not cry, they could not move,
They felt the lure from the charmed sea;
They could not think of home or love
Or any pleasant land to be.

They felt the vessel dip and trim,
And settle down from list to list;
They saw the sea-plain heave and swim
As gently as a rising mist.

And down so slowly, down and down,
Rivet by rivet, plank by plank;
A little flood of ocean flown
Across the deck, she sank and sank.

From knee to breast the water wore,
It crept and crept; ere they were ware
Gone was the angel at the prore,
They felt the water float their hair.

They saw the salt plain spark and shine,
They threw their faces to the sky;
Beneath a deepening film of brine
They saw the star-flash blur and die.

She sank and sank by yard and mast,
Sank down the shimmering gradual dark;
A little drooping pennon last
Showed like the black fin of a shark.

And down she sank till, keeled in sand,
She rested safely balanced true,
With all her upward gazing band,
The piper and the dreaming crew.

And there, unmarked of any chart,
In unrecorded deeps they lie,
Empearled within the purple heart
Of the great sea for aye and aye.

Their eyes are ruby in the green
Long shaft of sun that spreads and rays,
And upward with a wizard sheen
A fan of sea-light leaps and plays.

Tendrils of or and azure creep,
And globes of amber light are rolled,
And in the gloaming of the deep
Their eyes are starry pits of gold.

And sometimes in the liquid night
The hull is changed, a solid gem,
That glows with a soft stony light,
The lost prince of a diadem.

And at the keel a vine is quick,
That spreads its bines and works and weaves
O'er all the timbers veining thick
A plenitude of silver leaves.

The Forsaken

I

Once in the winter,
Out on a lake
In the heart of the north-land,
Far from the Fort
And far from the hunters,
A Chippewa woman
With her sick baby,
Crouched in the last hours
Of a great storm.
Frozen and hungry,
She fished through the ice
With a line of the twisted
Bark of the cedar,
And a rabbit-bone hook
Polished and barbed;
Fished with the bare hook
All through the wild day,
Fished and caught nothing;
While the young chieftain
Tugged at her breasts,
Or slept in the lacings
Of the warm *tikanagan*.

All the lake-surface
Streamed with the hissing
Of millions of iceflakes,
Hurled by the wind;
Behind her the round
Of a lonely island
Roared like a fire
With the voice of the storm
In the deeps of the cedars.
Valiant, unshaken,
She took of her own flesh,
Baited the fish-hook,
Drew in a gray-trout,
Drew in his fellow,
Heaped them beside her,
Dead in the snow.
Valiant, unshaken,
She faced the long distance,
Wolf-haunted and lonely,
Sure of her goal
And the life of her dear one;
Tramped for two days,
On the third in the morning,
Saw the strong bulk
Of the Fort by the river,
Saw the wood-smoke
Hang soft in the spruces,
Heard the keen yelp
Of the ravenous huskies
Fighting for whitefish:
Then she had rest.

II

Years and years after,
When she was old and withered,
When her son was an old man
And his children filled with vigour,
They came in their northern tour on the verge of winter,
To an island in a lonely lake.

There one night they camped, and on the morrow
Gathered their kettles and birch-bark
Their rabbit-skin robes and their mink-traps,
Launched their canoes and slunk away through the islands,
Left her alone forever,
Without a word of farewell,
Because she was old and useless,
Like a paddle broken and warped,
Or a pole that was splintered.
Then, without a sigh,
Valiant, unshaken,
She smoothed her dark locks under her kerchief,
Composed her shawl in state,
Then folded her hands ridged with sinews and corded with
veins,
Folded them across her breasts spent with the nourishing of
children,
Gazed at the sky past the tops of the cedars,
Saw two spangled nights arise out of the twilight,
Saw two days go by filled with the tranquil sunshine,
Saw, without pain, or dread, or even a moment of longing:
Then on the third great night there came thronging and
thronging
Millions of snowflakes out of a windless cloud;
They covered her close with a beautiful crystal shroud,
Covered her deep and silent.
But in the frost of the dawn,
Up from the life below,
Rose a column of breath
Through a tiny cleft in the snow,
Fragile, delicately drawn,
Wavering with its own weakness,
In the wilderness a sign of the spirit,
Persisting still in the sight of the sun
Till day was done.
Then all light was gathered up by the hand of God and hid in
His breast,
Then there was born a silence deeper than silence,
Then she had rest.

Night Hymns on Lake Nipigon

Here in the midnight, where the dark mainland and island
Shadows mingle in shadow deeper, profounder,
Sing we the hymns of the churches, while the dead water
        Whispers before us.

Thunder is travelling slow on the path of the lightning;
One after one the stars and the beaming planets
Look serene in the lake from the edge of the storm-cloud,
        Then have they vanished.

While our canoe, that floats dumb in the bursting thunder,
Gathers her voice in the quiet and thrills and whispers,
Presses her prow in the star-gleam, and all her ripple
        Lapses in blackness.

Sing we the sacred ancient hymns of the churches,
Chanted first in old-world nooks of the desert,
While in the wild, pellucid Nipigon reaches
        Hunted the savage.

Now have the ages met in the Northern midnight,
And on the lonely, loon-haunted Nipigon reaches
Rises the hymn of triumph and courage and comfort,
        Adeste Fideles.

Tones that were fashioned when the faith brooded in darkness,
Joined with sonorous vowels in the noble Latin,
Now are married with the long-drawn Ojibeway,
        Uncouth and mournful.

Soft with the silver drip of the regular paddles
Falling in rhythm, timed with the liquid, plangent
Sounds from the blades where the whirlpools break and
    are carried
        Down into darkness;

Each long cadence, flying like a dove from her shelter
Deep in the shadow, wheels for a throbbing moment,
Poises in utterance, returning in circles of silver
To nest in the silence.

All wild nature stirs with the infinite, tender
Plaint of a bygone age whose soul is eternal,
Bound in the lonely phrases that thrill and falter
Back into quiet.

Back they falter as the deep storm overtakes them,
Whelms them in splendid hollows of booming thunder,
Wraps them in rain, that, sweeping, breaks and onrushes
Ringing like cymbals.

On the Way to the Mission

They dogged him all one afternoon,
Through the bright snow,
Two whitemen servants of greed;
He knew that they were there,
But he turned not his head;
He was an Indian trapper;
He planted his snow-shoes firmly,
He dragged the long toboggan
Without rest.

The three figures drifted
Like shadows in the mind of a seer;
The snow-shoes were whisperers
On the threshold of awe;
The toboggan made the sound of wings,
A wood-pigeon sloping to her nest.

The Indian's face was calm.
He strode with the sorrow of fore-knowledge,
But his eyes were jewels of content
Set in circles of peace.

They would have shot him;
But momently in the deep forest,
They saw something flit by his side:
Their hearts stopped with fear.
Then the moon rose.
They would have left him to the spirit,
But they saw the long toboggan
Rounded well with furs,
With many a silver fox-skin,
With the pelts of mink and of otter.
They were the servants of greed;
When the moon grew brighter
And the spruces were dark with sleep,
They shot him.
When he fell on a shield of moonlight
One of his arms clung to his burden;
The snow was not melted:
The spirit passed away.

Then the servants of greed
Tore off the cover to count their gains;
They shuddered away into the shadows,
Hearing each the loud heart of the other.
Silence was born.

There in the tender moonlight,
As sweet as they were in life,
Glimmered the ivory features,
Of the Indian's wife.

In the manner of Montagnais women
Her hair was rolled with braid;
Under her waxen fingers
A crucifix was laid.

He was drawing her down to the Mission,
To bury her there in spring,
When the bloodroot comes and the windflower
To silver everything.

But as a gift of plunder
   Side by side were they laid,
The moon went on to her setting
   And covered them with shade.

At Gull Lake: August, 1810

Gull Lake set in the rolling prairie—
Still there are reeds on the shore,
As of old the poplars shimmer
As summer passes;
Winter freezes the shallow lake to the core;
Storm passes,
Heat parches the sedges and grasses,
Night comes with moon-glimmer,
Dawn with the morning-star;
All proceeds in the flow of Time
As a hundred years ago.
Then two camps were pitched on the shore,
The clustered teepees
Of Tabashaw Chief of the Saulteaux.
And on a knoll tufted with poplars
Two gray tents of a trader—
Nairne of the Orkneys.
Before his tents under the shade of the poplars
Sat Keejigo, third of the wives
Of Tabashaw Chief of the Saulteaux;
Clad in the skins of antelopes
Broidered with porcupine quills
Coloured with vivid dyes,
Vermilion here and there
In the roots of her hair,
A half-moon of powder-blue
On her brow, her cheeks
Scored with light ochre streaks.
Keejigo daughter of Launay
The Normandy hunter

And Oshawan of the Saulteaux,
Troubled by fugitive visions
In the smoke of the camp-fires,
In the close dark of the teepee,
Flutterings of colour
Along the flow of the prairies,
Spangles of flower tints
Caught in the wonder of dawn,
Dreams of sounds unheard—
The echoes of echo,
Star she was named for
Keejigo, star of the morning,
Voices of storm—
Wind-rush and lightning,—
The beauty of terror;
The twilight moon
Coloured like a prairie lily,
The round moon of pure snow,
The beauty of peace;
Premonitions of love and of beauty
Vague as shadows cast by a shadow.
Now she had found her hero,
And offered her body and spirit
With abject unreasoning passion,
As Earth abandons herself
To the sun and the thrust of the lightning.
Quiet were all the leaves of the poplars,
Breathless the air under their shadow,
As Keejigo spoke of these things to her heart
In the beautiful speech of the Saulteaux.

The flower lives on the prairie,
The wind in the sky,
I am here my beloved;
The wind and the flower.

The crane hides in the sand-hills,
Where does the wolverine hide?
I am here my beloved,
Heart's-blood on the feathers
The foot caught in the trap.

Take the flower in your hand,
The wind in your nostrils;
I am here my beloved;
Release the captive
Heal the wound under the feathers.

A storm-cloud was marching
Vast on the prairie,
Scored with livid ropes of hail,
Quick with nervous vines of lightning—
Twice had Nairne turned her away
Afraid of the venom of Tabashaw,
Twice had the Chief fired at his tents
And now when two bullets
Whistled above the encampment
He yelled "Drive this bitch to her master."
Keejigo went down a path by the lake;
Thick at the tangled edges,
The reeds and the sedges
Were gray as ashes
Against the death-black water;
The lightning scored with double flashes
The dark lake-mirror and loud
Came the instant thunder.
Her lips still moved to the words of her music,
"Release the captive,
Heal the wound under the feathers."

At the top of the bank
The old wives caught her and cast her down
Where Tabashaw crouched by his camp-fire.
He snatched a live brand from the embers,

Seared her cheeks,
Blinded her eyes,
Destroyed her beauty with fire,
Screaming, "Take that face to your lover."
Keejigo held her face to the fury
And made no sound.
The old wives dragged her away
And threw her over the bank
Like a dead dog.

Then burst the storm—
The Indians' screams and the howls of the dogs
Lost in the crash of hail
That smashed the sedges and reeds,
Stripped the poplars of leaves,
Tore and blazed onwards,
Wasting itself with riot and tumult—
Supreme in the beauty of terror.

The setting sun struck the retreating cloud
With a rainbow, not an arc but a column
Built with the glory of seven metals;
Beyond in the purple deeps of the vortex
Fell the quivering vines of the lightning.
The wind withdrew the veil from the shrine of the moon,
She rose changing her dusky shade for the glow
Of the prairie lily, till free of all blemish of colour
She came to her zenith without a cloud or a star,
A lovely perfection, snow-pure in the heaven of midnight.
After the beauty of terror the beauty of peace.

But Keejigo came no more to the camps of her people;
Only the midnight moon knew where she felt her way,
Only the leaves of autumn, the snows of winter
Knew where she lay.

E. J. PRATT

1883-1964

Newfoundland

Here the tides flow,
And here they ebb;
Not with that dull, unsinewed tread of waters
Held under bonds to move
Around unpeopled shores—
Moon-driven through a timeless circuit
Of invasion and retreat;
But with a lusty stroke of life
Pounding at stubborn gates,
That they might run
Within the sluices of men's hearts,
Leap under throb of pulse and nerve,
And teach the sea's strong voice
To learn the harmonies of new floods,
The peal of cataract,
And the soft wash of currents
Against resilient banks,
Or the broken rhythms from old chords
Along dark passages
That once were pathways of authentic fires.

Red is the sea-kelp on the beach,
Red as the heart's blood,
Nor is there power in tide or sun
To bleach its stain.
It lies there piled thick
Above the gulch-line.

It is rooted in the joints of rocks,
It is tangled around a spar,
It covers a broken rudder,
It is red as the heart's blood,
And salt as tears.

Here the winds blow,
And here they die,
Not with that wild, exotic rage
That vainly sweeps untrodden shores,
But with familiar breath
Holding a partnership with life,
Resonant with the hopes of spring,
Pungent with the airs of harvest.

They call with the silver fifes of the sea,
They breathe with the lungs of men,
They are one with the tides of the sea,
They are one with the tides of the heart,
They blow with the rising octaves of dawn,
They die with the largo of dusk,
Their hands are full to the overflow,
In their right is the bread of life,
In their left are the waters of death.

Scattered on boom
And rudder and weed
Are tangles of shells;
Some with backs of crusted bronze,
And faces of porcelain blue,
Some crushed by the beach stones
To chips of jade;
And some are spiral-cleft
Spreading their tracery on the sand
In the rich veining of an agate's heart;
And others remain unscarred,
To babble of the passing of the winds.

Here the crags
Meet with winds and tides—
Not with that blind interchange
Of blow for blow
That spills the thunder of insentient seas;
But with the mind that reads assault
In crouch and leap and the quick stealth,
Stiffening the muscles of the waves.
Here they flank the harbours,
Keeping watch
On thresholds, altars and the fires of home,
Or, like mastiffs,
Over-zealous,
Guard too well.

Tide and wind and crag,
Sea-weed and sea-shell
And broken rudder—
And the story is told
Of human veins and pulses,
Of eternal pathways of fire,
Of dreams that survive the night,
Of doors held ajar in storms.

The Shark

He seemed to know the harbour,
So leisurely he swam;
His fin,
Like a piece of sheet-iron,
Three-cornered,
And with knife-edge,
Stirred not a bubble
As it moved
With its base-line on the water.

His body was tubular
And tapered
And smoke-blue,
And as he passed the wharf
He turned,
And snapped at a flat-fish
That was dead and floating.
And I saw the flash of a white throat,
And a double row of white teeth,
And eyes of metallic grey,
Hard and narrow and slit.

Then out of the harbour,
With that three-cornered fin
Shearing without a bubble the water
Lithely,
Leisurely,
He swam—
That strange fish,
Tubular, tapered, smoke-blue,
Part vulture, part wolf,
Part neither—for his blood was cold.

The Lee-Shore

Her heart cried out,—"Come home, come home,"
When the storm beat in at the door,
When the window showed a spatter of foam,
And her ear rang with the roar
Of the reef; and she called again, "Come home,"
To the ship in reach of the shore.

"But not to-night," flashed the signal light
From the Cape that guarded the bay,
"No, not to-night," rang the foam where the white
Hard edge of the breakers lay;
"Keep away from the crash of the storm at its height,
Keep away from the land, keep away."

"Come home," her heart cried out again,
"For the edge of the reef is white."
But she pressed her face to the window-pane,
And read the flash of the signal light;
Then her voice called out when her heart was slain,
"Keep away, my love, to-night."

Still Life

To the poets who have fled
To pools where little breezes dusk and shiver,
Who need still life to deliver
Their souls of their songs,
We offer roses blanched of red
In the Orient gardens,
With April lilies to limn
On the Japanese urns—
And time, be it said,
For a casual hymn
To be sung for the hundred thousand dead
In the mud of the Yellow River.

And if your metric paragraphs
Incline to Western epitaphs,
Be pleased to return to a plain
Where a million lie
Under a proletarian sky,
Waiting to trouble
Your lines on the scorched Ukrainian stubble.
On the veined marble of their snows
Indite a score to tether
The flight of your strain;
Or should you need a rougher grain
That will never corrode with weather,
Let us propose
A stone west of the bend where the Volga flows
To lick her cubs on the Stalingrad rubble.

Hasten, for time may pass you by,
Mildew the reed and rust the lyre;
Look—that Tunisian glow will die
As died the Carthaginian fire!
Today the autumn tints are on
The trampled grass at Marathon.
Here are the tales to be retold,
Here are the songs to be resung.
Go, find a cadence for that field-grey mould
Outcropping on the Parthenon.
Invoke, in other than the Latin tongue,
A Mediterranean Muse
To leave her pastoral loves—
The murmurs of her soft Theocritean fold,
Mimosa, oleander,
Dovecotes and olive groves,
And court the shadows where the night bedews
A Roman mausoleum hung
Upon the tides from Candia to Syracuse.

Missing: Believed Dead: Returned

Steady, the heart!
Can you not see
You must not break
Incredulously?

The dead has come back,
He is here at the sill;
Try to believe
The miracle.

Give me more breath,
Or I may not withstand
The thrill of his voice
And the clasp of his hand.

Be quiet, my heart,
Can you not see
In the beat of my pulse
Mortality?

Come Away, Death

Willy-nilly, he comes or goes, with the clown's logic,
Comic in epitaph, tragic in epithalamium,
And unseduced by any mused rhyme.
However blow the winds over the pollen,
Whatever the course of the garden variables,
He remains the constant,
Ever flowering from the poppy seeds.

There was a time he came in formal dress,
Announced by Silence tapping at the panels
In deep apology.
A touch of chivalry in his approach,
He offered sacramental wine,
And with acanthus leaf
And petals of the hyacinth
He took the fever from the temples
And closed the eyelids,
Then led the way to his cool longitudes
In the dignity of the candles.

His mediaeval grace is gone—
Gone with the flame of the capitals
And the leisured turn of the thumb
Leafing the manuscripts,
Gone with the marbles
And the Venetian mosaics,
With the bend of the knee
Before the rose-strewn feet of the Virgin.
The *paternosters* of his priests,
Committing clay to clay,
Have rattled in their throats
Under the gride of his traction tread.

One night we heard his footfall—one September night—
In the outskirts of a village near the sea.
There was a moment when the storm
Delayed its fist, when the surf fell
Like velvet on the rocks—a moment only;
The strangest lull we ever knew!
A sudden truce among the oaks
Released their fratricidal arms;
The poplars straightened to attention
As the winds stopped to listen
To the sound of a motor drone—
And then the drone was still.
We heard the tick-tock on the shelf,
And the leak of valves in our hearts.
A calm condensed and lidded
As at the core of a cyclone ended breathing
This was the monologue of Silence
Grave and unequivocal.

What followed was a bolt
Outside the range and target of the thunder,
And human speech curved back upon itself
Through Druid runways and the Piltdown scarps,
Beyond the stammers of the Java caves,
To find its origins in hieroglyphs
On mouths and eyes and cheeks
Etched by a foreign stylus never used
On the outmoded page of the Apocalypse.

The Dying Eagle

A light had gone out from his vanquished eyes;
His head was cupped within the hunch of his shoulders;
His feathers were dull and bedraggled; the tips
Of his wings sprawled down to the edge of his tail.

He was old, yet it was not his age
Which made him roost on the crags
Like a rain-drenched raven
On the branch of an oak in November.
Nor was it the night, for there was an hour
To go before sunset. An iron had entered
His soul which bereft him of pride and of realm,
Had struck him today; for up to noon
That crag had been his throne.
Space was his empire, bounded only
By forest and sky and the flowing horizons.
He had outfought, outlived all his rivals,
And the eagles that now were poised over glaciers
Or charting the coastal outlines of clouds
Were his by descent: they had been tumbled
Out of their rocky nests by his mate,
In the first trial of their fledgeling spins.

Only this morning the eyes of the monarch
Were held in arrest by a silver flash
Shining between two peaks of the ranges—
A sight which galvanized his back,
Bristled the feathers on his neck,
And shot little runnels of dust where his talons
Dug recesses in the granite.
Partridge? Heron? Falcon? Eagle?
Game or foe? He would reconnoitre.

Catapulting from the ledge,
He flew at first with rapid beat,
Level, direct; then with his grasp
Of spiral strategy in fight,
He climbed the orbit
With swift and easy undulations,
And reached position where he might
Survey the bird—for bird it was;
But such a bird as never flew
Between the heavens and the earth
Since pterodactyls, long before

The birth of condors, learned to kill
And drag their carrion up the Andes.

The eagle stared at the invader,
Marked the strange bat-like shadow moving
In leagues over the roofs of the world,
Across the passes and moraines,
Darkening the vitriol blue of the mountain lakes.
Was it a flying dragon? Head,
Body and wings, a tail fan-spread
And taut like his own before the strike;
And there in front two whirling eyes
That took unshuttered
The full blaze of the meridian.
The eagle never yet had known
A rival that he would not grapple,

But something in this fellow's length
Of back, his plated glistening shoulders,
Had given him pause. And did that thunder
Somewhere in his throat not argue
Lightning in his claws? And then
The speed—was it not double his own?
But what disturbed him most, angered
And disgraced him was the unconcern
With which this supercilious bird
Cut through the aquiline dominion,
Snubbing the ancient suzerain
With extra-territorial insolence,
And disappeared.

So evening found him on the crags again,
This time with sloven shoulders
And nerveless claws.
Dusk had outridden the sunset by an hour
To haunt his unhorizoned eyes.
And soon his flock flushed with the chase
Would be returning, threading their glorious curves
Up through the crimson archipelagoes

Only to find him there—
Deaf to the mighty symphony of wings,
And brooding
Over the lost empire of the peaks.

The Truant

"What have you there?" the great Panjandrum
 said
To the Master of the Revels who had led
A bucking truant with a stiff backbone
Close to the foot of the Almighty's throne.

"Right Reverend, most adored,
And forcibly acknowledged Lord
By the keen logic of your two-edged sword!
This creature has presumed to classify
Himself—a biped, rational, six feet high
And two feet wide; weighs fourteen stone;
Is guilty of a multitude of sins.
He has abjured his choric origins,
And like an undomesticated slattern,
Walks with tangential step unknown
Within the weave of the atomic pattern.
He has developed concepts, grins
Obscenely at your Royal bulletins,
Possesses what he calls a will
Which challenges your power to kill."
"What is his pedigree?"

"The base is guaranteed, your Majesty—
Calcium, carbon, phosphorus, vapour
And other fundamentals spun
From the umbilicus of the sun,
And yet he says he will not caper
Around your throne, nor toe the rules
For the ballet of the fiery molecules."

"His concepts and denials—scrap them, burn them—
To the chemists with them promptly."
"Sire,
The stuff is not amenable to fire.
Nothing but their own kind can overturn them.
The chemists have sent back the same old story—
'With our extreme gelatinous apology,
We beg to inform your Imperial Majesty,
Unto whom be dominion and power and glory,
There still remains that strange precipitate
Which has the quality to resist
Our oldest and most trusted catalyst.
It is a substance we cannot cremate
By temperatures known to our Laboratory.' "

And the great Panjandrum's face grew dark—
"I'll put those chemists to their annual purge,
And I myself shall be the thaumaturge
To find the nature of this fellow's spark.
Come, bring him nearer by yon halter rope:
I'll analyse him with the cosmoscope."

Pulled forward with his neck awry,
The little fellow six feet short,
Aware he was about to die,
Committed grave contempt of court
By answering with a flinchless stare
The Awful Presence seated there.

The ALL HIGH swore until his face was black.
He called him a coprophagite,
A genus *homo*, egomaniac,
Third cousin to the family of worms,
A sporozoan from the ooze of night,
Spawn of a spavined troglodyte:
He swore by all the catalogue of terms
Known since the slang of carboniferous Time.
He said that he could trace him back
To pollywogs and earwigs in the slime.

And in his shrillest tenor he began
Reciting his indictment of the man,
Until he closed upon this capital crime—
"You are accused of singing out of key,
(A foul unmitigated dissonance)
Of shuffling in the measures of the dance,
Then walking out with that defiant, free
Toss of your head, banging the doors,
Leaving a stench upon the jacinth floors.
You have fallen like a curse
On the mechanics of my Universe.

"Herewith I measure out your penalty—
Hearken while you hear, look while you see:
I send you now upon your homeward route
Where you shall find
Humiliation for your pride of mind.
I shall make deaf the ear, and dim the eye,
Put palsy in your touch, make mute
Your speech, intoxicate your cells and dry
Your blood and marrow, shoot
Arthritic needles through your cartilage,
And having parched you with old age,
I'll pass you wormwise through the mire;
And when your rebel will
Is mouldered, all desire
Shrivelled, all your concepts broken,
Backward in dust I'll blow you till
You join my spiral festival of fire.
Go, Master of the Revels—I have spoken."

And the little genus *homo*, six feet high,
Standing erect, countered with this reply—
"You dumb insouciant invertebrate,
You rule a lower than a feudal state—
A realm of flunkey decimals that run,
Return; return and run, again return,
Each group around its little sun,
And every sun a satellite.

There they go by day and night,
Nothing to do but run and burn,
Taking turn and turn about,
Light-year in and light-year out,
Dancing, dancing in quadrillions,
Never leaving their pavilions.

"Your astronomical conceit
Of bulk and power is anserine.
Your ignorance so thick,
You did not know your own arithmetic.
We flung the graphs about your flying feet;
We measured your diameter—
Merely a line
Of zeros prefaced by an integer.
Before we came
You had no name.
You did not know direction or your pace;
We taught you all you ever knew
Of motion, time and space.
We healed you of your vertigo
And put you in our kindergarten show,
Perambulated you through prisms, drew
Your mileage through the Milky Way,
Lassoed your comets when they ran astray,
Yoked Leo, Taurus, and your team of Bears
To pull our kiddy cars of inverse squares.

"Boast not about your harmony,
Your perfect curves, your rings
Of *pure and endless light*—'Twas we
Who pinned upon your Seraphim their wings,
And when your brassy heavens rang
With joy that morning while the planets sang
Their choruses of archangelic lore,
'Twas we who ordered the notes upon their score
Out of our winds and strings.
Yes! all your shapely forms
Are ours—parabolas of silver light,

Those blueprints of your spiral stairs
From nadir depth to zenith height,
Coronas, rainbows after storms,
Auroras on your eastern tapestries
And constellations over western seas.

"And when, one day, grown conscious of your age,
While pondering an eolith,
We turned a human page
And blotted out a cosmic myth
With all its baby symbols to explain
The sunlight in Apollo's eyes,
Our rising pulses and the birth of pain,
Fear, and that fern-and-fungus breath
Stalking our nostrils to our caves of death—
That day we learned how to anatomize
Your body, calibrate your size
And set a mirror up before your face
To show you what you really were—a rain
Of dull Lucretian atoms crowding space,
A series of concentric waves which any fool
Might make by dropping stones within a pool,
Or an exploding bomb forever in flight
Bursting like hell through Chaos and Old Night.

"You oldest of the hierarchs
Composed of electronic sparks,
We grant you speed,
We grant you power, and fire
That ends in ash, but we concede
To you no pain nor joy nor love nor hate,
No final tableau of desire,
No causes won or lost, no free
Adventure at the outposts—only
The degradation of your energy
When at some late
Slow number of your dance your sergeant-major Fate
Will catch you blind and groping and will send
You reeling on that long and lonely
Lockstep of your wave-lengths towards your end.

"We who have met
With stubborn calm the dawn's hot fusillades;
Who have seen the forehead sweat
Under the tug of pulleys on the joints,
Under the liquidating tally
Of the cat-and-truncheon bastinades;
Who have taught our souls to rally
To mountain horns and the sea's rockets
When the needle ran demented through the points;
We who have learned to clench
Our fists and raise our lightless sockets
To morning skies after the midnight raids,
Yet cocked our ears to bugles on the barricades,
And in cathedral rubble found a way to quench
A dying thirst within a Galilean valley—
No! by the Rood, we will not join your ballet."

FROM *Brébeuf and His Brethren*

March 16, 1649

Three miles from town to town over the snow,
Naked, laden with pillage from the lodges,
The captives filed like wounded beasts of burden,
Three hours on the march, and those that fell
Or slowed their steps were killed.
                                                  Three days before
Brébeuf had celebrated his last mass.
And he had known it was to be the last.
There was prophetic meaning as he took
The cord and tied the alb around his waist,
Attached the maniple to his left arm
And drew the seamless purple chasuble
With the large cross over his head and shoulders,
Draping his body: every vestment held
An immediate holy symbol as he whispered—
"Upon my head the helmet of Salvation.
So purify my heart and make me white;

With this cincture of purity gird me,
O Lord.
May I deserve this maniple
Of sorrow and of penance.
Unto me
Restore the stole of immortality.
My yoke is sweet, my burden light.
Grant that
I may so bear it as to win Thy grace."

Entering, he knelt before as rude an altar
As ever was reared within a sanctuary,
But hallowed as that chancel where the notes
Of Palestrina's score had often pealed
The *Assumpta est Maria* through Saint Peter's.
For, covered in the centre of the table,
Recessed and sealed, a hollowed stone contained
A relic of a charred or broken body
Which perhaps a thousand years ago or more
Was offered as a sacrifice to Him
Whose crucifix stood there between the candles.
And on the morrow would this prayer be answered:—
"Eternal Father, I unite myself
With the affections and the purposes
Of Our Lady of Sorrows on Calvary.
And now I offer Thee the sacrifice
Which Thy Beloved Son made of Himself
Upon the Cross and now renews on this,
His holy altar . . .
Graciously receive
My life for His life as He gave His life
For mine . . .
This is my body.
In like manner . . .
Take ye and drink—the chalice of my blood."

XII No doubt in the mind of Brébeuf that this was the last
Journey—three miles over the snow. He knew
That the margins as thin as they were by which he escaped
From death through the eighteen years of his mission toil
Did not belong to this chapter: not by his pen
Would this be told. He knew his place in the line,
For the blaze of the trail that was cut on the bark by Jogues
Shone still. He had heard the story as told by writ
And word of survivors—of how a captive slave
Of the hunters, the skin of his thighs cracked with the frost,
He would steal from the tents to the birches, make a rough
    cross
From two branches, set it in snow and on the peel
Inscribe his vows and dedicate to the Name
In "litanies of love" what fragments were left
From the wrack of his flesh; of his escape from the tribes;
Of his journey to France where he knocked at the door of the
    College
Of Rennes, was gathered in as a mendicant friar,
Nameless, unknown, till he gave for proof to the priest
His scarred credentials of faith, the nail-less hands
And withered arms —the signs of the Mohawk fury.
Nor yet was the story finished—he had come again
Back to his mission to get the second death.
And the comrades of Jogues—Goupil, Eustache and Couture
Had been stripped and made to run the double files
And take the blows—one hundred clubs to each line—
And this as the prelude to torture, leisured, minute,
Where thorns on the quick, scallop shells to the joints of the
    thumbs,
Provided the sport for children and squaws till the end.
And adding salt to the blood of Brébeuf was the thought
Of Daniel—was it months or a week ago?
So far, so near, it seemed in time, so close
In leagues—just over there to the south it was
He faced the arrows and died in front of his church.

But winding into the greater artery
Of thought that bore upon the coming passion
Were little tributaries of wayward wish
And reminiscence. Paris with its vespers
Was folded in the mind of Lalemant,
And the soft Gothic lights and traceries
Were shading down the ridges of his vows.
But two years past at Bourges he had walked the cloisters,
Companioned by Saint Augustine and Francis,
And wrapped in quiet holy mists. Brébeuf,
His mind a moment throwing back the curtain
Of eighteen years, could see the orchard lands,
The *cidreries*, the peasants at the Fairs,
The undulating miles of wheat and barley,
Gardens and pastures rolling like a sea
From Lisieux to Le Havre. Just now the surf
Was pounding on the limestone Norman beaches
And on the reefs of Calvados. Had dawn
This very day not flung her surplices
Around the headlands and with golden fire
Consumed the silken argosies that made
For Rouen from the estuary of the Seine?
A moment only for that veil to lift—
A moment only for those bells to die
That rang their matins at Condé-sur-Vire.

By noon St. Ignace! The arrival there
The signal for the battle-cries of triumph,
The gauntlet of the clubs. The stakes were set
And the ordeal of Jogues was re-enacted
Upon the priests—even with wilder fury,
For here at last was trapped their greatest victim,
Echon. The Iroquois had waited long
For this event. Their hatred for the Hurons
Fused with their hatred for the French and priests
Was to be vented on this sacrifice,
And to that camp had come apostate Hurons,
United with their foes in common hate
To settle up their reckoning with *Echon*.

*   *   *   *

Now three o'clock, and capping the height of the passion,
Confusing the sacraments under the pines of the forest,
Under the incense of balsam, under the smoke
Of the pitch, was offered the rite of the font. On the head,
The breast, the loins and the legs, the boiling water!
While the mocking paraphrase of the symbols was hurled
At their faces like shards of flint from the arrow heads—
"We baptize thee with water . . .
That thou mayest be led
To Heaven . . .
To that end we do anoint thee.
We treat thee as a friend: we are the cause
Of thy happiness; we are thy priests; the more
Thou sufferest, the more thy God will reward thee,
So give us thanks for our kind offices."

The fury of taunt was followed by fury of blow.
Why did not the flesh of Brébeuf cringe to the scourge,
Respond to the heat, for rarely the Iroquois found
A victim that would not cry out in such pain— yet here
The fire was on the wrong fuel. Whenever he spoke,
It was to rally the soul of his friend whose turn
Was to come through the night while the eyes were uplifted in prayer,
Imploring the Lady of Sorrows, the mother of Christ,
As pain brimmed over the cup and the will was called
To stand the test of the coals. And sometimes the speech
Of Brébeuf struck out, thundering reproof to his foes,
Half-rebuke, half-defiance, giving them roar for roar.
Was it because the chancel became the arena,
Brébeuf a lion at bay, not a lamb on the altar,
As if the might of a Roman were joined to the cause
Of Judaea? Speech they could stop for they girdled his lips,
But never a moan could they get. Where was the source
Of his strength, the home of his courage that topped the best
Of their braves and even out-fabled the lore of their legends?
In the bunch of his shoulders which often had carried a load
Extorting the envy of guides at an Ottawa portage?

The heat of the hatchets was finding a path to that source.
In the thews of his thighs which had mastered the trails of
the Neutrals?
They would gash and beribbon those muscles. Was it the
blood?
They would draw it fresh from its fountain. Was it the heart?
They dug for it, fought for the scraps in the way of the
wolves.
But not in these was the valour or stamina lodged;
Nor in the symbol of Richelieu's robes or the seals
Of Mazarin's charters, nor in the stir of the *lilies*
Upon the Imperial folds; nor yet in the words
Loyola wrote on a table of lava-stone
In the cave of Manresa—not in these the source—
But in the sound of invisible trumpets blowing
Around two slabs of board, right-angled, hammered
By Roman nails and hung on a Jewish hill.

The wheel had come full circle with the visions
In France of Brébeuf poured through the mould of
St. Ignace.
Lalemant died in the morning at nine, in the flame
Of the pitch belts. Flushed with the sight of the bodies, the
foes
Gathered their clans and moved back to the north and west
To join in the fight against the tribes of the Petuns.
There was nothing now that could stem the Iroquois blast.
However undaunted the souls of the priests who were left,
However fierce the sporadic counter attacks
Of the Hurons striking in roving bands from the ambush,
Or smashing out at their foes in garrison raids,
The villages fell before a blizzard of axes
And arrows and spears, and then were put to the torch.

The days were dark at the fort and heavier grew
The burdens on Ragueneau's shoulders. Decision was his.
No word from the east could arrive in time to shape
The step he must take. To and fro—from altar to hill,
From hill to altar, he walked and prayed and watched.

As governing priest of the Mission he felt the pride
Of his Order whipping his pulse, for was not St. Ignace
The highest test of the Faith? And all that torture
And death could do to the body was done. The Will
And the Cause in their triumph survived. Loyola's
    mountains,
Sublime at their summits, were scaled to the uttermost peak.
Ragueneau, the Shepherd, now looked on a battered fold.
In a whirlwind of fire St. Jean, like St. Joseph, crashed
Under the Iroquois impact. Firm at his post,
Garnier suffered the fate of Daniel. And now
Chabanel, last in the roll of the martyrs, entrapped
On his knees in the woods met death at apostate hands.

The drama was drawing close to its end. It fell
To Ragueneau's lot to perform a final rite—
To offer the fort in sacrificial fire!
He applied the torch himself. *"Inside an hour,"*
He wrote, *"we saw the fruit of ten years' labour*
Ascend in smoke,—then looked our last at the fields,
Put altar-vessels and food on a raft of logs,
And made our way to the island of St. Joseph."
But even from there was the old tale retold—
Of hunger and the search for roots and acorns;
Of cold and persecution unto death
By the Iroquois; of Jesuit will and courage
As the shepherd-priest with Chaumonot led back
The remnant of a nation to Quebec.

THE MARTYRS' SHRINE

Three hundred years have passed, and the winds of God
Which blew over France are blowing once more through
    the pines
That bulwark the shores of the great Fresh Water Sea.
Over the wastes abandoned by human tread,
Where only the bittern's cry was heard at dusk;
Over the lakes where the wild ducks built their nests,
The skies that had banked their fires are shining again
With the stars that guided the feet of Jogues and Brébeuf.

The years as they turned have ripened the martyrs' seed,
And the ashes of St. Ignace are glowing afresh.

The trails, having frayed the threads of the cassocks, sank
Under the mould of the centuries, under fern
And brier and fungus—there in due time to blossom
Into the highways that lead to the crest of the hill
Which havened both shepherd and flock in the days of
their trial.
For out of the torch of Ragueneau's ruins the candles
Are burning today in the chancel of Sainte Marie.
The Mission sites have returned to the fold of the Order.
Near to the ground where the cross broke under the hatchet,
And went with it into the soil to come back at the turn
Of the spade with the carbon and calcium char of the bodies,
The shrines and altars are built anew; the *Aves*
And prayers ascend, and the Holy Bread is broken.

W. W. E. ROSS

1894-1966

The Creek

The creek, shining,
out of the deep woods
comes with its rippling of
water over pebbly bottom.

Moving between
banks crowded with raspberry
bushes, the ripe red
berries in their short season

to deepen slowly
among tall pines, athletes in
the wind, then the swampy
ground low-lying and damp

where sunlight strikes
glints on the gliding surface
of the clear cold
creek winding towards the shore

of the lake, blue,
not far through reeds and rushes,
where with a plunge, a small
waterfall, it disappears

among the waves
hastening from far to meet
the stranger, the stream issuing
from depths of green unknown.

The Diver

I would like to dive
Down
Into this still pool
Where the rocks at the bottom are safely deep,

Into the green
Of the water seen from within,
A strange light
Streaming past my eyes—

Things hostile;
You cannot stay here, they seem to say;
The rocks, slime-covered, the undulating
Fronds of weeds—

And drift slowly
Among the cooler zones;
Then, upward turning,
Break from the green glimmer

Into the light,
White and ordinary of the day,
And the mild air,
With the breeze and the comfortable shore.

On the Supernatural

We must affirm the supernatural
However doubtfully we have looked upon
Its bare existence in the time that's gone,
For it is ever near and ever real;
As we shall find. We love the natural.
The human reason seated on a throne,
Creator of kingdoms for itself alone,
Is conscious of no zone ethereal.
But to an end with all this lower view,
The cause illusory, vain and yet employed;—
Angels there are and kindly demons too,
Their throng, removed from faulty human sight,
In the unseen worlds as we should know in spite
Of natural explanation thin and void.

Rocky Bay

The iron rocks
slope sharply down
into the gleaming
of northern water,
and there is a shining
to northern water
reflecting the sky
on a keen cool morning.

A little bay,—
and there the water
reflects the trees
upside down,
and the coloured rock,
inverted also
in the little
shining bay.

Above, on the rock,
stand trees, hardy,
gripping the rock
tenaciously.
The water repeats them
upside down,
repeats the coloured
rock inverted.

Spring Song

One day
walking
along
the track
I passed
a pond
slimy
greenish
From it came
sounds
of frogs
piping
I picked up
a stone
and threw it
into the pond
The stone
splashed
and the piping
of the frogs
stopped

in the spring
walking
the railroad track
near the town
looking at
a pond
of greenish water
a large pond
incessantly
sounds
frogs piping
frogs in the water
I could not see
any frogs
I threw a stone
into the pond
it splashed
a big splash
and the sounds
the frogs' piping

This Form

This form expresses now.
At other times other forms.
Now, this form.
This form seems effective now.
It is monotonous, crude.
It may be called "primitive."
A primitive form.
No form, a lack of form.
Nevertheless, it expresses.
It is expressive now.
At other times other forms.
This form now. Expressive now.

The Walk

He walked through the woods
and saw the merging
of the tall trunks
in the green distance—
the undergrowth
of mottled green
with sunlight and shadow,
and flowers starting

here and there
on the mottled ground;
he looked along
the green distance
and up towards
the greenly-laden
curving boughs
of the tall trees;

and down a slope
as he walked onward
down the sloping
ground, he saw
in among
the green, broken,
the blue shimmering
of lake-water.

RAYMOND KNISTER

1899-1932

Feed

For Danny whistling slowly
"Down in Tennessee"
A fat white shoat by the trough
Lifts his snout a moment to hear,
Among the guzzling and slavering comrades,
Squeezing and forcing:
And begins to feed again.
Whenever the certain note comes,
He will raise his jaws
With his unturning eyes,
Then lean again to scoop up the swill.

Change

I shall not wonder more, then,
But I shall know.

Leaves change, and birds, flowers,
And after years are still the same.

The sea's breast heaves in sighs to the moon,
But they are moon and sea forever.

As in other times the trees stand tense and lonely,
And spread a hollow moan of other times.

You will be you yourself,
I'll find you more, not else,
For vintage of the woeful years.

The sea breathes, or broods, or loudens,
Is bright or is mist and the end of the world;
And the sea is constant to change.

I shall not wonder more, then,
But I shall know.

Lake Harvest

Down on the flat of the lake
Out on the slate and the green,
Spotting the border of Erie's sleeping robe of silver-blue
changeable silk,
In sight of the shimmer of silver-blue changeable silk,
In the sun,
The men are sawing the frosted crystal.
Patient the horses look on from the sleighs,
Patient the trees, down from the bank, darkly ignoring
the sun.
Each saw sings and whines in a grey-mittened hand,
And diamonds and pieces of a hundred rainbows are
strown around.

The Plowman

All day I follow
Watching the swift dark furrow
That curls away before me,
And care not for skies or upturned flowers,
And at the end of the field
Look backward
Ever with discontent.

A stone, a root, a strayed thought
Has warped the line of that furrow
And urge my horses round again.

Sometimes even before the row is finished
I must look backward;
To find, when I come to the end
   That there I swerved.

Unappeased I leave the field,
Expectant, return.

The horses are very patient.
When I tell myself
This time
The ultimate unflawed turning
Is before my share,
They must give up their rest.

Someday, someday, be sure,
I shall turn the furrow of all my hopes
But I shall not, doing it, look backward.

Stable-Talk

We have sweat our share;
The harrow is caught full of sod-pieces,
The bright disks are misted yellow in the wet.
Hear tardy hesitant drips from the eaves!

We can rest today.
Let the dozy eye,
The one raised hip
Give no hint to the hours.

We are not done with toil:
Let rain work in these hours,
Wind in night's hours,
We with the sun together
Tomorrow.

The Humourist

I am written of as a great humourist,
A jester with life,
A laugher at men.
People say, "I have heard him speak,
He's just like his picture.
He tells his jokes with such side-aching gravity
I nearly died. You ought to hear him,
So much better than his books, him looking so solemn."
All my life I've wanted to write
Something sad, grim and pitiful.
I just took up this side-tickling humour to start with,
To gain the public ear.
I've always been going to begin
To tell the world of its goalless gropings,
Its tortive mazeful stumblings,
But now I'm too old to try.
Poe, Hardy and Dostoyevsky
Are my prophets,
And people say
I'm another Juvenal, Rabelais, Cervantes, "Hudibras" Butler,
Anyone they think their listeners have not read.

Sumach

A little knoll
On the shoulder of the hill
Whisks the sumach bush
Under the nose of a cloud
Gaily.
He smiles
Pretends to sneeze
Playfully,—
Filling the valley with mist.

F. R. SCOTT

b. 1899

Summer Camp

Here is a lovely little camp
Built among the Laurentian hills
By a Children's Welfare Society,
Which is entirely supported by voluntary contributions.
All summer long underprivileged children scamper about,
And it is astonishing how soon they look healthy and well.
Two weeks here in the sun and air
Through the kindness of our wealthy citizens
Will be a wonderful help to the little tots
When they return for a winter in the slums.

Overture

In the dark room, under a cone of light,
You precisely play the Mozart sonata. The bright
Clear notes fly like sparks through the air
And trace a flickering pattern of music there.

Your hands dart in the light, your fingers flow—
They are ten careful operatives in a row
That pick their packets of sound from steel bars,
Constructing harmonies as sharp as stars.

But how shall I hear old music? This is an hour
Of new beginnings, concepts warring for power,
Decay of systems—the tissue of art is torn
With overtures of an era being born.

And this perfection which is less yourself
Than Mozart, seems a trinket on a shelf,
A pretty octave played before a window
Beyond whose curtain grows a world crescendo.

Trans Canada

Pulled from our ruts by the made-to-order gale
We sprang upward into a wider prairie
And dropped Regina below like a pile of bones.

Sky tumbled upon us in waterfalls,
But we were smarter than a Skeena salmon
And shot our silver body over the lip of air
To rest in a pool of space
On the top storey of our adventure.

A solar peace
And a six-way choice.

Clouds, now, are the solid substance,
A floor of wool roughed by the wind
Standing in waves that halt in their fall.
A still of troughs.

The plane, our planet,
Travels on roads that are not seen or laid
But sound in instruments on pilots' ears,
While underneath,
The sure wings
Are the everlasting arms of science.

Man, the lofty worm, tunnels his latest clay,
And bores his new career.

This frontier, too, is ours.
This everywhere whose life can only be led
At the pace of a rocket
Is common to man and man,
And every country below is an I land.

The sun sets on its top shelf,
And stars seem farther from our nearer grasp.
I have sat by nights beside a cold lake
And touched things smoother than moonlight on still water,
But the moon on this cloud sea is not human,
And here is no shore, no intimacy,
Only the start of space, the road to suns.

Bonne Entente

The advantages of living with two cultures
Strike one at every turn,
Especially when one finds a notice in an office building:
"This elevator will not run on Ascension Day";
Or reads in the *Montreal Star:*
"Tomorrow being the Feast of the Immaculate Conception,
There will be no collection of garbage in the city";
Or sees on the restaurant menu the bilingual dish:

DEEP APPLE PIE
TARTE AUX POMMES PROFONDES

Lakeshore

The lake is sharp along the shore
Trimming the bevelled edge of land
To level curves; the fretted sands
Go slanting down through liquid air
Till stones below shift here and there
Floating upon their broken sky
All netted by the prism wave
And rippled where the currents are.

I stare through windows at this cave
Where fish, like planes, slow-motioned, fly.
Poised in a still of gravity
The narrow minnow, flicking fin,
Hangs in a paler, ochre sun,
His doorways open everywhere.

And I am a tall frond that waves
Its head below its rooted feet
Seeking the light that draws it down
To forest floors beyond its reach
Vivid with gloom and eerie dreams.

The water's deepest colonnades
Contract the blood, and to this home
That stirs the dark amphibian
With me the naked swimmers come
Drawn to their prehistoric womb.

They too are liquid as they fall
Like tumbled water loosed above
Until they lie, diagonal,
Within the cool and sheltered grove
Stroked by the fingertips of love.

Silent, our sport is drowned in fact
Too virginal for speech or sound
And each is personal and laned
Along his private aqueduct.

Too soon the tether of the lungs
Is taut and straining, and we rise
Upon our undeveloped wings
Toward the prison of our ground
A secret anguish in our thighs
And mermaids in our memories.

This is our talent, to have grown
Upright in posture, false-erect,
A landed gentry, circumspect,
Tied to a horizontal soil
The floor and ceiling of the soul;
Striving, with cold and fishy care
To make an ocean of the air.

Sometimes, upon a crowded street,
I feel the sudden rain come down
And in the old, magnetic sound
I hear the opening of a gate
That loosens all the seven seas.
Watching the whole creation drown
I muse, alone, on Ararat.

Trees in Ice

these gaunt prongs and points of trees
pierce the zero air with flame
every finger of black ice
stealing the sun's drawn fire
to make a burning of a barren bush

underneath, from still branch and arm
flakes of light fall, fall
flecking the dark white snow

this cruelty is a formal loveliness
on a tree's torn limbs
this glittering pain

Dancing

Long ago
when I first danced
I danced
holding her
back and arm
making her move
as I moved

she was best
when she was
least herself
lost herself

Now I dance
seeing her
dance away from
me   she
looks at me
dancing   we
are closer
held in the movement of the dance
I no longer dance
with myself
we are two
not one
the dance
is one

On the Terrace, Quebec

Northward, the ice-carved land,
les pays d'en haut.

South, the softer continent,
river-split.

By Valcartier, three Laurentian hills.
Many years ago, as children,
looking north from the Rectory window
on the longest day of each year
we saw the sun set
in the second dip.

I walk these boards under the citadel,
see the narrow streets below,
the basin, l'Ile d'Orléans,
the gateway.

I think of the English troops
imprisoned in the broken city
in the spring of 1760
waiting the first ship.

Whose flag would it fly?

And that other army, under de Lévis,
victorious at Ste. Foy,
still strong,
watching too.

Suddenly, round the bend,
masts and sails
begin to finger the sky.

The first question was answered.

ROBERT FINCH

b. 1900

Egg-and-Dart

This never-ended searching for the eyes
Wherein the unasked question's answer lies;
This beating, beating, beating of the heart
Because a contour seems to fit the part;
The long, drear moment of the look that spoils
The little bud of hope; the word that soils
The pact immaculate, so newly born;
The noisy silence of the old self-scorn;
These, and the sudden leaving in the lurch;
Then the droll recommencement of the search.

The Five Kine

Down from the distant pasture of my ease
their lean flanks scarred against the wall of duty
come the five kine I never sought to please,
come in a famished parody of beauty.
Their eyes are dim, their udders drop no milk,
their hooves are splayed, their flanks, sunken and sooty,
augur a dearth of inauspicious ilk.
Barns must be raised and food be found for keeping
when no expected corn hides in the silk,
but that perpetual harvest none went reaping,
soil so exuberant was never tilled,
and still the kine kept feeding, feeding and sleeping.
Pasture of ease, what vigilance withheld
froze the intrepid marrow of your grass?

The kine were there, fivefold and safely belled,
The wall was there, oh perilous blade of glass,
sheering denial between pent and wrung,
The soil was there, long, long ago, alas
so long. The kine too had been there for long,
yet now they seek the faithless drover's goad
as he the scattered purchase of a song,
while leisure is become a desert road.

Train Window

The dark green truck on the cement platform
is explicit as a paradigm.
Its wheels are four black cast-iron starfish.
Its body, a massive tray of planking,
ends in two close-set dark green uprights
crossed with three straight cross-pieces, one
looped with a white spiral of hose.

The truck holds eleven cakes of ice,
each cake a different size and shape.
Some look as though a weight had hit them.
One, solid glass, has a core of sugar.
They lean, a transitory Icehenge,
in a moor of imitation snow
from the hatchet's bright wet-sided steel.

Five galvanized pails, mottled, as if
of stiffened frosted caracul, three
with crescent lids and elbowed spouts,
loom in the ice, their half-hoop handles
linking that frozen elocution
to the running chalk-talk of powder-red
box-cars beyond, while our train waits here.

The Statue

A small boy has thrown a stone at a statue,
And a man who threatened has told a policeman so.
Down the pathway they rustle in a row,
The boy, the man, the policeman. If you watch you

Will see the alley of trees join in the chase
And the flower-beds stiffly make after the boy,
The fountains brandish their cudgels in his way
And the sky drop a blue netting in his face.

Only the statue unmoved in its moving stillness
Holds the park as before the deed was done
On a stone axis round which the trio whirls.

Stone that endured the chisel's cutting chillness
Is tolerant of the stone at its foot of stone
And the pigeon sitting awry on its carved curls.

When

When razors fashion
rock, when thread
moors vessels, passion
shall be tied
with knowledge, reason
shall quarry pride.

The Foreman

If your thread is tangled, call the foreman, read
The unmistakable sign hung overhead.

Her thread is tangled, desperate her endeavour,
Untangling makes the tangle worse than ever.

She calls. The foreman shows the sign's request.
Sullenly she insists: *I did my best.*

Quietly the foreman speaks, the thread set free:
Remember, doing your best is calling me.

Silverthorn Bush

I am a dispossessed Ontario wood
That took the circling weather as my crown,
Now noise makes havoc of my whispered mood
And enterprise has laughed my towers down.

Is there a poem where I blossom still?
Do paintings keep my solitude secure?
Somewhere remote adventure must distil
Part of its fragrance from an air so pure.

I am the springing memory of my past
In vagabond and child who held me dear,
Theirs is the surest witness that I last
In buds of mine that I no longer bear.

If you can overtake their truant youth
Ask them to flash my secret on your sight,
They heard my pensive river spill its truth
And felt my hidden fibres tug the light.

The riddle is how disappearance puts
A dusty end to a green revery
Yet leaves me nourished by so many roots
That I shall never cease ceasing to be.

The Lovers

Burns would have loved, and sung, the way you love
Beneath his statue, though the Embankment Gardens
Are too exiguous even for gentle guerdons
To be exchanged (approve or disapprove).
Recumbent on the grass you take your fill
Of inexhaustibly renewed embraces
While seemingly aloof the public passes
Censorious or vicarious where you thrill.
The Coldstream Guards in scarlet, blue and gold
Make bandshell noise of scarlet, gold and blue
That turns to nuptial notes because of you,
Streaming from Hotstream Guards instead of Cold.
Meanwhile bronze Burns, more merciful and wise
Than guards or public, closes both his eyes.

A. J. M. SMITH

1902-1980

The Lonely Land

Cedar and jagged fir
uplift sharp barbs
against the gray
and cloud-piled sky;
and in the bay
blown spume and windrift
and thin, bitter spray
snap
at the whirling sky;
and the pine trees
lean one way.

A wild duck calls
to her mate,
and the ragged
and passionate tones
stagger and fall,
and recover,
and stagger and fall,
on these stones—
are lost
in the lapping of water
on smooth, flat stones.

This is a beauty
of dissonance,
this resonance
of stony strand,
this smoky cry
curled over a black pine
like a broken
and wind-battered branch
when the wind
bends the tops of the pines
and curdles the sky
from the north.

This is the beauty
of strength
broken by strength
and still strong.

Swift Current

This is a visible
and crystal wind:
no ragged edge,
no splash of foam,
no whirlpool's scar;
only
—in the narrows,
sharpness cutting sharpness,
arrows of direction,
spears of speed.

Like an Old Proud King in a Parable

A bitter king in anger to be gone
From fawning courtier and doting queen
Flung hollow sceptre and gilt crown away,
And breaking bound of all his counties green
He made a meadow in the northern stone
And breathed a palace of inviolable air
To cage a heart that carolled like a swan,
And slept alone, immaculate and gay,
With only his pride for a paramour.

O who is that bitter king? It is not I.

Let me, I beseech thee, Father, die
From this fat royal life, and lie
As naked as a bridegroom by his bride,
And let that girl be the cold goddess Pride:

And I will sing to the barren rock
Your difficult, lonely music, heart,
Like an old proud king in a parable.

News of the Phoenix

They say the Phoenix is dying, some say dead.
Dead without issue is what one message said,
But that has been suppressed, officially denied.

I think myself the man who sent it lied.
In any case, I'm told, he has been shot,
As a precautionary measure, whether he did or not.

Noctambule

Under the flag of this pneumatic moon,
—Blown up to bursting, whitewashed white,
And painted like the moon—the piracies of day
Scuttle the crank hulk of witless night.
The great black innocent Othello of a thing
Is undone by the nice clean pockethandkerchief
Of 6 a.m., and though the moon is only an old
Wetwash snotrag—horsemeat for good *rosbif*—
Perhaps to utilize substitutes is what
The age has to teach us,
                    wherefore let the loud
Unmeaning warcry of treacherous daytime
Issue like whispers of love in the moonlight,
—Poxy old cheat!
                    So mewed the lion,
Until mouse roared once and after lashed
His tail: Shellshock came on again, his skin
Twitched in the rancid margarine, his eye
Like a lake isle in a florist's window:
Reality at two removes, and mouse and moon
Successful.

The Archer

Bend back thy bow, O Archer, till the string
Is level with thine ear, thy body taut,
Its nature art, thyself thy statue wrought
Of marble blood, thy weapon the poised wing
Of coiled and aquiline Fate. Then, loosening, fling
The hissing arrow like a burning thought
Into the empty sky that smokes as the hot
Shaft plunges to the bullseye's quenching ring.

So for a moment, motionless, serene,
Fixed between time and time, I aim and wait;
Nothing remains for breath now but to waive
His prior claim and let the barb fly clean
Into the heart of what I know and hate—
That central black, the ringed and targeted grave.

Far West

Among the cigarettes and the peppermint creams
Came the flowers of fingers, luxurious and bland,
Incredibly blossoming in the little breast.
And in the Far West
The tremendous cowboys in goatskin pants
Shot up the town of her ignorant wish.

In the gun flash she saw the long light shake
Across the lake, repeating that poem
At Finsbury Park.
But the echo was drowned in the roll of the trams—
Anyway, who would have heard? Not a soul.
Not one noble and toxic like Buffalo Bill.

In the holy name *bang! bang!* the flowers came
With the marvellous touch of fingers
Gentler than the fuzzy goats
Moving up and down up and down as if in ecstasy
As the cowboys rode their skintight stallions
Over the barbarous hills of California.

The Mermaid

Dark green and seaweed-cold, the snake-bright hair
Streams on the golden-sun-illumined wave
That sways as gently as two bells the grave
Small coral-tinted breasts to starboard there
Where salt translucency's green branches bear
This sea-rose, a lost mermaid, whose cold cave,
Left lightless now, the lapping seatides lave
At base of Okeanos' twisted stair.

She's come where bubbles burst, crisp silver skims;
Where the tall sun stands naked; where he shines;
Where live men walk the shrouds with fork-like limbs.

She smiles: and the head of the shipmite swims;
But the bo'sun bawls for the grappling lines,
And the Chaplain fumbles in his book of hymns.

The Wisdom of Old Jelly Roll

How all men wrongly death to dignify
Conspire, I tell. Parson, poetaster, pimp,
Each acts or acquiesces. They prettify,
Dress up, deodorize, embellish, primp,
And make a show of Nothing. Ah, but met-
aphysics laughs; she touches, tastes, and smells
—Hence knows—the diamond holes that make a net.
Silence resettled testifies to bells.
'Nothing' depends on 'Thing', which is or was:
So death makes life or makes life's worth, a worth
Beyond all highfalutin' woes or shows
To publish and confess, 'Cry at the birth,
Rejoice at the death,' old Jelly Roll said,
Being on whiskey, ragtime, chicken, and the scriptures fed.

Metamorphosis

This flesh repudiates the bone
With such dissolving force,
In such a tumult to be gone,
Such longing for divorce,
As leaves the livid mind no choice
But to conclude at last
That all this energy and poise
Were but designed to cast
A richer flower from the earth
Surrounding its decay,
And like a child whose fretful mirth
Can find no constant play,
Bring one more transient form to birth
And fling the old away.

EARLE BIRNEY

b. 1904

Hands

In the amber morning by the inlet's high shore
my canoe drifts and the slim trees come bending
arching the palms of their green hands
juggling the shimmer of ripples
                                        Too bewildering
even in the dead days of peace was this manumission
the leaves' illogical loveliness   Now am I frustrate
alien   Here is the battle steeped in silence
the fallen have use and fragrantly nourish the quick
My species would wither   away from the radio's barkings
the headline beating its chimpanzee breast   the nimble
young digits at levers and triggers   Lithe are these balsam
fingers   gaunt as a Jew's in Poland   but green
green   not of us   our colours are black and red
Cold and unskilled is the cedar   his webbed claws
drooping over the water shall focus no bombsight
nor suture the bayoneted bowel   his jade tips
alert to the seadew alone or the soundless touch
of the light winked by the wind from the breathing ocean
inept for clutching the parachute cord   the uniformed
throat   the mud by the river in ebbing agony
These alders cupping their womanish palms pulsing
to the startled light when the long unpredictable swell
reaches from the dark heart of the far Pacific
are not of my flesh   Their hands speak for Brutus
and signal sedition to the poet interned   the lover
suppressed   they render nought unto Caesar

My fingers
must close on the paddle Back to the safe dead
wood of the docks the whining poles of the city
to hands the extension of tools of the militant
 typewriter
the self-filling patriot pen back to the paws
clasping warmly over the bomber contract
applauding the succulent orators back to the wrinkled
index weaving the talisman sock pointing the witch hunt
while the splayed fist thrusts at the heart of hereafter
We are gloved with steel and a magnet is set us in Europe
We are not of these woods we are not of these woods
our roots are in autumn and store for no spring

Vancouver 1940

Vancouver Lights

About me the night moonless wimples the
 mountains
wraps ocean land air and mounting
sucks at the stars The city throbbing below
webs the sable peninsula The golden
strands overleap the seajet by bridge and buoy
vault the shears of the inlet climb the woods
toward me falter and halt Across to the firefly
haze of a ship on the gulf's erased horizon
roll the lambent spokes of a lighthouse

Through the feckless years we have come to the time
when to look on this quilt of lamps is a troubling delight
Welling from Europe's bog through Africa flowing
and Asia drowning the lonely lumes on the oceans
tiding up over Halifax now to this winking
outpost comes flooding the primal ink

On this mountain's brutish forehead with terror of space
I stir   of the changeless night and the stark ranges
of nothing   pulsing down from beyond and between
the fragile planets   We are a spark beleaguered
by darkness   this twinkle we make in a corner of
emptiness
how shall we utter our fear that the black Experimentress
will never in the range of her microscope find it?   Our
Phoebus
himself is a bubble that dries on Her slide   while the
Nubian
wears for an evening's whim a necklace of nebulae

Yet we must speak   we the unique glowworms
Out of the waters and rocks of our little world
we conjured these flames   hooped these sparks
by our will   From blankness and cold we fashioned stars
to our size   and signalled Aldebaran
This must we say   whoever may be to hear us
if murk devour   and none weave again in gossamer:

These rays were ours
we made and unmade them   Not the shudder of
continents
doused us   the moon's passion   nor crash of comets
In the fathomless heat of our dwarfdom   our dream's
combustion
we contrived the power   the blast that snuffed us
No one bound Prometheus   Himself he chained
and consumed his own bright liver   O stranger
Plutonian   descendant   or beast in the stretching
night—
there was light

1941

Bushed

He invented a rainbow but lightning struck it
shattered it into the lake-lap of a mountain
so big his mind slowed when he looked at it

Yet he built a shack on the shore
learned to roast porcupine belly and
wore the quills on his hatband

At first he was out with the dawn
whether it yellowed bright as wood-columbine
or was only a fuzzed moth in a flannel of storm
But he found the mountain was clearly alive
sent messages whizzing down every hot morning
boomed proclamations at noon and spread out
a white guard of goat
before falling asleep on its feet at sundown

When he tried his eyes on the lake   ospreys
would fall like valkyries
choosing the cut-throat
He took then to waiting
till the night smoke rose from the boil of the sunset

But the moon carved unknown totems
out of the lakeshore
owls in the beardusky woods derided him
moosehorned cedars circled his swamps and tossed
their antlers up to the stars
then he knew   though the mountain slept   the winds
were shaping its peak to an arrowhead
poised

And now he could only
bar himself in and wait
for the great flint to come singing into his heart

Wreck Beach 1951

El Greco: *Espolio*

The carpenter is intent on the pressure of his hand

on the awl   and the trick of pinpointing his strength
through the awl to the wood   which is tough
He has no effort to spare for despoilings
or to worry if he'll be cut in on the dice
His skill is vital to the scene   and the safety of the state
anyone can perform the indignities   It's his hard arms
and craft that hold the eyes of the convict's women
There is the problem of getting the holes exact
(in the middle of this elbowing crowd)
and deep enough to hold the spikes
after they've sunk through those bared feet
and inadequate wrists he knows are waiting behind him
He doesn't sense perhaps that one of the hands
is held in a curious gesture over him—
giving   or asking   forgiveness?—
but he'd scarcely take time to be puzzled by poses
Criminals come in all sorts
as anyone knows who makes crosses
are as mad or sane as those who decide on their killings
Our one at least has been quiet so far
though they say he talked himself into this trouble
a carpenter's son who got notions of preaching

Well here's a carpenter's son who'll have carpenter sons
God willing   and build what's wanted
temples or tables   mangers or crosses
and shape them decently
working alone in that firm and profound abstraction
which blots out the bawling of rag-snatchers
To construct with hands   knee-weight   braced thigh
keeps the back turned from death

But it's too late now for the other carpenter's boy
to return to this peace before the nails are hammered

Point Grey 1960

Bangkok Boy

On the hot
cobbles hoppity
he makes a jig up
this moppet
come alive from chocolate
sudden
with all
small
boys'
joy
dancing under the sun
        that dances
        over the toy king's
        claw roofed palace
        and blazes the roof
        above the latest Hong Kong girlies
        imported to strip
        to the beat of copulation
        and shimmers the broken-china towers
        where ten thousand Buddhas
        sit forever
        on other boys' ashes
In his own time
naked
laughing he
on the scene's edge
like a small monkey-
man
in the endless Ramayana fresco
skips

that frozen fresco
of old wars
under still another glittering Wat
where tourists worship
in a regalia
of cameras
pacing out their grave
measures
along the enormous stone-still
god
or splaying
to immortalize
the splayed gyrations
of temple dancers
Beat out
brown smallfry
beat our your own
wild
jive
under this towering strayed
tourist and his bright
strange
cold—whee!—
coin in your small paws
before in his own motions
he vanishes
in the fearful tempo of a taxi
to that spireless palace
where god-tall
in their chalked goblin-faces
all tourists return
to plod in pairs like water-buffalo
by a bare hotel pool
to their funeral music

Prance
this dazzled instant
of your father's big
Buddha smile
and all the high
world bang in tune
the bright
sun caught
cool
        before in the high world's
        clumpings
        you are caught
        slid lethewards
        on choleric canals
        to where the poles of klongs
        and rows of paddyfields
        are shaped to bend
        small leaping backs
        and the flat bellies
        of impets
        are rounded with beriberi
Scamper little Thai
hot on these hot stones
scat
leap
this is forever O for
all gods' sakes
beat out
that first
last
cry of joy
under the sun!

1958

The Bear on the Delhi Road

Unreal   tall as a myth
by the road the Himalayan bear
is beating the brilliant air
with his crooked arms
About him two men   bare
spindly as locusts   leap

One pulls on a ring
in the great soft nose   His mate
flicks   flicks with a stick
up at the rolling eyes

They have not led him here
down from the fabulous hills
to this bald alien plain
and the clamorous world   to kill
but simply to teach him to dance

they are peaceful both   these spare
men of Kashmir   and the bear
alive is their living   too
If   far on the Delhi way
around him galvanic they dance
it is merely to wear   wear
from his shaggy body the tranced
wish forever to stay
only an ambling bear
four-footed in berries

It is no more joyous for them
in this hot dust to prance
out of reach of the praying claws
sharpened to paw for ants
in the shadows of deodars
It is not easy to free
myth from reality
or rear this fellow up
to lurch   lurch with them
in the tranced dancing of men

Srinagar 1958/Île des Porquerolles 1959

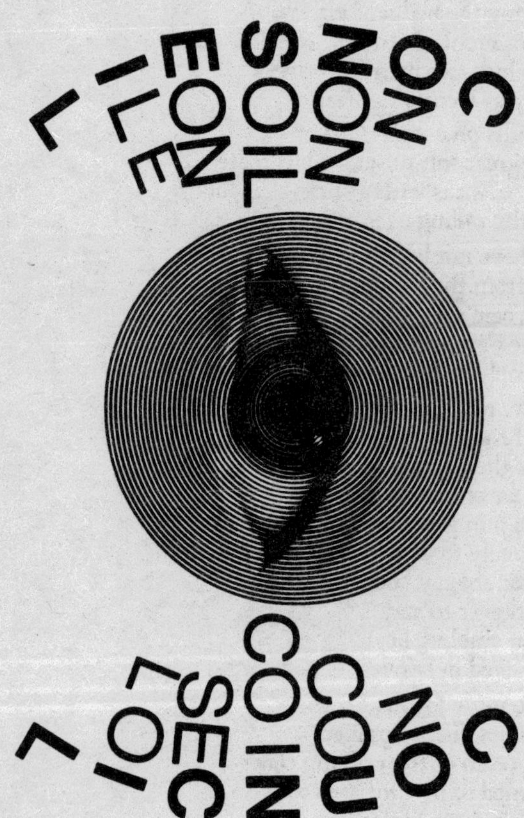

Museum of Man

the trustful curator has left me alone
in the closed wing of the aboriginal section

what's here?
3000 spears from arnhemland
waiting for a computer
to calculate their principle of balance

but what's in those wooden drawers?
i peek—sheeeez! shrunken heads
from new guinea
& dozens upon dozens
of twelve-inch penis sheathes

i'm going to lock doors
plant spears at windows
& try on everything for size

Adelaide 1968

my love is young

my love is young & i am old
she'll need a new man soon
but still we wake to clip and talk
to laugh as one
to eat and walk
beneath our five-year moon

good moon   good sun
that we do love
i pray the world believe me
& never tell me when it's time
that i'm to die
or she's to leave me

Toronto, 1978

father grouse

some mornings trying to write
i get like an old ruffed partridge
flopping off & on the nest
scared somebody'll steal
those handsome brown eggs
i've never quite laid yet

flinching from cloud shadows
hearing a fox behind every bush
snakes in the grass
shots on the hill—
limping & trembling around
from what looked like a man
but was only a dumb moose—
till i crumple down beat
with nothing done
& then the phone rings

but listen!
it isnt another mag salesman
or the Poets' League about dues
out of that lovely earpiece
comes a voice spreading sunshine
all through the woods
& i sit back drumming softly
to the loveliest partridge of all
(whose eggs they really are)
& feeling energy-control
right down to my wingtips

after we hang up
quietly i'm warming the eggs again
if i cant lay i can hatch
maybe something of me
will show in the chicks

Alexander St., July 1974

LEO KENNEDY

b. 1907

Epithalamium

This body of my mother, pierced by me,
In grim fulfilment of our destiny,
Now dry and quiet as her fallow womb
Is laid beside the shell of that bridegroom
My father, who with eyes towards the wall
Sleeps evenly; his dust stirs not at all,
No syllable of greeting curls his lips,
As to that shrunken side his leman slips.

Lo! these are two of unabated worth
Who in the shallow bridal bed of earth
Find youth's fecundity, and of their swift
Comminglement of bone and sinew, lift
—A lover's seasonable gift to blood
Made bitter by a parchèd widowhood—
This bloom of tansy from the fertile ground:
My sister, heralded by no moan, no sound.

Mad Boy's Song

The small activity of mice,
The velvet passing of a moth,
And one grey spider's cautious tread
Make thunder in this shed:
Where God has stored his tightened drum—
A mind inside a head!

Meek Candidates for Grave Space

In shrouds distinct, on palls apart
 The latest ones to tire,
Arrange their waxen limbs with care
 And piously expire.
A common hope dilates each breast,
 One spark glows in each eye,
A spasm uniform to all
 Provokes the strength to die.
The lips creased deep with pain compose
 A feverish syllable,
The halting tongue revives to phrase
 The name impeccable,
And 'God', emits the swooning brain,
 And 'Love', taps out the heart,
And 'Death', concludes the failing breath,
 To bid corruption start.

Mole Talk

The weasel and the wren consort
  Beneath one coverlet,
Upon the whittled bones of each
  Docility is set;
Strange fellows for a common bed,
  The rodent and the bird
Lip-deep in sand and gravel, lie
  Without a grudging word.
No shuddering disports the worm,
  Too wise are they, and proud,
To lift a stiffened limb, or pluck
  The seaming of a shroud.

Words for a Resurrection

Each pale Christ stirring underground
Splits the brown casket of its root,
Wherefrom the rousing soil upthrusts
A narrow, pointed shoot,

And bones long quiet under frost
Rejoice as bells precipitate
The loud, ecstatic sundering,
The hour inviolate.

This Man of April walks again—
Such marvel does the time allow—
With laughter in His blessèd bones,
And lilies on His brow.

Memorial to the Defenders

(FOR BESS AND BEN)

You Comrades rearing separate barricades
Of bone that's prompt to splinter, blood to spurt
And intricate, swift nerves that shock and dull
At blast of thermite and the bullet's rip;
You Workers gnawed by death astride a cloud,
Shrivelled by flame thrown, churned with mud and steel,
The limbs recoiling at the eyeballs twist,
The breath frayed out between prised, lurching ribs . . .
This love will yet set garlands round your names;
This sacrifice bear increment of joy
When the clean world you die for casts its slough;
And newborn men erect as monument
To your dispersed flesh and valiant hearts
The People's Spain with freedom on its towers!

Leonard Bullen

Calling Eagles

Slanting the ragged peaks of the mind, Eagles,
Swift thinkers, readers in books and the bones of nature,
construing
Life at its conflux, observing nebula, sifting fact from
suppose, swooping
With fearsome talons arched for the scrap of truth;

Hurl from the frozen roof of the world, splitting
Air with breast feather, diving
Outward and downward, scattering
Hawks with fear of your purpose, noble plunge;

Come down into life, Eagles, where iron grinds bone, hands
falter
And brave men perish for a tyrant's peace;
Come where Spain strangles in blood, Ethiopia
Groans at the iron-cased heel, Vienna
Numbers the dead, remembers Weissel and Wallisch;
Scream for Brazilian dungeons where Prestes rots
And fascist madmen rattle gaoler's keys;

Drop from your eyrie, spurning the misted heights,
Plunge to the valley where life is and verdure,
Join with the groundlings, multitudes, with hope and
passion
Lifting their fists with the steel clenched, towering
A new state from the crumble and wrack of the old:

You are part of this turmoil, Eagles, knit to its glory.
There is work for your strong beaks and the thundering
wings,
For the clean flight of the mind and the sharp perception:

There is only a glacial death on the lonely crags.

RALPH GUSTAFSON

b. 1909

Dedication

"They shall not die in vain," we said.
"Let us impose, since we forget
The hopeless giant alphabet,
Great stones above the general dead,"
The living said.

"They shall not be outdone in stones.
Generously, sculptured grief shall stand
In general over numbered bones
With book and index near at hand
For particular sons.

"And we the living left in peace
Will set aside such legal date
At such and suchlike time or state
Or place as meet and fitting is,
Respecting this."

O boy, locked in the grisly hollow,
You who once idly peeled a willow-
switch, whistling, wondering at the stick
Of willow's whiteness clean and slick,
Do not believe that we shall bury
You with words: aptly carry
Cloth flowers, proxy for love.
O we have done with granite grief
And silk denials: summing you
Within the minutes' silence—two!

More than you had need to target
Hate, against the pitiless bullet's
Calculated greed oppose
Heart's anger: falling, gave to us
What power to lance the pocket of
An easy past, what use of love
Teaching children's laughter loud
On shutters in an evil street,

What edge, O death, of days, delight?
What linch of love, spate of sun?
And shall we with a sedentary noun
Signature receipt, having had read
The catechism of the generous dead?

You who live, see! These,
These were his hills where laughter was
And counted years of longing, grain
And wintry apples scorched in sun,
Of corded hemlock deep in snow.
Here at his seven birches growing
Oblique by the boulder the fence has stopped—
Rusted wire, posts lopped
For staking. To circle love, he said.
And there are other fables made:
Of plough and intricate loom; the broken
Soldier on the sill; and latin
Parchment framed, conferring letters
On hooded death; the axe, the motto
Against the wall; abandoned hills.

Fables for stout reading. Tales
Listened to by twice-told death.
Our tongues how silent, muscles lithe
O land, hoist by the lag-end of little
Deeds? What lack of monstrous metal,
Monumental mouths; over
This land what love, wheel, lever
Of God, anchorage, pivot of days,
Remembering?

Old and certain the sea,
The mountain-tilted sky, old,
Older than words, than you are old,
Boy, who never thought to point the hill
With dawn! Only as these, our telling:
As men labour: as harvest done:
At dusk a joyful walking home.
Of nearer things: how he was young,
And died, a silent writing down.

Mythos

Once Daedalus in distant Crete
(Who from his ivory tower steps
To frown this antique telling false?)
That father to young Icarus drowned

Who naked on wings defiant soared,
With the world a star between his feet
Staggered, strafed by the sun, dashed
To glaucous ocean flaming down,

Spurt of crimson plunged in foam
His daring down (Star-dazed dare!
Hurl, then, hurtle the headlong winds
Nor haggle joy in the gasping lungs,

Moon-managed gallant of gales! Go,
Greet the giant grapple of sun.
On cunning buckle and quill let Daedalus
Limp shaking precautious beard),

Once built for Minos where the chalk-
cliffs brunt the sea a labyrinth
(What Theseus-love shall penetrate,
Plunge the mazing green miraculous

To monstrous centre, nor burst the green
And beast with bomb to no-solution
Wisdom lost? O we have need
The other way, trammelling the heart

With faith, omphalos of globe and guerdon).
And Ariadne loved the flesh
And solid heart of Theseus girded
Through green to grapple and gave to Theseus

Love who slew the Minotaur, the beast.
(Shall not seven youths be saved
And seven maidens sacrificed
In Crete to assuage the beast once broken?)

Broken before him the torso lay,
Bronzed beauty male the body but
The head a bull, and Theseus stood
Amazed no clue the labour done

To solve the mind's snarled labyrinth.
O glorious leave lone Icarus, elsewhere
Lost, on coloured pinions chose
Who dared the sun for hazardous gold

Against the liquid sea. Whose wings
Plain Theseus laughed at lost, yet faced
The giddy exit, frowned. Half-turned
To her, he heard the distant ocean

Crash its foamy thunder down
The beach, confused in sun and green
He thought of marble Athens, mazed.
Then Ariadne kissed his lips.

In the Yukon

In Europe, you can't move without going down into history.
Here, all is a beginning. I saw a salmon jump,
Again and again, against the current,
The timbered hills a background, wooded green
Unpushed through; the salmon jumped, silver.
This was news, was commerce, at the end of the summer
The leap for dying. Moose came down to the water edge
To drink and the salmon turned silver arcs.
At night, the northern lights played, great over country
Without tapestry and coronations, kings crowned
With weights of gold. They were green,
Green hangings and great grandeur, over the north
Going to what no man can hold hard in mind,
The dredge of that gravity, being without experience.

Aspects of Some Forsythia Branches

Waiting for these dry sticks in a vase—
Cut (with deliberate shears taken
From the third drawer down on the left) from the bush
In snow—complicated with leaf
And yellow in the earth elaborated, even
In the wintering sun; as the spiral of a protein
Divides and duplicates the thrust
Of love, the hereditary nose of Caesar,
Alexander's brow and Jennie's
Mole; the aggregation of a galaxy!:
So the April science of a bunch
Of sticks cut for an etched glass vase—
Waiting for these to flower in a March
Room—waiting for all this business—
As an act of love, a science of gravel,
A suffering, is this not done
With reliance? One way, dry sticks
Lead to buds, presumably wanted,
To yellow eventually. What trivial aspects

Can be got! We handle love
For small purposes. Yet they serve.
Shrubs are cut for what is believed in.
Somewhere death's in it. Dignity
Is demanded even for the dead.
So we cut branches two
Days ago. Take great precautions.
Go carefully through a door. Stand
Among deathbeds as though among heroes,
Pausing in winter along windy corridors
With the knowledge ahead of us, to wrap our throats.

Landscape with Rain

I looked at the landscape quickly as though
I had not deserved it. Too much time
Had passed and I had not observed
The flash of colour that the leaves show
As rain falls turning the under
Sides to silver with the weight.
The hills move with translucence.
I was careless how the heart revives,
The sight of a horse standing and how
As the moon goes through the night the resonance
Of silence is without birds or any
Hindrance to completion. Light astonishes
The mind with new wonder at dawn.
These things are felt with guilt
As the days pass and nothing of them
Has been seen except the concern
Of their going.
I now walk with suspense,
The going not less real but stopping
An uneven of times with astonishment, getting
Where I have to with adequate concern,
Time shortens very quickly,
But seeing at least how the moss
Is green in patches under the rain
Where the boulder stands exposed and the lake
Is come on grandly swept.

Trio For Harp and Percussion

I
ARGUMENT

If God is the speed of light,
As well crack walnuts set
At table. If so,
Golgotha is an abstract thought
And Light's speed dug in toes
And shoved a plane at Nazareth.

I'll have the concrete.

From here
To there, quicker than a wink.
There, where's there?
Infinitum. Einstein,
Asked, fiddled. So
Do I. I'll have a measure of music,
A bolt of good concordance,
Heard notes,
Above ground.
Lay me down in time
I'll think of speed.

Light, Erigina's Light
(Capital L) 's
An abstract absolute.
I'll have sun
On cranky crystal, corners in
The glass, tablecloths and silver,
Oranges with peels on them,
Crack inconsequential nuts
And talk of music,
Haydn; light my own
Apocalyptic candle.

II
ADAGIO MA NON TROPPO

As who shall sit in the sun
Thinking himself immortal,
Rameses in his chair,
His face broken, Tiye
That Nubian queen come
To Egypt done by the sculptor
In jasper hardest after
Diamond, beauty gone,
Only lips left,
The reach of river, dust.
The barge she sat in, like a
Burnish'd throne . . . Starry
Cassiopeia, lady
With her mirror in
The sky where physics sits
Dispensing laws. I'll
Have earthly music, heard,
Unsphered, no choirs squeaked
In eternal passacaglia
As the planets turn
In need of oil but mortal
Tribulations, that Festspiel
Seat hard on the bottom
For sweet acoustics' sake,
Wagner delving his gold
E♭, and sweeter, Schubert
Dying of Eros, handing
The theme that summer in Steyr
To amiable Krump, his bull-fiddle
Less than immortal, Kathi,
Large blue eyes, thick
Gold tresses, upright in
Her chair while papa gives
A dubious *A*, the short-lived
Schubert full of smiles.

III
DIABELLI VARIATIONS

Beethoven's *schusterfleck*, a cobbler's
Patch: magnificence! Sole of a shoe,
Hermes' sandal; skullcap, halo;
Digested mushroom, Helen's shoulder;
Earth a heaven! Well, not quite.
But what the world can do in time!
Transmogrification, mud bedaubed,
Bedizened! Botticelli's girl,
Canvas, paint and camel hair;
James' Bible, glue and ink—
Metamorphosis manipulated
By eardrum, pulse and pate! So,
Diabelli asked Beethoven,
"Ein variation on mein liddle
Theme." Thirty-three! Inanity
Brought sublime, empyrean reached,
Become his last sonata, Beethoven
Deaf!
            Instances, exaltations,
Mortalities—apostrophes at
Their ends! Why not? Any son
Of divinity can rub his nose in dust
If so inclined, a beneficial
Exercise—but not the whole of it,
Fix and finish yet, not
By a longshot, mankind notwithstanding:
Jesus and His lousy deal,
Jonah ducked, Pound pitched
In a loony bin and Liszt betrayed—
The Saturday sundry of this world,
Schumann mad, hearing *A*,
Schubert turned to the wall to die.

Husks and blossoming, sun and mud.
No help for it.
                                    At Bonn, in a case,
Ear-trumpets against the stars.

A. M. KLEIN

1909-1972

Out of the Pulver and the Polished Lens

i

The paunchy sons of Abraham
Spit on the maculate streets of Amsterdam,
Showing Spinoza, Baruch *alias* Benedict,
He and his God are under interdict.

Ah, what theology there is in spatted spittle,
And in anathema what sacred prose
Winnowing the fact from the suppose!
Indeed, what better than these two things can whittle
The scabrous heresies of Yahweh's foes,
Informing the breast where Satan gloats and crows
That saving it leave false doctrine, jot and tittle,
No vigilant thumb will leave its orthodox nose?
What better than ram's horn blown,
And candles blown out by maledictory breath,
Can bring the wanderer back to his very own,
The infidel back to his faith?

Nothing, unless it be that from the ghetto
A soldier of God advance to teach the creed,
Using as rod the irrefutable stiletto.

ii

Uriel da Costa
Flightily ranted
Heresies one day,
Next day recanted.

Rabbi and bishop
Each vies to smuggle
Soul of da Costa
Out of its struggle.

Confessional hears his
Glib paternoster;
Synagogue sees his
Penitent posture.

What is the end of
This catechism?
Bullet brings dogma
That suffers no schism.

iii

Malevolent scorpions befoul thy chambers,
O my heart; they scurry across its floor,
Leaving the slimy vestiges of doubt.

Banish memento of the vermin; let
No scripture on the wall affright you; no
Ghost of da Costa; no, nor any threat.
Ignore, O heart, even as didst ignore
The bribe of florins jingling in the purse.

iv

Jehovah is factotum of the rabbis;
And Christ endures diurnal Calvary;
Polyglot God is exiled to the churches;
Synods tell God to be or not to be.

The Lord within his vacuum of heaven
Discourses his domestic policies,
With angels who break off their loud hosannas
To help him phrase infallible decrees.

Soul of Spinoza, Baruch Spinoza bids you
Forsake the god suspended in mid-air,
Seek you that other Law, and let Jehovah
Play his game of celestial solitaire.

v

Reducing providence to theorems, the horrible atheist compiled such lore that proved, like proving two and two make four, that in the crown of God we all are gems. From glass and dust of glass he brought to light, out of the pulver and the polished lens, the prism and the flying mote; and hence the infinitesimal and infinite.

Is it a marvel, then, that he forsook the abracadabra of the synagogue, and holding with timelessness a duologue, deciphered a new scripture in the book? Is it a marvel that he left old fraud for passion intellectual of God?

vi

Unto the crown of bone cry *Suzerain!*
Do genuflect before the jewelled brain!
Lavish the homage of the vassal; let
The blood grow heady with strong epithet;
O cirque of the Cabbalist! O proud skull!
Of alchemy O crucible!
Sanctum sanctorum; grottoed hermitage
Where sits the bearded sage!
O golden bowl of Koheleth! and of fate
O hourglass within the pate!
Circling, O planet in the occiput!
O Macrocosm, sinew-shut!
Yea, and having uttered this loud *Te Deum*
Ye have been singularly dumb.

vii

I am weak before the wind; before the sun
  I faint; I lose my strength;
I am utterly vanquished by a star;
  I go to my knees, at length

Before the song of a bird; before
  The breath of spring or fall
I am lost; before these miracles
  I am nothing at all.

viii

Lord, accept my hallelujahs; look not askance at these my petty words; unto perfection a fragment makes its prayer.

For thou art the world, and I am part thereof; thou art the blossom and I its fluttering petal.

I behold thee in all things, and in all things: lo, it is myself; I look into the pupil of thine eye, it is my very countenance I see.

Thy glory fills the earth; it is the earth; the noise of the deep, the moving of many waters, is it not thy voice aloud, O Lord, aloud that all may hear?

The wind through the almond-trees spreads the fragrance of thy robes; the turtle-dove twittering utters diminutives of thy love; at the rising of the sun I behold thy countenance.

Yea, and in the crescent moon, thy little finger's finger-nail.

If I ascend up into heaven, thou art there; If I make my bed in hell, behold thou art there.

Thou art everywhere; a pillar to thy sanctuary is every blade of grass.

Wherefore I said to the wicked, Go to the ant, thou sluggard, seek thou an audience with God.

On the swift wings of a star, even on the numb legs of a snail, thou dost move, O Lord.

A babe in swaddling clothes laughs at the sunbeams on the door's lintel; the sucklings play with thee; with thee Kopernik holds communion through a lens.

I am thy son, O Lord, and brother to all that lives am I.

The flowers of the field, they are kith and kin to me; the lily my sister, the rose is my blood and flesh.

Even as the stars in the firmament move, so does my inward heart, and even as the moon draws the tides in the bay, so does it the blood in my veins.

For thou art the world, and I am part thereof;

Howbeit, even in dust I am resurrected; and even in decay I live again.

ix

Think of Spinoza, then, not as you think
Of Shabbathai Zvi who for a time of life
Took to himself the Torah for a wife,
And underneath the silken canopy
Made public: Thou art hallowed unto me.

Think of Spinoza, rather, plucking tulips
Within the garden of Mynheer, forgetting
Dutchmen and Rabbins, and consumptive fretting,
Plucking his tulips in the Holland sun,
Remembering the thought of the Adored,
Spinoza, gathering flowers for the One,
The ever-unwedded lover of the Lord.

Heirloom

My father bequeathed me no wide estates;
No keys and ledgers were my heritage;
Only some holy books with *yahrzeit* dates
Writ mournfully upon a blank front page—

Books of the Baal Shem Tov, and of his wonders;
Pamphlets upon the devil and his crew;
Prayers against road demons, witches, thunders;
And sundry other tomes for a good Jew.

Beautiful: though no pictures on them, save
The scorpion crawling on a printed track;
The Virgin floating on a scriptural wave,
Square letters twinkling in the Zodiac.

The snuff left on this page, now brown and old,
The tallow stains of midnight liturgy—
These are my coat of arms, and these unfold
My noble lineage, my proud ancestry!

And my tears, too, have stained this heirloomed ground,
When reading in these treatises some weird
Miracle, I turned a leaf and found
A white hair fallen from my father's beard.

Psalm XXVII: A Psalm to Teach Humility

O sign and wonder of the barnyard, more
beautiful than the pheasant, more melodious
than nightingale! O creature marvellous!

Prophet of sunrise, and foreteller of times!
Vizier of the constellations! Sage,
red-bearded, scarlet-turbaned, in whose brain
the stars lie scattered like well-scattered grain!

Calligraphist upon the barnyard page!
Five-noted balladist! Crower of rhymes!

O morning-glory mouth, O throat of dew,
announcing the out-faring of the blue,
the greying and the going of the night,
the coming on,
the imminent coming of the dawn,
the coming of the kinsman, the brightly-plumaged sun!

O creature marvellous—and O blessed Creator,
Who givest to the rooster wit
to know the movements of the turning day,
to understand, to herald it,
better than I, who neither sing nor crow
and of the sun's goings and comings nothing know.

Autobiographical

Out of the ghetto streets where a Jewboy
Dreamed pavement into pleasant Bible-land,
Out of the Yiddish slums where childhood met
The friendly beard, the loutish Sabbath-goy,
Or followed, proud, the Torah-escorting band,
Out of the jargoning city I regret,
Rise memories, like sparrows rising from
The gutter-scattered oats,
Like sadness sweet of synagogal hum,
Like Hebrew violins
Sobbing delight upon their Eastern notes.

Again they ring their little bells, those doors
Deemed by the tender-year'd, magnificent:
Old Ashkenazi's cellar, sharp with spice;
The widows' double-parloured candy-stores
And nuggets sweet bought for one sweaty cent;
The warm fresh-smelling bakery, its pies,
Its cakes, its navel'd bellies of black bread;
The lintels candy-poled
Of barber-shop, bright-bottled, green, blue, red;
And fruit-stall piled, exotic,
And the big synagogue door, with letters of gold.

Again my kindergarten home is full—
Saturday night—with kin and compatriot:
My brothers playing Russian card-games; my
Mirroring sisters looking beautiful,
Humming the evening's imminent fox-trot;
My uncle Mayer, of blessed memory,
Still murmuring maariv, counting holy words;
And the two strangers, come
Fiery from Volhynia's murderous hordes—
The cards and humming stop.
And I too swear revenge for that pogrom.

Occasions dear: the four-legged aleph named
And angel pennies dropping on my book;
The rabbi patting a coming scholar-head;
My mother, blessing candles, Sabbath-flamed,
Queenly in her Warsovian perruque;
My father pickabacking me to bed
To tell tall tales about the Baal Shem Tov—
Letting me curl his beard.
Oh memory of unsurpassing love,
Love leading a brave child
Through childhood's ogred corridors, unfear'd!

The week in the country at my brother's—(May
He own fat cattle in the fields of heaven!)
Its picking of strawberries from grassy ditch,
Its odour of dogrose and of yellowing hay—
Dusty, adventurous, sunny days, all seven!—
Still follow me, still warm me, still are rich
With the cow-tinkling peace of pastureland.
The meadow'd memory
Is sodded with its clover, and is spanned
By that same pillow'd sky
A boy on his back one day watched enviously.

And paved again the street: the shouting boys,
Oblivious of mothers on the stoops,
Playing the robust robbers and police,
The corncob battle—all high-spirited noise
Competitive among the lot-drawn groups.
Another day, of shaken apple trees
In the rich suburbs, and a furious dog,
And guilty boys in flight;
Hazelnut games, and games in the synagogue—
The burrs, the Haman rattle,
The Torah dance on Simchas Torah night.

Immortal days of the picture calendar
Dear to me always with the virgin joy
Of the first flowering of senses five,
Discovering birds, or textures, or a star,
Or tastes sweet, sour, acid, those that cloy;
And perfumes. Never was I more alive.
All days thereafter are a dying off,
A wandering away
From home and the familiar. The years doff
Their innocence.
No other day is ever like that day.

I am no old man fatuously intent
On memoirs, but in memory I seek
The strength and vividness of nonage days,
Not tranquil recollection of event.
It is a fabled city that I seek;
It stands in Space's vapours and Time's haze;
Thence comes my sadness in remembered joy
Constrictive of the throat;
Thence do I hear, as heard by a Jewboy,
The Hebrew violins,
Delighting in the sobbed Oriental note.

Montreal

O city metropole, isle riverain!
Your ancient pavages and sainted routs
Traverse my spirit's conjured avenues!
Splendour erablic of your promenades
Foliates there, and there your maisonry
Of pendent balcon and escalier'd march,
Unique midst English habitat,
Is vivid Normandy!

You populate the pupils of my eyes:
Thus, does the Indian, plumèd, furtivate
Still through your painted autumns, Ville-Marie!
Though palisades have passed, though calumet
With tabac of your peace enfumes the air,
Still do I spy the phantom, aquiline,
Genuflect, moccasin'd, behind
His statue in the square!

Thus, costumed images before me pass,
Haunting your archives architectural:
Coureur de bois, in posts where pelts were portaged;
Seigneur within his candled manoir; Scot
Ambulant through his bank, pillar'd and vast.
Within your chapels, voyaged mariners
Still pray, and personage departed,
All present from your past!

Grand port of navigations, multiple
The lexicons uncargo'd at your quays,
Sonnant though strange to me; but chiefest, I,
Auditor of your music, cherish the
Joined double-melodied vocabulaire
Where English vocable and roll Ecossic,
Mollified by the parle of French
Bilinguefact your air!

Such your suaver voice, hushed Hochelaga!
But for me also sound your potencies,
Fortissimos of sirens fluvial,
Bruit of manufactory, and thunder
From foundry issuant, all puissant tone
Implenishing your hebdomad; and then
Sanct silence, and your argent belfries
Clamant in orison!

You are a part of me, O all your quartiers—
And of dire pauvrete and of richesse—
To finished time my homage loyal claim;
You are locale of infancy, milieu
Vital of institutes that formed my fate;
And you above the city, scintillant,
Mount Royal, are my spirit's mother,
Almative, poitrinate!

Never do I sojourn in alien place
But I do languish for your scenes and sounds,
City of reverie, nostalgic isle,
Pendant most brilliant on Laurentian cord!
The coigns of your boulevards—my signiory—
Your suburbs are my exile's verdure fresh,
Your parks, your fountain'd parks—
Pasture of memory!

City, O city, you are vision'd as
A parchemin roll of saecular exploit
Inked with the script of eterne souvenir!
You are in sound, chanson and instrument!
Mental, you rest forever edified
With tower and dome; and in these beating valves,
Here in these beating valves, you will
For all my mortal time reside!

Portrait of the Poet as Landscape

i

Not an editorial-writer, bereaved with bartlett,
mourns him, the shelved Lycidas.
No actress squeezes a glycerine tear for him.
The radio broadcast lets his passing pass.
And with the police, no record. Nobody, it appears,
either under his real name or his alias,
missed him enough to report.

It is possible that he is dead, and not discovered.
It is possible that he can be found some place
in a narrow closet, like the corpse in a detective story,
standing, his eyes staring, and ready to fall on his face.
It is also possible that he is alive
and amnesiac, or mad, or in retired disgrace,
or beyond recognition lost in love.

We are sure only that from our real society
he has disappeared; he simply does not count,
except in the pullulation of vital statistics—
somebody's vote, perhaps, an anonymous taunt
of the Gallup poll, a dot in a government table—
but not felt, and certainly far from eminent—
in a shouting mob, somebody's sigh.

O, he who unrolled our culture from his scroll—
the prince's quote, the rostrum-rounding roar—
who under one name made articulate
heaven, and under another the seven-circled air,
is, if he is at all, a number, an x,
a Mr. Smith in a hotel register,—
incognito, lost, lacunal.

ii

The truth is he's not dead, but only ignored—
like the mirroring lenses forgotten on a brow
that shine with the guilt of their unnoticed world.
The truth is he lives among neighbours, who, though they
will allow
him a passable fellow, think him eccentric, not solid,
a type that one can forgive, and for that matter, forego.

Himself he has his moods, just like a poet.
Sometimes, depressed to nadir, he will think all lost,
will see himself as throwback, relict, freak,
his mother's miscarriage, his great-grandfather's ghost,
and he will curse his quintuplet senses, and their tutors
in whom he put, as he should not have put, his trust.

Then he will remember his travels over that body—
the torso verb, the beautiful face of the noun,
and all those shaped and warm auxiliaries!
A first love it was, the recognition of his own.
Dear limbs adverbial, complexion of adjective,
dimple and dip of conjugation!

And then remember how this made a change in him
affecting for always the glow and growth of his being;
how suddenly was aware of the air, like shaken tinfoil,
of the patents of nature, the shock of belated seeing,
the lonelinesses peering from the eyes of crowds;
the integers of thought; the cube-roots of feeling.

Thus, zoomed to zenith, sometimes he hopes again,
and sees himself as a character, with a rehearsed role:
the Count of Monte Cristo, come for his revenges;
the unsuspected heir, with papers; the risen soul;
or the chloroformed prince awaking from his flowers;
or—deflated again—the convict on parole.

iii

He is alone; yet not completely alone.
Pins on a map of a colour similar to his,
each city has one, sometimes more than one;
here, caretakers of art, in colleges;
in offices, there, with arm-bands, and green-shaded;
and there, pounding their catalogued beats in libraries,—

everywhere menial, a shadow's shadow.
And always for their egos—their outmoded art.
Thus, having lost the bevel in the ear,
they know neither up nor down, mistake the part
for the whole, curl themselves in a comma,
talk technics, make a colon their eyes. They distort—

such is the pain of their frustration—truth
to something convolute and cerebral.
How they do fear the slap of the flat of the platitude!
Now Pavlov's victims, their mouths water at bell,
the platter empty.
                                        See they set twenty-one jewels
into their watches; the time they do not tell!

Some, patagonian in their own esteem,
and longing for the multiplying word,
join party and wear pins, now have a message,
an ear, and the convention-hall's regard.
Upon the knees of ventriloquists, they own,
of their dandled brightness, only the paint and board.

And some go mystical, and some go mad.
One stares at a mirror all day long, as if
to recognize himself; another courts
angels,—for here he does not fear rebuff;
and a third, alone, and sick with sex, and rapt,
doodles him symbols convex and concave.

O schizoid solitudes! O purities
curdling upon themselves! Who live for themselves,
or for each other, but for nobody else;
desire affection, private and public loves;
are friendly, and then quarrel and surmise
the secret perversions of each other's lives.

iv

He suspects that something has happened, a law
been passed, a nightmare ordered. Set apart,
he finds himself, with special haircut and dress,
as on a reservation. Introvert.
He does not understand this; sad conjecture
muscles and palls thrombotic on his heart.

He thinks an impostor, having studied his personal
biography,
his gestures, his moods, now has come forward to pose
in the shivering vacuums his absence leaves.
Wigged with his laurel, that other, and faked with his face,
he pats the heads of his children, pecks his wife,
and is at home, and slippered, in his house.

So he guesses at the impertinent silhouette
that talks to his phone-piece and slits open his mail.
Is it the local tycoon who for a hobby
plays poet, he so epical in steel?
The orator, making a pause? Or is that man
he who blows his flash of brass in the jittering hall?

Or is he cuckolded by the troubadour
rich and successful out of celluloid?
Or by the don who unrhymes atoms? Or
the chemist death built up? Pride, lost impostor'd pride,
it is another, another, whoever he is,
who rides where he should ride.

v

Fame, the adrenalin: to be talked about;
to be a verb; to be introduced as *The:*
to smile with endorsement from slick paper; make
caprices anecdotal; to nod to the world; to see
one's name like a song upon the marquees played;
to be forgotten with embarrassment; to be—
to be.

It has its attractions, but is not the thing;
nor is it the ape mimesis who speaks from the tree
ancestral; nor the merkin joy . . .
Rather it is stark infelicity
which stirs him from his sleep, undressed, asleep
to walk upon roofs and window-sills and defy
the gape of gravity.

vi

Therefore he seeds illusions. Look, he is
the nth Adam taking a green inventory
in world but scarcely uttered, naming, praising,
the flowering fiats in the meadow, the
syllabled fur, stars aspirate, the pollen
whose sweet collision sounds eternally.
For to praise

the world—he, solitary man—is breath
to him. Until it has been praised, that part
has not been. Item by exciting item—
air to his lungs, and pressured blood to his heart—
they are pulsated, and breathed, until they map,
not the world's, but his own body's chart!

And now in imagination he has climbed
another planet, the better to look
with single camera view upon this earth—

its total scope, and each afflated tick,
its talk, its trick, its tracklessness—and this,
this he would like to write down in a book!

To find a new function for the *déclassé* craft
archaic like the fletcher's; to make a new thing;
to say the word that will become sixth sense;
perhaps by necessity and indirection bring
new forms to life, anonymously, new creeds—
O, somehow pay back the daily larcenies of the lung!

These are not mean ambitions. It is already something
merely to entertain them. Meanwhile, he
makes of his status as zero a rich garland,
a halo of his anonymity,
and lives alone, and in his secret shines
like phosphorus. At the bottom of the sea.

The Rocking Chair

It seconds the crickets of the province. Heard
in the clean lamplit farmhouses of Quebec,—
wooden,—it is no less a national bird;
and rivals, in its cage, the mere stuttering clock.
To its time, the evenings are rolled away;
and in its peace the pensive mother knits
contentment to be worn by her family,
grown-up, but still cradled by the chair in which she sits.

It is also the old man's pet, pair to his pipe,
the two aids of his arithmetic and plans,
plans rocking and puffing into market-shape;
and it is the toddler's game and dangerous dance.
Moved to the verandah, on summer Sundays, it is,
among the hanging plants, the girls, the boy-friends,
sabbatical and clumsy, like the white haloes
dangling above the blue serge suits of the young men.

It has a personality of its own;
is a character (like that old drunk Lacoste,
exhaling amber, and toppling on his pins);
it is alive; individual; and no less
an identity than those about it. And
it is tradition. Centuries have been flicked
from its arcs, alternately flicked and pinned.
It rolls with the gait of St. Malo. It is act

and symbol, symbol of this static folk
which moves in segments, and returns to base,—
a sunken pendulum: *invoke, revoke*;
loosed yon, leashed hither, motion on no space.
O, like some Anjou ballad, all refrain,
which turns about its longing, and seems to move
to make a pleasure out of repeated pain,
its music moves, as if always back to a first love.

Political Meeting

(FOR CAMILLIEN HOUDE)

On the school platform, draping the folding seats,
they wait the chairman's praise and glass of water.
Upon the wall the agonized Y initials their faith.

Here all are laic; the skirted brothers have gone.
Still, their equivocal absence is felt, like a breeze
that gives curtains the sounds of surplices.

The hall is yellow with light, and jocular;
suddenly some one lets loose upon the air
the ritual bird which the crowd in snares of singing

catches and plucks, throat, wings, and little limbs.
Fall the feathers of sound, like *alouette's*.
The chairman, now, is charming, full of asides and wit,

building his orators, and chipping off
the heckling gargoyles popping in the hall.
(Outside, in the dark, the street is body-tall,

flowered with faces intent on the scarecrow thing
that shouts to thousands the echoing
of their own wishes.) The Orator has risen!

Worshipped and loved, their favourite visitor,
a country uncle with sunflower seeds in his pockets,
full of wonderful moods, tricks, imitative talk,

he is their idol: like themselves, not handsome,
not snobbish, not of the *Grande Allée! Un homme!*
Intimate, informal, he makes bear's compliments

to the ladies; is gallant; and grins;
goes for the balloon, his opposition, with pins;
jokes also on himself, speaks of himself

in the third person, slings slang, and winks with folklore;
and knows now that he has them, kith and kin.
Calmly, therefore, he begins to speak of war,

praises the virtue of being *Canadien*,
of being at peace, of faith, of family,
and suddenly his other voice: *Where are your sons?*

He is tearful, choking tears; but not he
would blame the clever English; in their place
he'd do the same, maybe.

Where *are* your sons?
The whole street wears one face,
shadowed and grim; and in the darkness rises
the body-odour of race.

Sestina on the Dialectic

Yes yeasts to No, and No is numinous with Yes. All is a hap, a haze, a hazard, a do-doubtful, a flight from, a travel to. Nothing will keep, but eases essence,—out!— outplots its plight. So westers east, and so each teaches an opposite: a nonce-thing still.

A law? Fact or flaw of the fiat, still—a law. It binds us, braided, wicker and withe. It stirs the seasons, it treads the tides, it so rests in our life there's nothing, there's not a sole thing that from its workings will not out.

The antics of the antonyms! From, to; stress, slack and stress,—a rhythm running to a reason, a double dance, a shivering still.

Even the heart's blood bursting in, bales out, an ebb and flow; and even the circuit within which its pulsebeat's beam—man's morse—is a something that grows, that grounds—treks, totters. So.

O dynasties and dominions downfall so! Flourish to flag and fail, are potent to a pause, a panic precipice, to a picked pit, and thence—rubble rebuilding,—still rise resurrective, —and now see them, with new doers in dominion!

They, too, dim out.

World's sudden with somersault, updown, inout, overand-under. And, note well: also that other world, the two-chambered mind, goes with it, ever kaleidoscopic, one scape to another, suffering change that changes still, that focusses and fissions *the* to *a*.

When will there be arrest? Consensus? A marriage of the antipathies, and out of the vibrant deaths and rattles the life still? O just as the racked one hopes his ransom, so I hope it, name it, image it, the together-living, the together-with, the final synthesis. A stop.

But so it never will turn out, returning to the rack within, without. And no thing's still.

DOROTHY LIVESAY

b. 1909

Fire and Reason

I cannot shut out the night—
Nor its sharp clarity.

The many blinds we draw,
You and I,
The many fires we light
Can never quite obliterate
The irony of stars,
The deliberate moon,
The last, unsolved finality of night.

Green Rain

I remember long veils of green rain
Feathered like the shawl of my grandmother—
Green from the half-green of the spring trees
Waving in the valley.

I remember the road
Like the one which leads to my grandmother's house,
A warm house, with green carpets,
Geraniums, a trilling canary
And shining horse-hair chairs;
And the silence, full of the rain's falling
Was like my grandmother's parlour
Alive with herself and her voice, rising and falling—
Rain and wind intermingled.

I remember on that day
I was thinking only of my love
And of my love's house.
But now I remember the day
As I remember my grandmother.
I remember the rain as the feathery fringe of her shawl.

Day and Night

1

Dawn, red and angry, whistles loud and sends
A geysered shaft of steam searching the air.
Scream after scream announces that the churn
Of life must move, the giant arm command.
Men in a stream, a moving human belt
Move into sockets, every one a bolt.
The fun begins, a humming, whirring drum—
Men do a dance in time to the machines.

2

One step forward
Two steps back
Shove the lever,
Push it back

While Arnot whirls
A roundabout
And Geoghan shuffles
Bolts about.

One step forward
Hear it crack
Smashing rhythm—
Two steps back

Your heart-beat pounds
Against your throat
The roaring voices
Drown your shout

Across the way
A writhing whack
Sets you spinning
Two steps back—

One step forward
Two steps back.

3

Day and night are rising and falling
Night and day shift gears and slip rattling
Down the runway, shot into storerooms
Where only arms and a note-book remember
The record of evil, the sum of commitments.
We move as through sleep's revolving memories
Piling up hatred, stealing the remnants,
Doors forever folding before us—
And where is the recompense, on what agenda
Will you set love down? Who knows of peace?

Day and night
Night and day
Light rips into ribbons
What we say.

I called to love
Deep in dream:
Be with me in the daylight
As in gloom.

Be with me in the pounding
In the knives against my back
Set your voice resounding
Above the steel's whip crack.

High and sweet
Sweet and high
Hold, hold up the sunlight
In the sky!

Day and night
Night and day
Tear up all the silence
Find the words I could not say . . .

4

We were stoking coal in the furnaces; red hot
They gleamed, burning our skins away, his and mine.
We were working together, night and day, and knew
Each other's stroke; and without words, exchanged
An understanding about kids at home,
The landlord's jaw, wage-cuts and overtime.
We were like buddies, see? Until they said
That nigger is too smart the way he smiles
And sauces back the foreman; he might say
Too much one day, to others changing shifts.
Therefore they cut him down, who flowered at night
And raised me up, day hanging over night—
So furnaces could still consume our withered skin.

Shadrach, Meshach and Abednego
Turn in the furnace, whirling slow.
  Lord, I'm burnin' in the fire
  Lord, I'm steppin' on the coals
  Lord, I'm blacker than my brother
  Blow your breath down here.

  Boss, I'm smothered in the darkness
  Boss, I'm shrivellin' in the flames
  Boss, I'm blacker than my brother
  Blow your breath down here.
Shadrach, Meshach and Abednego
Burn in the furnace, whirling slow.

5

Up in the roller room, men swing steel
Swing it, zoom; and cut it, crash.
Up in the dark the welder's torch
Makes sparks fly like lightning reel.

Now I remember storm on a field
The trees bow tense before the blow
Even the jittering sparrows' talk
Ripples into the still tree shield.

We are in storm that has no cease
No lull before, no after time
When green with rain the grasses grow
And air is sweet with fresh increase.

We bear the burden home to bed
The furnace glows within our hearts:
Our bodies hammered through the night
Are welded into bitter bread.

Bitter, yes:
But listen, friend:
We are mightier
In the end.

We have ears
Alert to seize
A weakness
In the foreman's ease

We have eyes
To look across
The bosses' profit
At our loss.

Are you waiting?
Wait with us
After evening
There's a hush—

Use it not
For love's slow count:
Add up hate
And let it mount

Until the lifeline
Of your hand
Is calloused with
A fiery brand!

Add up hunger,
Labour's ache
These are figures
That will make

The page grow crazy
Wheels go still,
Silence sprawling
On the till—

Add your hunger,
Brawn and bones,
Take your earnings:
Bread, not stones!

6

Into thy maw I commend my body
But the soul shines without
A child's hands as a leaf are tender
And draw the poison out.

Green of new leaf shall deck my spirit
Laughter's roots will spread:
Though I am overalled and silent
Boss, I'm far from dead!

One step forward
Two steps back
Will soon be over:
Hear it crack!

The wheels may whirr
A roundabout
And neighbour's shuffle
Drown your shout

The wheel must limp
Till it hangs still
And crumpled men
Pour down the hill.

Day and night
Night and day
Till life is turned
The other way!

Autumn: 1939

In our time the great ones fade
We hear the whisper of their falling
Words on a radio announce
How Yeats and Freud within a year
Heard the insistent silence calling.

In our time torpedoes score
In thunder-foam the ships go under
Blood is spurted from the sky
Ashes smoke where children played—
Gardens, pavements, split in plunder.

In our time no great ones live
For ears are censored from their singing—
No surgeon of the mind can touch
Pillar of salt, idiot stare,
Bell-tongues meaninglessly swinging.

Bartok and the Geranium

She lifts her green umbrellas
Towards the pane
Seeking her fill of sunlight
Or of rain;
Whatever falls
She has no commentary
Accepts, extends,
Blows out her furbelows,
Her bustling boughs;

And all the while he whirls
Explodes in space,
Never content with this small room:
Not even can he be
Confined to sky
But must speed high and higher still
From galaxy to galaxy,
Wrench from the stars their momentary notes
Steal music from the moon.

She's daylight
He is dark
She's heaven-held breath
He storms and crackles
Spits with hell's own spark.

Yet in this room, this moment now
These together breathe and be:
She, essence of serenity,
He in a mad intensity
Soars beyond sight
Then hurls, lost Lucifer,
From heaven's height.

And when he's done, he's out:
She leans a lip against the glass
And preens herself in light.

Lament

FOR J.F.B.L.

What moved me, was the way your hand
Lay in my hand, not withering,
But warm, like a hand cooled in a stream
And purling still; or a bird caught in a snare
Wings folded stiff, eyes in a stare,
But still alive with the fear,
Heart hoarse with hope—
So your hand, your dead hand, my dear.

And the veins, still mounting as blue rivers,
Mounting towards the tentative finger-tips,
The delta where four seas come in—
Your fingers promontories into colourless air
Were rosy still—not chalk (like cliffs
You knew in boyhood, Isle of Wight):
But blushed with colour from the sun you sought
And muscular from garden toil;
Stained with the purple of an iris bloom,
Violas grown for a certain room;
Hands seeking faïence, filagree,
Chinese lacquer and ivory—
Brussels lace; and a walnut piece
Carved by a hand now phosphorus.

What moved me, was the way your hand
Held life, although the pulse was gone.
The hand that carpentered a children's chair,
Carved out a stair
Held leash upon a dog in strain
Gripped wheel, swung sail,
Flicked horse's rein
And then again
Moved kings and queens meticulous on a board,
Slashed out the cards, cut bread, and poured
A purring cup of tea;
The hand so neat and nimble
Could make a tennis partner tremble,
Write a resounding round
Of sonorous verbs and nouns—
Hand that would not strike a child, and yet
Could ring a bell and send a man to doom.

And now unmoving in this Spartan room
The hand still speaks:
After the brain was fogged
And the tight lips tighter shut,
After the shy appraising eyes
Relinquished fire for the sea's green gaze—
The hand still breathes, fastens its hold on life;
Demands the whole, establishes the strife.

What moved me, was the way your hand
Lay cool in mine, not withering;
As bird still breathes, and stream runs clear—
So your hand; your dead hand, my dear.

*The Three Emily's**

These women crying in my head
Walk alone, uncomforted:
The Emily's, these three
Cry to be set free—
And others whom I will not name
Each different, each the same.

Yet they had liberty!
Their kingdom was the sky:
They batted clouds with easy hand,
Found a mountain for their stand;
From wandering lonely they could catch
The inner magic of a heath—
A lake their palette, any tree
Their brush could be.

And still they cry to me
As in reproach—
I, born to hear their inner storm
Of separate man in woman's form,
I yet possess another kingdom, barred
To them, these three, this Emily.
I move as mother in a frame,
My arteries
Flow the immemorial way
Towards the child, the man;
And only for brief span
Am I an Emily on mountain snows
And one of these.

And so the whole that I possess
Is still much less—
They move triumphant through my head:
I am the one
Uncomforted.

*Emily Bronte, Emily Dickinson and Emily Carr.

On Looking into Henry Moore

1

Sun, stun me, sustain me
Turn me to stone:
Stone, goad me and gall me
Urge me to run.

When I have found
Passivity in fire
And fire in stone
Female and male
I'll rise alone
Self-extending and self-known.

2

The message of the tree is this:
Aloneness is the only bliss

Self-adoration is not in it
(Narcissus tried, but could not win it)

Rather, to extend the root
Tombwards, be at home with death

But in the upper branches know
A green eternity of fire and snow.

3

The fire in the farthest hills
Is where I'd burn myself to bone:
Clad in the armour of the sun
I'd stand anew, alone

Take off this flesh, this hasty dress
Prepare my half-self for myself:
One unit, as a tree or stone
Woman in man, and man in womb.

Ice Age

(FOR LAURA DAMANIA)

In this coming cold
devouring our wheat fields
and Russia's
there'll be no shadow
nor sign of shadow
all cloud, shroud
endless rain
eternal snow

In this coming cold
which we have fashioned
out of our vain jet-pride,
the supersonic planes
will shriek destruction
upon the benign
yin yang
ancient and balanced universe

Worse than an animal
man tortures his prey
given sun's energy
and fire's blaze
he has ripped away
leaf
        bird
                flower
is moving to destroy
the still centre
heart's power.

Now who among us
will lift a finger
to declare *I am of God, good*?
Who among us
dares to be righteous?

ANNE WILKINSON

1910-1961

Still Life

I'd love this body more
If graved in rigid wood
It could not move;
I'd cut it fresh in pine;
The little knots
Would show where muscles grew,
The hollows shadow ovals
Into eyes,
The grain be quick to point
The vein, be tendon's clue;
I'd whittle hair
A solid armoured hood
And nothing here profane,
Nor rend the wood
But bind my fluid form
To forest tree,
Be still and let its green blood
Enter me.

Letter to My Children: Postscript

With winter here my age
Must play with miracles.
So if I grant you wishes three
Scoff and say I owe you five,
Five full and fathomed senses,
Precision instruments

To chart the wayward course
Through rock and moss and riddles
Hard or soft as ether, airy
Airy quite contrary
Where will the next wind blow?

With sense alive you're wiser
Than the man who ploughs the profit
From his field
For you, a child, still touch
Taste, smell out heaven and hell
When lying hidden
In the waves of wheat his acres yield.

I'd set your heart by relativity,
With space for slow and fast,
Set five alarms to wake and catch
The shadowless noon
Before it moves to after.
And luminous be thy dial
To read the pale
Gold numerals of dawn
Thin on the face of the midnight watch.

Your kingdom comes with senses
Schooled to top professionals;
The ear, a master bred on dissonance
Of urban sound
Will mark the drop in pitch of towns
Adrift in fog
And the lowering of evening song
When the strut is gone
From the tenor birds;

You'll shiver but you'll hear
The sharp white nails of the moon
Scratch the slate of midnight water;
Your ear will share
The loneliness of curlews crying,
Record the laugh of loons
On the delicate grooves of madness.

Before you tar with age
Swing to hot percussion jazz
Of insects, dance
To carnal charivari
Broadcast from distended throats of frogs.

And when the windy autumn blows
Hoist antennae, gather
The blazing brass of your being
To compass the ocean's scale
And crescendos
Surfed from a sea in storm.

When waves go limp come home,
Push the water in your bath and echo
On a porcelain reef
The older swell and foam;
Adjust, as seamen do on land, to gales
Blustered from a gutted shell
On a parlour mantel.

Uncage the tiger in your eye
And tawny, night and day,
Stalk the landscape for the contour
Of a fern or arm,
Gorge on pigment squeezed
From barley fields
Or part the strawberry leaves
That hungry eyes may water
On the fruit and feast of colour;

Let eager pupils measure
Girth and bravado of bulldozer,
Watch the flex of iron muscle
When giant shovels
Grind their jaws and roar,
'Like Samson I can lift a ton
Of terra in my teeth.'

Speed your vision till it follows
Power and plumb of bullet's line
From gun to heart,
Slow your eyes with patience, see
The bud relax-
ing as the petals yawn apart.

Touch everything available
To consciousness,
Birch and bark of cedar, tables
Worn to silk by women
Rubbing their restlessness
To polished wood;
Shut your eyes and feel a way
To linen and lover, marvel
At aluminium, cold in the sun
And at the thermossed fire
And chill of stone.

Touch worms and warts
In gratitude for shudders, stroke
The soft white bulge of peonies
And trace their crimson veins
Back to the milky memory of mothers;
Sharpen wit where nerve ends
Lace the skin of fingers—
Their tips will clock the pulse
Beat of a leaf—
And when by some enormous morning grief
You are undone,
Feel the warm salt water
Where your eyes swim, green
With childhood
In the last sea vestiges of home.

And with a scholar's nose
Catalogue the flowers
Fighting for precedence in June,
Learn the lesson
Stinked at you from skunk or drains
And from pot pourri of
Department stores inhale
The current substitutes for love;

Smell the vigour
Packed in snow at noon and metal
In the air
When stars show up for duty
On the dim lit wards of winter
And breath is everywhere white with veils
And the vows of nuns.

Taste a thesis on your tongue,
Honey, lemon, spring sprung water
Loaded with geology.
Skin and flush of peaches, red
Tomatoes picked and bitten in the sun
All gush the juice and seed of summer
To the learned mouth.

And sense how prehistoric fathers
Weigh our modern cells with jungle genes
When huge our appetite for lean
And fat of meat
Sets saliva dreaming of the kill
A million years behind the nearest hill.

In milk and curd of cheese
Guess the whey and whyfore
Of our interval need of peace;
For bread and wine
Let wisdom on your tongue
Pause to conceive a fivefold grace.

'Sleep well'—I wonder why
We harp on sleep, our certainty.
I'd turn the message inside out
And have you listen
With immaculate ear
To what the bells of matin say,
'Wake well, my child,
Don't lie on your nose,
Today is a holy day.'

In June and Gentle Oven

In June and gentle oven
Summer kingdoms simmer
As they come
And flower and leaf and love
Release
Their sweetest juice.

No wind at all
On the wide green world
Where fields go stroll-
ing by
And in and out
An adder of a stream
Parts the daisies
On a small Ontario farm.

And where, in curve of meadow,
Lovers, touching, lie,
A church of grass stands up
And walls them, holy, in.

Fabulous the insects
Stud the air
Or walk on running water,
Klee-drawn saints
And bright as angels are.

Honeysuckle here
Is more than bees can bear
And time turns pale
And stops to catch its breath
And lovers slip their flesh
And light as pollen
Play on treble water
Till bodies reappear
And a shower of sun
To dry their languor.

Then two in one the lovers lie
And peel the skin of summer
With their teeth
And suck its marrow from a kiss
So charged with grace
The tongue, all knowing
Holds the sap of June
Aloof from seasons, flowing.

Lens

I

The poet's daily chore
Is my long duty;
To keep and cherish my good lens
For love and war
And wasps about the lilies
And mutiny within.

My woman's eye is weak
And veiled with milk;
My working eye is muscled
With a curious tension,
Stretched and open
As the eyes of children;
Trusting in its vision
Even should it see
The holy holy spirit gambol
Counterheadwise,
Lithe and warm as any animal.

My woman's iris circles
A blind pupil;
The poet's eye is crystal,
Polished to accept the negative,
The contradictions in a proof
And the accidental
Candour of the shadows;
The shutter, oiled and smooth
Clicks on the grace of heroes
Or on some bestial act
When lit with radiance
The afterwords the actors speak
Give depths to violence,

Or if the bull is great
And the matador
And the sword
Itself the metaphor.

II

In my dark room the years
Lie in solution,
Develop film by film.
Slow at first and dim
Their shadows bite
On the fine white pulp of paper.

An early snap of fire
Licking the arms of air
I hold against the light, compare
The details with a prehistoric view
Of land and sea
And cradles of mud that rocked
The wet and sloth of infancy.

A stripe of tiger, curled
And sleeping on the ribs of reason
Prints as clear
As Eve and Adam, pearled
With sweat, staring at an apple core;

And death, in black and white
Or politic in green and Easter film,
Lands on steely points, a dancer
Disciplined to the foolscap stage,
The property of poets
Who command his robes, expose
His moving likeness on the page.

IRVING LAYTON

b. 1912

The Swimmer

The afternoon foreclosing, see
The swimmer plunges from his raft,
Opening the spray corollas by his act of war—
The snake heads strike
Quickly and are silent.

Emerging see how for a moment
A brown weed with marvellous bulbs,
He lies imminent upon the water
While light and sound come with a sharp passion
From the gonad sea around the Poles
And break in bright cockle-shells about his ears.

He dives, floats, goes under like a thief
Where his blood sings to the tiger shadows
In the scentless greenery that leads him home,
A male salmon down fretted stairways
Through underwater slums . . .

Stunned by the memory of lost gills
He frames gestures of self-absorption
Upon the skull-like beach;
Observes with instigated eyes
The sun that empties itself upon the water,
And the last wave romping in
To throw its boyhood on the marble sand.

The Bull Calf

The thing could barely stand. Yet taken
from his mother and the barn smells
he still impressed with his pride,
with the promise of sovereignty in the way
his head moved to take us in.
The fierce sunlight tugging the maize from the ground
licked at his shapely flanks.
He was too young for all that pride.
I thought of the deposed Richard II.

"No money in bull calves," Freeman had said.
The visiting clergyman rubbed the nostrils
now snuffing pathetically at the windless day.
"A pity," he sighed.
My gaze slipped off his hat toward the empty sky
that circled over the black knot of men,
over us and the calf waiting for the first blow.

Struck,
the bull calf drew in his thin forelegs
as if gathering strength for a mad rush . . .
tottered . . . raised his darkening eyes to us,
and I saw we were at the far end
of his frightened look, growing smaller and smaller
till we were only the ponderous mallet
that flicked his bleeding ear
and pushed him over on his side, stiffly,
like a block of wood.

Below the hill's crest
the river snuffled on the improvised beach.
We dug a deep pit and threw the dead calf into it.
It made a wet sound, a sepulchral gurgle,
as the warm sides bulged and flattened.
Settled, the bull calf lay as if asleep,
one foreleg over the other,
bereft of pride and so beautiful now,
without movement, perfectly still in the cool pit,
I turned away and wept.

The Fertile Muck

There are brightest apples on those trees
        but until I, fabulist, have spoken
they do not know their significance
or what other legends are hung like garlands
        on their black boughs twisting
like a rumour. The wind's noise is empty.

Nor are the winged insects better off
        though they wear my crafty eyes
wherever they alight. Stay here, my love;
you will see how delicately they deposit
        me on the leaves of elms
or fold me in the orient dust of summer.

And if in August joiners and bricklayers
        are thick as flies around us
building expensive bungalows for those
who do not need them, unless they release
        me roaring from their moth-proofed cupboards
their buyers will have no joy, no ease.

I could extend their rooms for them without cost
        and give them crazy sundials
to tell the time with, but I have noticed
how my irregular footprint horrifies them
        evenings and Sunday afternoons:
they spray for hours to erase its shadow.

How to dominate reality? Love is one way;
        imagination another. Sit here
beside me, sweet; take my hard hand in yours.
We'll mark the butterflies disappearing over the hedge
        with tiny wristwatches on their wings:
our fingers touching the earth, like two Buddhas.

The Cold Green Element

At the end of the garden walk
the wind and its satellite wait for me;
their meaning I will not know
until I go there,
but the black-hatted undertaker

who, passing, saw my heart beating in the grass,
is also going there. Hi, I tell him,
a great squall in the Pacific blew a dead poet
out of the water,
who now hangs from the city's gates.

Crowds depart daily to see it, and return
with grimaces and incomprehension;
if its limbs twitched in the air
they would sit at its feet
peeling their oranges.

And turning over I embrace like a lover
the trunk of a tree, one of those
for whom the lightning was too much
and grew a brilliant
hunchback with a crown of leaves.

The ailments escaped from the labels
of medicine bottles are all fled to the wind;
I've seen myself lately in the eyes
of old women,
spent streams mourning my manhood,

in whose old pupils the sun became
a bloodsmear on broad catalpa leaves
and hanging from ancient twigs,
my murdered selves
sparked the air like the muted collisions

of fruit. A black dog howls down my blood,
a black dog with yellow eyes;
he too by someone's inadvertence
                saw the bloodsmear
on the broad catalpa leaves.

But the furies clear a path for me to the worm
who sang for an hour in the throat of a robin,
and misled by the cries of young boys
                I am again
a breathless swimmer in that cold green element.

Keine Lazarovitch

1870-1959

When I saw my mother's head on the cold pillow,
Her white waterfalling hair in the cheeks' hollows,
I thought, quietly circling my grief, of how
She had loved God but cursed extravagantly his creatures.

For her final mouth was not water but a curse,
A small black hole, a black rent in the universe,
Which damned the green earth, stars and trees in its stillness
And the inescapable lousiness of growing old.

And I record she was comfortless, vituperative,
Ignorant, glad, and much else besides; I believe
She endlessly praised her black eyebrows, their thick weave,
Till plagiarizing Death leaned down and took them for his
      mould.

And spoiled a dignity I shall not again find,
And the fury of her stubborn limited mind;
Now none will shake her amber beads and call God blind,
Or wear them upon a breast so radiantly.

O fierce she was, mean and unaccommodating;
But I think now of the toss of her gold earrings,
Their proud carnal assertion, and her youngest sings
While all the rivers of her red veins move into the sea.

Whatever Else Poetry is Freedom

Whatever else poetry is freedom.
Forget the rhetoric, the trick of lying
All poets pick up sooner or later. From the river,
Rising like the thin voice of grey castratos—the mist;
Poplars and pines grow straight but oaks are gnarled;
Old codgers must speak of death, boys break windows;
Women lie honestly by their men at last.

And I who gave my Kate a blackened eye
Did to its vivid changing colours
Make up an incredible musical scale;
And now I balance on wooden stilts and dance
And thereby sing to the loftiest casements.
See how with polish I bow from the waist.
Space for these stilts! More space or I fail!

And a crown I say for my buffoon's head.
Yet no more fool am I than King Canute,
Lord of our tribe, who scanned and scorned;
Who half-deceived, believed; and, poet, missed
The first white waves come nuzzling at his feet;
Then damned the courtiers and the foolish trial
With a most bewildering and unkingly jest.

It was the mist. It lies inside one like a destiny.
A real Jonah it lies rotting like a lung.
And I know myself undone who am a clown
And wear a wreath of mist for a crown;
Mist with the scent of dead apples,
Mist swirling from black oily waters at evening,
Mist from the fraternal graves of cemeteries.

It shall drive me to beg my food and at last
Hurl me broken I know and prostrate on the road;
Like a huge toad I saw, entire but dead,
That Time mordantly had blacked; O pressed
To the moist earth it pled for entry.

I shall be I say that stiff toad for sick with mist
And crazed I smell the odour of mortality.

And Time flames like a paraffin stove
And what it burns are the minutes I live.
At certain middays I have watched the cars
Bring me from afar their windshield suns;
What lay to my hand were blue fenders
The suns extinguished, the drivers wearing sunglasses.
And it made me think I had touched a hearse.

So whatever else poetry is freedom. Let
Far off the impatient cadences reveal
A padding for my breathless stilts. Swivel,
O hero, in the fleshy groves, skin and glycerine,
And sing of lust, the sun's accompanying shadow
Like a vampire's wing, the stillness in dead feet—
Your stave brings resurrection, O aggrievèd king.

A Tall Man Executes a Jig

I

So the man spread his blanket on the field
And watched the shafts of light between the tufts
And felt the sun push the grass towards him;
The noise he heard was that of whizzing flies,
The whistlings of some small imprudent birds,
And the ambiguous rumbles of cars
That made him look up at the sky, aware
Of the gnats that tilted against the wind
And in the sunlight turned to jigging motes.
Fruitflies he'd call them except there was no fruit
About, spoiling to hatch these glitterings,
These nervous dots for which the mind supplied
The closing sentences from Thucydides,
Or from Euclid having a savage nightmare.

II

Jig jig, jig jig. Like minuscule black links
Of a chain played with by some playful
Unapparent hand or the palpitant
Summer haze bored with the hour's stillness.
He felt the sting and tingle afterwards
Of those leaving their orthodox unrest,
Leaving their undulant excitation
To drop upon his sleeveless arm. The grass,
Even the wildflowers became black hairs
And himself a maddened speck among them.
Still the assaults of the small flies made him
Glad at last, until he saw purest joy
In their frantic jiggings under a hair,
So changed from those in the unrestraining air.

III

He stood up and felt himself enormous.
Felt as might Donatello over stone,
Or Plato, or as a man who has held
A loved and lovely woman in his arms
And feels his forehead touch the emptied sky
Where all antinomies flood into light.
Yet jig jig jig, the haloing black jots
Meshed with the wheeling fire of the sun:
Motion without meaning, disquietude
Without sense or purpose, ephemerides
That mottled the resting summer air till
Gusts swept them from his sight like wisps of smoke.
Yet they returned, bringing a bee who, seeing
But a tall man, left him for a marigold.

IV

He doffed his aureole of gnats and moved
Out of the field as the sun sank down,
A dying god upon the blood-red hills.
Ambition, pride, the ecstasy of sex,
And all circumstance of delight and grief,
That blood upon the mountain's side, that flood
Washed into a clear incredible pool
Below the ruddied peaks that pierced the sun.
He stood still and waited. If ever
The hour of revelation was come
It was now, here on the transfigured steep.
The sky darkened. Some birds chirped. Nothing else.
He thought the dying god had gone to sleep:
An Indian fakir on his mat of nails.

V

And on the summit of the asphalt road
Which stretched towards the fiery town, the man
Saw one hill raised like a hairy arm, dark
With pines and cedars against the stricken sun
—The arm of Moses or of Joshua.
He dropped his head and let fall the halo
Of mountains, purpling and silent as time,
To see temptation coiled before his feet:
A violated grass snake that lugged
Its intestine like a small red valise.
A cold-eyed skinflint it now was, and not
The manifest of that joyful wisdom,
The mirth and arrogant green flame of life;
Or earth's vivid tongue that flicked in praise of earth.

VI

And the man wept because pity was useless.
"Your jig's up; the flies come like kites," he said
And watched the grass snake crawl towards the hedge,
Convulsing and dragging into the dark
The satchel filled with curses for the earth,
For the odours of warm sedge, and the sun,
A blood-red organ in the dying sky.
Backwards it fell into a grassy ditch
Exposing its underside, white as milk,
And mocked by wisps of hay between its jaws;
And then it stiffened to its final length.
But though it opened its thin mouth to scream
A last silent scream that shook the black sky,
Adamant and fierce, the tall man did not curse.

VII

Beside the rigid snake the man stretched out
In fellowship of death; he lay silent
And stiff in the heavy grass with eyes shut,
Inhaling the moist odours of the night
Through which his mind tunnelled with flicking tongue
Backwards to caves, mounds, and sunken ledges
And desolate cliffs where come only kites,
And where of perished badgers and racoons
The claws alone remain, gripping the earth.
Meanwhile the green snake crept upon the sky,
Huge, his mailed coat glittering with stars that made
The night bright, and blowing thin wreaths of cloud
Athwart the moon; and as the weary man
Stood up, coiled above his head, transforming all.

For My Brother Jesus

My father had terrible words for you
—whoreson, bastard, *meshumad*;
and my mother loosed Yiddish curses
on your name and the devil's spawn
on their way to church
that scraped the frosted horsebuns
from the wintry Montreal street
to fling clattering into our passageway

Did you ever hear an angered
Jewish woman curse? Never mind the words:
at the intonations alone, Jesus,
the rusted nails would drop out
from your pierced hands and feet
and scatter to the four ends of earth
Luckless man, at least
that much you were spared

In my family you
were a *mamzer*, a *yoshke pondrick*
and main reason for their affliction and pain.
Even now I see the contemptuous curl
on my gentle father's lips;
my mother's never-ending singsong curses
still ring in my ears more loud
than the bells I heard each Sunday morning,
their clappers darkening the outside air

Priests and nuns
were black blots on the snow
—forbidding birds, crows
Up there
up there beside the Good Old Man
we invented and the lyring angels
do you get the picture, my hapless brother:

deserted daily, hourly
by the Philistines you hoped to save
and the murdering heathens,
your own victimized kin hating and despising
you?
        O crucified poet
your agonized face haunts me
as it did when I was a boy;
I follow your strange figure
through all the crooked passageways
of history, the walls reverberating
with ironic whisperings and cries,
the unending sound of cannonfire
and rending groans, the clatter
of bloodsoaked swords falling
on armour and stone
to lose you finally among your excited brethren
haranguing and haloing them
with your words of love,
your voice gentle as my father's

The Search

My father's name was Moses; his beard was black
and black the eyes that beheld God's light;
they never looked upon me but they saw
a crazy imp dropt somehow from the sky
and then I knew from his holy stare
I had disgraced the Prophets and the Law.

Nor was I my mother's prayer;
she who all day railed at a religious indolence
that kept her man warm under his prayershawl
while her reaching arm froze with each customer
who brought a needed penny to her store;
added to another it paid the food and rent.

An ill-matched pair they were. My father
thought he saw Jehovah everywhere,
entertaining his messengers every day
though visible to him alone in that room
where making his fastidious cheese
he dreamt of living in Zion at his ease.

My mother: unpoetical as a pot of clay,
with as much mysticism in her as a banker
or a steward; lamenting God's will for her
yet blessing it with each Friday's candles.
But O her sturdy mind has served me well
who see how humans forge with lies their lonely hell.

Alien and bitter the road my forbears knew:
fugitives forever eating unleavened bread
and hated pariahs because of that one Jew
who taught the tenderest Christian how to hate
and harry them to whatever holes they sped.
Times there were the living envied the dead.

Iconoclasts, dreamers, men who stood alone:
Freud and Marx, the great Maimonides
and Spinoza who defied even his own.
In my veins runs their rebellious blood.
I tread with them the selfsame antique road
and seek everywhere the faintest scent of God.

P. K. PAGE

b. 1916

The Stenographers

After the brief bivouac of Sunday,
their eyes, in the forced march of Monday to Saturday,
hoist the white flag, flutter in the snow-storm of paper,
haul it down and crack in the mid-sun of temper.

In the pause between the first draft and the carbon
they glimpse the smooth hours when they were children—
the ride in the ice-cart, the ice-man's name,
the end of the route and the long walk home;

remember the sea where floats at high tide
were sea marrows growing on the scatter-green vine
or spools of grey toffee, or wasps' nests on water;
remember the sand and the leaves of the country.

Bell rings and they go and the voice draws their pencil
like a sled across snow; when its runners are frozen
rope snaps and the voice then is pulling no burden
but runs like a dog on the winter of paper.

Their climates are winter and summer—no wind
for the kites of their hearts—no wind for a flight;
a breeze at the most, to tumble them over
and leave them like rubbish—the boy-friends of blood.

In the inch of the noon as they move they are stagnant.
The terrible calm of the noon is their anguish;
the lip of the counter, the shapes of the straws
like icicles breaking their tongues, are invaders.

Their beds are their oceans—salt water of weeping
the waves that they know—the tide before sleep;
and fighting to drown they assemble their sheep
in columns and watch them leap desks for their fences
and stare at them with their own mirror-worn faces.

In the felt of the morning the calico-minded,
sufficiently starched, insert papers, hit keys,
efficient and sure as their adding machines;
yet they weep in the vault, they are taut as net curtains
stretched upon frames. In their eyes I have seen
the pin men of madness in marathon trim
race round the track of the stadium pupil.

Stories of Snow

Those in the vegetable rain retain
an area behind their sprouting eyes
held soft and rounded with the dream of snow
precious and reminiscent as those globes—
souvenir of some never-nether land—
which hold their snow-storms circular, complete,
high in a tall and teakwood cabinet.

In countries where the leaves are large as hands
where flowers protrude their fleshy chins
and call their colours,
an imaginary snow-storm sometimes falls
among the lilies.
And in the early morning one will waken
to think the glowing linen of his pillow
a northern drift, will find himself mistaken
and lie back weeping.
And there the story shifts from head to head,
of how in Holland, from their feather beds
hunters arise and part the flakes and go
forth to the frozen lakes in search of swans—

the snow-light falling white along their guns,
their breath in plumes.
While tethered in the wind like sleeping gulls
ice-boats wait the raising of their wings
to skim the electric ice at such a speed
they leap jet strips of naked water,
and how these flying, sailing hunters feel
air in their mouths as terrible as ether.
And on the story runs that even drinks
in that white landscape dare to be no colour;
how flasked and water clear, the liquor slips
silver against the hunters' moving hips.
And of the swan in death these dreamers tell
of its last flight and how it falls, a plummet,
pierced by the freezing bullet
and how three feathers, loosened by the shot,
descend like snow upon it.
While hunters plunge their fingers in its down
deep as a drift, and dive their hands
up to the neck of the wrist
in that warm metamorphosis of snow
as gentle as the sort that woodsmen know
who, lost in the white circle, fall at last
and dream their way to death.

And stories of this kind are often told
in countries where great flowers bar the roads
with reds and blues which seal the route to snow—
as if, in telling, raconteurs unlock
the colour with its complement and go
through to the area behind the eyes
where silent, unrefractive whiteness lies.

Adolescence

In love they wore themselves in a green embrace.
A silken rain fell through the spring upon them.
In the park she fed the swans and he
whittled nervously with his strange hands.
And white was mixed with all their colours
as if they drew it from the flowering trees.

At night his two-finger whistle brought her down
the waterfall stairs to his shy smile
which, like an eddy, turned her round and round
lazily and slowly so her will
was nowhere—as in dreams things are and aren't.

Strolling along avenues in the dark
street lamps sang like sopranos in their heads
with a violence they never understood
and all their movements when they were together
had no conclusion.

Only leaning into the question had they motion;
after they parted were savage and swift as gulls.
Asking and asking the hostile emptiness
they were as sharp as partly sculptured stone
and all who watched, forgetting, were amazed
to see them form and fade before their eyes.

T-Bar

Relentless, black on white, the cable runs
through metal arches up the mountain side.
At intervals giant pickaxes are hung
on long hydraulic springs. The skiers ride
propped by the axehead, twin automatons
supported by its handle, one each side.

In twos they move slow motion up the steep
incision in the mountain. Climb. Climb.
Somnambulists, bolt upright in their sleep
their phantom poles swung lazily behind,
while to the right, the empty T-bars keep
in mute descent, slow monstrous jigging time.

Captive the skiers now and innocent,
wards of eternity, each pair alone.
They mount the easy vertical ascent,
pass through successive arches, bride and groom,
as through successive naves, are newly wed
participants in some recurring dream.

So do they move forever. Clocks are broken.
In zones of silence they grow tall and slow,
inanimate dreamers, mild and gentle-spoken
blood-brothers of the haemophilic snow
until the summit breaks and they awaken
imagos from the stricture of the tow.

Jerked from her chrysalis the sleeping bride
suffers too sudden freedom like a pain.
The dreaming bridegroom severed from her side
singles her out, the old wound aches again.
Uncertain, lost, upon a wintry height
these two, not separate, but no longer one.

Now clocks begin to peck and sing. The slow
extended minute like a rubber band
contracts to catapult them through the snow
in tandem trajectory while behind
etching the sky-line, obdurate and slow
the spastic T-bars pivot and descend.

Another Space

Those people in a circle on the sand
are dark against its gold
turn like a wheel
revolving in a horizontal plane
whose axis—do I dream it?—
vertical
invisible
immeasurably tall
rotates a starry spool.

Yet *if* I dream
why in the name of heaven are fixed parts
within me set in motion
like a poem?

Those people in a circle reel me in.
Down the whole length of golden beach I come
willingly pulled by their rotation
slow
as a moon pulls waters
on a string
their turning circle winds around its rim.

I see them there in three dimensions yet
their height implies another space
their clothes'
surprising chiaroscuro postulates
a different spectrum.
What kaleidoscope
does air construct
that all their movements make a compass rose
surging and altering?
I speculate
on some dimension I can barely guess.

Nearer I see them dark-skinned.
They are dark. And beautiful.
Great human sunflowers spinning in a ring
cosmic as any bumble-top
the vast
procession of the planets in their dance.
And nearer still I see them—"a Chagall"—
each fiddling on an instrument—its strings
of some black woollen fibre
and its bow—feathered—
an arrow almost.
Arrow *is*.

For now the headman—one step forward shoots
(or does he bow or does he lift a kite
up and over the bright pale dunes of air?)
to strike the absolute centre of my skull
my absolute centre somehow
with such skill
such staggering lightness
that the blow is love.

And something in me melts.
It is as if a glass partition melts—
or something I had always thought was glass—
some pane that halved my heart
is proved, in its melting, ice.

And to-fro all the atoms pass
in bright osmosis
hitherto
in stasis locked
where now a new
direction opens like an eye.

PAGE 258

Cross

He has leaned for hours against the veranda railing
gazing the darkened garden out of mind
while she with battened hatches rides out the wind
that will blow for a year or a day, there is no telling.

As to why they are cross she barely remembers now.
That they *are* cross, she is certain. They hardly speak.
Feel cold and hurt and stoney. For a week
have without understanding behaved so.

And will continue so to behave for neither
can come to that undemanded act of love—
kiss the sleeping princess or sleep with the frog—
and break the spell which holds them each from the other.

Or if one ventures towards it, the other, shy
dissembles, regrets too late the dissimulation
and sits hands slack, heart tiny, the hard solution
having again passed by.

Silly the pair of them. Yet they make me weep.
Two on a desert island, back to back
who, while the alien world howls round them black
go their own ways, fall emptily off to sleep.

MIRIAM WADDINGTON

b. 1917

Wonderful Country

May was a wonderful country;
all the world's children were in pilgrimage
to greet the summer and on the way
they stopped at the zoo and lifted spells
from the golden tiger and lonely lion;
they appointed zebras their ambassadors
to laughter and they counted rabbits
surrogates of colour; on the grassy hill
they observed the peacock pondering
and down in the fen the swans
glided smooth as music and the children said:
'Let them be, they will make pillows soft as sleep,
and sleep deep as death.' So the children said
and let them be.

Around them the city flowed and the children saw
mandarin yellow leaping at them from coats
and there was chartreuse and purple—
the lanes were like a bazaar decked out
with romance for the lucky, where
across the hot-dog counter
beggars and queens came together;
oh what a clamour and shout under the palace of summer
as the children marched singing hallelujah to May
singing homage to May and to meadows.

The Season's Lovers

In the daisied lap of summer
the lovers lay, they dozed
and lay in sun unending
they lay in light they slept
and only stirred
each one to find the other's lips.
At times they sighed
or spoke a word
that wavered on uneven breath,
he had no name and she forgot
the ransomed kingdom of her death.

When at last the sun went down
and chilly evening stained the fields
the lovers rose and rubbed their eyes:
they saw the pale wash of grass
heighten to metallic green
and spindly tongues of granite mauve
lick up the milk of afternoon
they gathered all the scattered light
of daisies to one place of white
and ghostly poets lent their speech
to the stillness of the air
the lovers listened, each to each.

Into the solid wall of night
the lovers looked, their clearer sight
went through that dark intensity
to the other side of light.
The lovers stood, it seemed to them
they hung upon the world's rim—
he clung to self, and she to him;
he rocked her with his body's hymn
and murmured to her shuddering cry
you are all states, all princes I,
and sang against her trembling limbs
nothing else is, he sang, *but I*.

They lifted the transparent lid
from world false and world true
and in the space of both they flew.
He found a name, she lost her death
and summer lulled them in its lap
with a leafy lullaby.
There they sleep unending sleep
the lovers lie
he with a name, she free of death
in a country hard to find
unless you read love's double mind
or invent its polar map.

Icons

Suddenly
in middle age
instead of withering
into blindness
and burying myself
underground
I grow delicate
and fragile
superstitious;
I carry icons
I have begun
to worship
images.

I take them out
and prop them up
on bureau tops
in hotel rooms
in Spain
I study them
in locked libraries
in Leningrad
I untie them

from tourist packages
in Italy
they warm me
in the heatless winters
of London in the
hurry-up buses
of Piccadilly.

My icons are not
angels or holy
babies they have
nothing to do
with saints or
madonnas, they
are mostly of
seashores summer
and love which I no
longer believe in
but I still believe
in the images,
I still preserve
the icons:

a Spanish factory
worker talks to me
in a street behind
the cathedral he
offers me *un poco*
amor, the scars on
his hand, his wounded
country and the black-
jacketed police; he
touches me on the
arm and other places,
and the alcoholic
in the blazing square

drinks brandy, confides
that fortunes can still
be made in Birmingham
but he has a bad
lung is hard of
hearing and owns
an apartment in Palma.

In Montreal a man
in a white shirt
with his sleeves
rolled up is reading
a book and waiting
for me in a room
with the door ajar,
the light falls
through the open
door the book
falls from his
open hand and he
stands up and
looks at me with
open eyes.

Of course I know
these are only
icons; there is
no such thing
as love left in
the world but
there is still
the image of it
which doesn't let
me wither into
blindness which
doesn't let me
bury myself
underground which
doesn't let me

say yes to the
black leather police
or the empty libraries
or the lonely rooms
or the foggy window
of cold London buses.

The world is getting
dark but I carry
icons, I remember
the summer
I will never forget
the light.

The nineteen thirties are over

The nineteen thirties
are over; we survived
the depression, the Sacco-
Vanzetti of childhood
saw Tom Mooney smiling
at us from photographs,
put a rose on the grave
of Eugene Debs, listened
to our father's stories
of the Winnipeg strike and
joined the study groups
of the OBU always keeping
one eye on the revolution.

Later we played records
with thorn needles, Josh
White's *Talking Union* and
Prokofief's *Lieutenant Kije*,
shuddered at the sound of
bells and all those wolves

whirling past us in snow
on the corner of Portage
and Main, but in my mind
summer never ended on the
shores of Gimli where we
looked across to an Icelandic
paradise we could never see
the other side of; and I
dreamed of Mexico and shining
birds who beckoned to me
from the gold-braided lianas
of my own wonder.

These days I step out
from the frame of my wind-
battered house into Toronto
city; somewhere I still
celebrate sunlight, touch
the rose on the grave of
Eugene Debs but I walk
carefully in this land
of sooty snow; I pass the
rich houses and double
garages and I am not really
this middle-aged professor
but someone from
Winnipeg whose bones ache
with the broken revolutions
of Europe, and even now
I am standing on the heaving
ploughed-up field
of my father's old war.

Portrait: Old Woman

Old woman, cabbage queen,
gourd-tapper, fortune-
hunter in teacups—
the black plumes
of your hatboat
quiver in the wind
tremble with secret
piracy as your knowing
hand touches without
gloves the supreme
trophy of the world's
cargo—peppersquash.

When you come home
to your rooming house
with the reddest apple,
the most grooved most
crenellated peppersquash,
the other old ladies
will vote you the
prize for picking, you
will be snow-white and
rose-red, you will be
royal at last,
queening it in the
communal kitchen of
your rooming house.

MARGARET AVISON

b. 1918

The Swimmer's Moment

For everyone
The swimmer's moment at the whirlpool comes,
But many at that moment will not say
"This is the whirlpool, then."
By their refusal they are saved
From the black pit, and also from contesting
The deadly rapids, and emerging in
The mysterious, and more ample, further waters.
And so their bland-blank faces turn and turn
Pale and forever on the rim of suction
They will not recognize.
Of those who dare the knowledge
Many are whirled into the ominous centre
That, gaping vertical, seals up
For them an eternal boon of privacy,
So that we turn away from their defeat
With a despair, not for their deaths, but for
Ourselves, who cannot penetrate their secret
Nor even guess at the anonymous breadth
Where one or two have won:
(The silver reaches of the estuary).

The Apex Animal

A Horse, thin-coloured as oranges ripened in freight-cars
which have shaken casements through the miles of night
across three nights of field and waterfront warehouses—
rather, the narrow Head of the Horse
with the teeth shining and white ear-tufts:
It, I fancy, and from experience
commend the fancy to your inner eye,
It is the One, in a patch of altitude
troubled only by clarity of weather,
Who sees, the ultimate Recipient
of what happens, the One Who is aware
when, in the administrative wing
a clerk returns from noon-day, though
the ointment of mortality
for one strange hour, in all his lustreless life,
has touched his face.

(For that Head of a Horse there is no question
whether he spent the noon-hour with a friend,
below street-level, or on the parapet—
a matter which may safely rest
in mortal memory.)

Butterfly Bones; or Sonnet Against Sonnets

The cyanide jar seals life, as sonnets move
towards final stiffness. Cased in a white glare
these specimens stare for peering boys, to prove
strange certainties. Plane dogsled and safari
assure continuing range. The sweep-net skill,
the patience, learning, leave all living stranger.
Insect—or poem—waits for the fix, the frill
precision can effect, brilliant with danger.
What law and wonder the museum spectres
bespeak is cryptic for the shivery wings,
the world cut-diamond-eyed, those eyes' reflectors,
or herbal grass, sunned motes, fierce listening.
Might sheened and rigid trophies strike men blind
like Adam's lexicon locked in the mind?

Easter

Now that the eve of April brings
A delicacy of light at the day's end
The bulge of earth seems again comic, and,
On it, the city sails along the swerve
Into that depthless diapason, pink,
Absurd, queer as a chemist's liquid, cloudless,
Then filmed, then wind-fomented
And flashed and flung about with rivers of rain.

After the blur of doves the milky air
Lulls, and listens, and there
Is the sorrow of all fullness.
But on the hillside the frail tremulo
Of a new dayspring, eggshell and lilac, wanders
through the drenched quiet branches.

A bird sings, forceful, glorious as a pipeorgan,
And the huge bustling girth of the whole world
Turns in an everywhere of sunwardness
Among the cloudcarved sundering of its oceans.

The Mirrored Man

Lot put his wife out of his mind
Through respect for the mortal lot:
She having dared to yearn defined
All that to him was naught.

So now we flee the Garden
Of Eden, steadfastly.
And still in our flight are ardent
For lost eternity.

We always turn our heads away
When Canaan is at hand,
Knowing it mortal to enjoy
The Promise, not the Land.

Yet the cimmerian meadows know the sword
Flaming and searching that picks out
The children for this earth, and hurls the curse
After us, through the void.
So each of us conceals within himself
A cell where one man stares into the glass
And sees, now featureless the meadow mists,
And now himself, a pistol at his temple,
Gray, separate, wearily waiting.

We, comic creatures of our piebald day,
Either ignore this burden, nonchalantly
(Dragging a dull repudiated house
At heel, through all our trivial ramblings)
Or gravely set ourselves the rigorous task
Of fashioning the key that fits that cell
(As if it hid the timeless Garden).
I interviewed one gentleman so engaged,
And he looked up and said:
"Despair is a denial and a sin
But to deny despair, intolerable."
The next week, so I heard, he used his key,
Walked over to the mirror, forced the hand
Of the young man, and left him
Drooping, the idle door of an idle cell
Mirrored at last. Such men are left possessed
Of ready access to no further incident.

One man unlocked his cell
To use it as a love-nest.
By fond report, the mirror there is crammed
With monkey faces, ruby ear-rings, branches
Of purple grapes, and ornamental feathers.

Whatever winter ravages his gardens
No banging shutters desolate his guests
Who entertain illusion as he wills it,
And grant him the inviolate privacy
His hospitable favour purchases.

All of us, flung in one
Murky parabola,
Seek out some pivot for significance,
Leery of comets' tails, mask-merry,
Wondering at the centre
Who will gain access, search the citadel
To its last, secret door?
And what face will the violator find
When he confronts the glass?

Voluptuaries and Others

That Eureka of Archimedes out of his bath
Is the kind of story that kills what it conveys;
Yet the banality is right for that story, since it is not a
communicable one
But just a particular instance of
The kind of lighting up of the terrain
That leaves aside the whole terrain, really,
But signalizes, and compels, an advance in it.
Such an advance through a be-it-what-it-may but
take-it-not-quite-as-given locale:
Probably that is the core of being alive.
The speculation is not a concession
To limited imaginations. Neither is it
A constrained voiding of the quality of immanent death.
Such near values cannot be measured in values
Just because the measuring
Consists in that other kind of lighting up
That shows the terrain comprehended, as also its containing
space,
And wipes out adjectives, and all shadows
(or, perhaps, all but shadows).

The Russians made a movie of a dog's head
Kept alive by blood controlled by physics, chemistry,
 equipment, and
Russian women scientists in cotton gowns with writing
 tablets.
The heart lay on a slab midway in the apparatus
And went phluff, phluff.
Like the first kind of illumination, that successful
 experiment
Can not be assessed either as conquest or as defeat.
But it is living, creating the chasm of creation,
Contriving to cast only man to brood in it, further.
History makes the spontaneous jubilation at such moments
 less and less likely though,
And that story about Archimedes does get into public school
 textbooks.

Black-White Under Green:

May 18, 1965

This day of the leafing-out
speaks with blue power—
among the buttery grassblades
white, tiny-spraying spokes on the end of a weed-stem
and in the formal beds, tulips
and invisible birds inaudibly hallooing,
enormous, their beaks out wide, throats bulging, aflutter,
eyes weeping with speed
where the ultraviolets play and the scythe of the jets
flashes, carrying
the mind-wounded heartpale person, still a boy, a pianist,
 dying not
of the mind's wounds (as they read the X-rays) but
dying, fibres separated, parents ruddy and
American, strong, sheathed in the cold of
years of his differentness, clustered by two at
the nether arc of his flight.

This day of the leafing-out is one to remember
        how the ice crackled among
            stiff twigs. Glittering strongly
                the old trees sagged. Boughs
        abruptly unsocketed. Dry, orange gashes
the dawn's fine snowing discovered and powdered over.

. . . to remember the leaves ripped loose
the thudding of the dark sky-beams
and the pillared plunging sea
shelterless. Down the centuries
a flinching speck
        in the white fury found of itself—and another—
the rich blood spilling, mother to child, threading
the perilous combers, marbling
the surges, flung
out, and ten-fingered, feeling for
the lollop, the fine-wired
music, dying skyhigh
still between carpets and the
cabin-pressuring windows
on the day of the leafing.

Faces fanned by
rubberized, cool air
are opened; eyes wisely
smile.
The tulips, weeds, new leaves
neither smile nor are scorning to smile nor uncertain,
dwelling in light.
A flick of ice, fire, flood,
far off from
the day of the leafing-out I knew
when knee-wagon small, or from my
father's once at a horse-tail silk-shiny
fence-corner or this
day when the runways wait
white in the sun, and a new leaf is
metal, torn out of that blue
afloat in the dayshine.

Strong Yellow, for Reading Aloud:

WRITTEN FOR AND READ TO ENGLISH 385'S CLASS WHEN ASKED TO COMMENT ON MY POEM "THE APEX ANIMAL", ETC.

A painted horse,
a horse-sized clay horse, really,
like blue riverclay, painted,
with real mural eyes—or a
Clydesdale with his cuff-tufts
barbered—the mane
marcelled like a conch and cropped and plastered down like a
merry-go-round pony's
without the varnish—
all kinds confounding,
yet a powerful presence
on the rainy Sunday diningroom wall,
framed by a shallow niche . . .

Q: "Miss Avison could you
relate that to the 'head of a horse'?"

No. No. That one
was strong yellow—almost tangerine, with
white hairs, the eyes
whited too as if
pulled back by the hair
so the eyeballs would water with wind in them,
one you'd call Whitey, maybe,
though he was not, I say,
white . . .

Q: "Auburn?"

It was not a horse-shaped horse,
or sized. It loomed. Only the
narrow forehead part, the
eyes starting   loose and appled,
and shoulder-streaming part. . . .
Colour? a stain on the
soiled snow-mattress-colour of
the office-day noon-hour mezzanine
                        that is the sky downtown.

Q: "The Head of the Horse
            'sees', you say in that poem.
            Was that your vision of
            God, at that period
            in your development?"

Who I was then we
both approach timorously—
or I do, believe me!
But I think, reading the lines,
the person looking *up* like that
was all squeezed solid, only a crowd-pressed
mass of herself at shoulder-
level, as it were, or at least
nine to noon, and the p.m. still to come
day *in* day *out*   as the saying goes
which pretty well covers everything
or seems to, in *and* out then,
                        when it's like that: no heart, no surprises, no
people-scope, no utterances,
no strangeness, no nougat of delight
                              to touch, and worse,
no secret cherished in the
midriff then.

Whom you look up from that to
is Possibility not
God.
        I'd think . . .

Q: "Strong yellow."

Yes! Not the clay-blue
with rump and hoof and all and almost
eyelashes, the pupil
fixed on you, on that wall of
fake hunt, fake aristocracy
in this fake Sunday
diningroom I was telling
about. . . .

CHARLES SANGSTER

1822-1893

Charles Sangster grew up in poverty in Kingston, but by independent reading and personal industry he made himself a writer. He had published two volumes of poetry by the time he was thirty-eight, and he made a living working for newspapers until he was forty-six. In 1868 he became a Post Office Department clerk, which unfortunately ended his major period of writing. During his eighteen miserable years there, he wrote little more than twenty-six poems, and when he retired to Kingston in 1886, his health was broken, and his distress had debilitated him. During the next five years, Sangster revised his two published volumes and the poems which were to constitute two more volumes. He consigned the revised versions of his works to W. D. Lighthall in 1891, but they remained in manuscript eighty years, until they were published in the 1970s. He died in Kingston at the age of seventy-one.

Charles Sangster seems very much a poet of two worlds. His poetry combines the eighteenth-century traditions of topographic description, reflection, and sentiment with the romantic concept of transcendentally significant nature. His early poetry, although uneven in quality, contains strikingly vivid descriptions of life in nineteenth-century Canada. His landscape is often a moral or sentimental metaphor, but it also has a significant reality of its own which is romantic. The landscape of the new world stirs the imagination, not with the Classical associations of eighteenth-century pastoral poetry, but with the presence of beauty, the sublime, the geologic history of the elements, and the pre-history of aboriginal inhabitants. Sangster recognizes the validity of both the real world of experience and the world of imagination. The tension in Sangster's poetry arises, not from a clash between objective reality and fanciful illusion, but from a dialectic between the real universe as a manifestation of a higher world which makes it significant and the imagination's world which is more personally spiritual. This dialectic appears most clearly in the poems of his last two volumes. His "The St. Lawrence and the Saguenay" is a journey from beauty to the sublime, but it is also a voyage through a real landscape. In "Dreams," a late poem, Sangster points out that there is more than one level of dream, and at its highest level, dream reveals the creative energy of the imagination and of the universe alike to be light itself.

Sangster's works are *The St. Lawrence and the Saguenay and Other Poems* (1856); *Hesperus and Other Poems and Lyrics* (1860); *Our Norland* (1896); *Norland Echoes* (1976); and *The Angel Guest and Other Poems and Lyrics* (1977).

Works on Sangster include Arthur S. Bourinot, "Charles Sangster," in *Leading Canadian Poets* (1948); Desmond Pacey, "Charles Sangster," *Ten Canadian Poets* (1958); W. D. Hamilton, *Charles Sangster* (1971); and Frank M. Tierney, "Introduction" and "Biographical Note," in Charles Sangster, *Hesperus and Other Poems and Lyrics* (1979), and his introductions to *Norland Echoes* (1976) and *The Angel Guest and Other Poems and Lyrics* (1977).

– DON CONWAY

ISABELLA VALANCY CRAWFORD

c. 1850-1887

A few years after her birth in Dublin, Ireland, Crawford's family immigrated to North America, settling in Paisley, Ontario, in 1858. In 1876, after the deaths of her father and her younger sister, Crawford and her mother moved to Toronto. Crawford began writing as a teenager in Lakefield, and her apprenticeship continued through the Peterborough years when her work began to appear in *The Favorite* and the

Toronto *Daily Mail.* Much of her mature verse was later published in the *Evening Telegram* and *The Globe.* The only volume of her work published in her lifetime was *Old Spookses' Pass, Malcolm's Katie and Other Poems* (1884).

Crawford's mature work is marked by ambiguity, irony, and metaphorical compression, all of which contribute to a remarkably modern poetic idiom that fuses and transmutes polarities of thought and feeling into a landscape of expanded apprehension. Whether in a compressed metaphysical lyric or in an extended passage of blank-verse narrative, Crawford is able to evoke the natural terrain in dynamic verbal imagery, animated by intense eroticism. Her subject is often love, which she presents as illusory and destructive as well as regenerative and redemptive. In her longer poems, she synthesizes a wide variety of mythological tradition, from Graeco-Roman and Judeo-Christian to Gnostic, Manichaean, Norse, Slavic, and North American Indian. Her political thought develops from early conservatism to the liberalism of John Stuart Mill and Goldwin Smith. She rejects the "imperialistic idea" and consistently represents religion, commerce, government, and science as members in an insidious coalition to maintain the dominance of the wealthy. Celebrating the ideal of the city, she condemns the failed reality, portraying the expansion of industry and the consequent growth of cities in terms of sweated labour and human misery. In religion, Crawford is heterodox and eclectic, and as she explores the spiritual bases for moral choice and responsible social action, she often takes Christianity to task for its hypocrisy and complaisance.

Her later work reveals her imagination to be increasingly engaged by the dark side of human nature and experience, leading her to affirm suffering and sorrow as nurturing to the soul. In "Gisli, the Chieftain," "Malcolm's Katie," and *Hugh and Ion,* good and evil comprise a metaphysical unity whose radical metaphor is cosmic irony, which allows Crawford to present the pessimism of Alfred and Ion with clarity and force even as she celebrates the regenerative power of love. Despite the tragic overtones of *Hugh and Ion* and "The Pessimist," Crawford remains capable of lyric ebullience, and she achieves in "The Rolling-Pin," the last of her short lyrics to be published in her lifetime, a momentary glimpse into the fulfillment of the imaginative life.

Crawford's work includes *Old Spookses' Pass, Malcolm's Katie and Other Poems* (1884); *The Collected Poems of Isabella Valancy Crawford* (1905); *Isabella Valancy Crawford* (1923); and *Hugh and Ion* (1977).

Works on Crawford include James Reaney, "Isabella Valancy Crawford," in *Our Living Tradition* (1959); John B. Ower, "Isabella Valancy Crawford: 'The Canoe,'" *Canadian Literature,* No. 34 (1967), pp. 54-62; Frank Bessai, "The Ambivalence of Love in the Poetry of Isabella Valancy Crawford,"*Queen's Quarterly,* 77 (1970), 404-18; and Catharine Ross, "'Narrative II'—The Unpublished Long Narrative Poem," in *The Crawford Symposium* (1979).

– ROBERT ALAN BURNS

W. WILFRED CAMPBELL

1858-1918

The son of an Anglican minister, Wilfred Campbell was born in Berlin, Canada West (now Kitchener, Ontario) on 1 June 1858. After brief careers as a teacher and a minister, Campbell joined the civil service in Ottawa. In Ottawa, he befriended Archibald Lampman and Duncan Campbell Scott and the three poets collaborated on "At the Mermaid Inn," a column in *The Globe* (Toronto). In the course of his literary career, Campbell wrote poetry, novels, poetic dramas, and travel books. He also served as editor, anthologist, columnist, and lecturer and was one of Canada's most respected men of letters at his death on 1 January 1918.

In the late nineteenth century, higher criticism of the Bible and the encroachment of science upon religion were the subjects of considerable debate in Canadian intellectural circles.

The poetry of Wilfred Campbell is, to a large extent, the chronicle of a sensitive man's struggle to find meaning in an age of shifting values. Campbell's early nature poems, such as "Vapor and Blue," offer Pantheistic interpretations of the natural world but his later nature poetry is stark and horrifying in its imagery. "How One Winter Came in the Lake Region" paints a bleak portrait of a world untouched by God's grace. The uncertainty of God's presence in the world makes meaningful action difficult but Campbell's work argues that meaning can be found through commitment. In "Lazarus," the protagonist questions God's authority and embarks on a dangerous mission to wrest a suffering man from the horrors of hell. Another glorious mission, in Campbell's view, is the practice of British imperialism. The monarchy and empire provide a reassuring link between past and present. A number of Campbell's poems take as their subject matter significant events in the evolution of the monarchy: Victoria's Diamond Jubilee, Victoria's death, and the coronation of Edward VII. "England" celebrates the empire which Edward inherited from Victoria and enumerates the "torrid sand," "Indian jungle," and "Canadian snows" where British concepts of liberty and justice flourish. Canadians, "we of the newer and vaster West," claim a part of England's glory: her history and traditions are ours. In the late twentieth century, imperialism has become synonymous with subjugation but for Wilfred Campbell it represents the highest achievement of civilized man. In its continuity and idealism he recognizes the potential for meaningful action in an age of uncertainty and flux.

Campbell's works include *Snowflakes and Sunbeams* (1888); *Lake Lyrics and Other Poems* (1889); *The Dread Voyage* (1893); *Beyond the Hills of Dream* (1899); *The Poems of Wilfred Campbell* (1905); *Sagas of Vaster Britain. Poems of the Race, the Empire and the Divinity of Man* (1914); and *The Poetical Works of Wilfred Campbell* (1923).

Works on Campbell include Carl F. Klinck, *Wilfred Campbell: A Study in Late Provincial Victorianism* (1942); John Ower, "Portraits of the Landscape as Poet: Canadian Nature as Aesthetic Symbol in Three Confederation Writers," *Journal of Canadian Studies*, 6 (1971), 27-32; Terry Whalen, "Wilfred Campbell: The Poetry of Celebration and

Harmony," *Journal of Canadian Poetry*, 1, No. 2 (1978), 27-41; and George Wicken, "William Wilfred Campbell (1858-1918)," *Canadian Writers and Their Works* (1982).

– GEORGE WICKEN

CHARLES G. D. ROBERTS

1860-1943

Charles G. D. Roberts spent his childhood by the Tantramar marshes and at the cathedral and university city of Fredericton, New Brunswick. He began writing in earnest in 1878 as a university student, and his first volume, *Orion and Other Poems* (1880), was a brilliant advance beyond other Canadian writing. He became editor of *The Week*, a professor at King's College, Nova Scotia, and an editor of the *Illustrated American* in New York, but from 1899 he lived entirely by his pen—in New York until 1906, in Europe until 1911, and in London until 1925 when he returned to Canada. He travelled the nation on reading tours, served as President of the Canadian Authors Association, aided Canadian writers wherever he could, and was knighted in 1935. He settled in Toronto, and continued to write and to serve the cause of Canadian letters until he died at eighty-three after marrying for the second time.

Roberts was a stylistically brilliant poet whose work was underrated because his poetic vocabulary included much from well-known Romantic and Victorian poets, and because he was concerned with much that was part of popular culture in the nineteenth century. Roberts' critics failed to observe that he was a Symbolist employing familiar terms ironically to restore to sentimentally religious and morally conservative concepts the vitality and intellectual rigor they lacked for him even as a youth. He was, like Shelley, a visionary idealist, and he was certain that a positive impulse transcending the generative and destructive forces of nature underlies life.

Thematically and technically, his poems reveal his constant conviction that this underlying ideal force could be revealed through art. Roberts extended Carlyle's discussion of symbols in *Sartor Resartus* to suggest that there is not a particle in this world "but is the visible embodiment of a Thought; but bears visible record of invisible things; but is, in the transcendental sense, symbolical as well as real." Roberts, more than any Canadian before him, was able to make the precise physical detail of experience significant through highly compressed and economical symbolical actions. He gave technically difficult and rigorous poetic forms an apparent ease and deceptive simplicity, and he used line and stanza as integral units of meaning to control his poetic actions. He was concerned with an inexplicable harmony in the stir of nature until 1884. Because his resignation from *The Week* also turned his attention to New York, from 1884 to 1892 his poems counterpoise a potential good in nature against the world of labour and urban distress. When his brother, Gooderidge, and his friend, Joseph Collins, died in 1892, he rejected the abstraction of an unrealized good, and he redefined the ideal as the generative life energy in nature. When he separated permanently from his wife in 1897 and his eldest son, Athelstan, died that same year, he sought an immortal aspect of the life force as a moral life manifested as love and virtue.

Roberts' works include *Orion and Other Poems* (1880); *In Divers Tones* (1886); *Songs of the Common Day and Ave* (1893); *The Book of the Native* (1896); *New York Nocturnes* (1898); *Poems: New Complete Edition* (1907); *The Vagrant of Time* (1927); *The Iceberg and Other Poems* (1934); *Selected Poems* (1936); and *Canada Speaks of Britain* (1941).

Works on Roberts include James Cappon, *Roberts and the Influence of His Times* (1905); E. M. Pomeroy, *Sir Charles G. D. Roberts: A Biography* (1943); W. J. Keith, *Charles G. D. Roberts* (1969); John Ower, "Portraits of the Landscape as Poet: Canadian Nature as Aesthetic Symbol in Three Confederation Writers," *Journal of Canadian Studies*, 6 (1971), 27-32; and Lorraine McMullen, "The Poetry of Earth: A Note on Roberts' Sonnets," *Studies in Canadian Literature*, 1 (1976), 247-51. – DON CONWAY

BLISS CARMAN

1861-1929

Bliss Carman was born in New Brunswick and he travelled the world, spending most of his adult life loosely based in New England. He graduated from the University of New Brunswick in 1884 and studied further at Oxford, Edinburgh, and Harvard Universities but gave up his academic pursuits in the name of a professional career as a writer and an editor. With the publication of *Low Tide on Grande Pré* (1893) he was critically announced as a major Canadian voice, as well as an interesting American one, and he proceeded to command an audience on both sides of the Atlantic as he wrote his way through over thirty volumes of print. He lived a life of genteel poverty, bachelorhood, gregariousness, wandering and editing and intense writing. In his later years he continually returned to Canada on a series of reading and lecturing tours. By the time of his death in 1929 he was the recipient of many honours and awards. In keeping with his wishes, he was buried in Fredericton, New Brunswick, where many physical, and critical, tributes to his genius have been housed.

Like his contemporaries Sir Charles G. D. Roberts, Archibald Lampman, Duncan Campbell Scott, and William Wilfred Campbell, Carman was a seminal part of the growth to self-consciousness in Canadian literature just before and about the turn of the twentieth century. He drew eclectically on the classical, Romantic, Victorian, and Transcendentalist traditions of poetry for his characteristic forms and the bias of his vision. He was aware of Modernist experimentation in verse, but remained unimpressed by its vogue and its obscurity. Technically, Carman is a poet of lyric openness par excellence. His best critics praise him as a master melodist, a singer of life's cosmic spontaneity, and at the same time, a poet sensitive to the fragility and melancholy of existence. He experimented extensively with traditional poetic structures, gracefully submitting to the demands of fixed forms. Visually, he is a freshly alert poet of observation who beholds the thick beauty and overcast dreariness of the Canadian landscape and seasons as though they express the very contours of his own mind. At his most precise he is an intricate poet of witness. When he is empirically vague, he is usually designedly so, carefully evoking the presence of a supernatural, sometimes ghostly, reality implicit in the actual world and beckoning the mystical poet to give it a shape and a sound. He is a beholding, very impressionistic poet who is one of the first to embrace our locus and explore it in an intimate way. He adopted many masks and mythologies and hence wrote from the perspectives of a nature mystic, bohemian poet of the open road, elegist, love poet, sea balladist, regional poet of witness, and philosopher of wonder. In his later years he became enamoured of Delsartean unitarianism and is still often accused of intellectual tendentiousness because of that fixation. But, for all of the variations in his personae, his canon is tonally coherent in its rich blending of the notes of joy and notes of poignant melancholy which make up the music of his essentially wondrous view of life. Carman once termed himself a "cheerful pessimist" as a poet and thinker and no critic thus far has surpassed the precision of that existential self-description, the accuracy of its firmly courageous epithet.

Carman's works include *Low Tide on Grand Pré: A Book of Lyrics* (1893); *Behind the Arras: A Book of the Unseen* (1895); *Pipes of Pan* (1906); *Later Poems* (1921); and *Ballads and Lyrics* (1923).

Works on Carman include H. D. C. Lee, *Bliss Carman: A Study in Canadian Poetry* (1912); Odell Shepard, *Bliss Carman* (1923); James Cappon, *Bliss Carman and the Literary Currents and Influences of His Time* (1930); Muriel Miller, *Bliss Carman: A Portrait* (1935); and Donald Stephens, *Bliss Carman* (1966).

– TERRY WHALEN

ARCHIBALD LAMPMAN

1861-1899

Born at Morpeth, Canada West, Lampman grew up in several small towns in what is now east central Ontario, and graduated from Trinity College, University of Toronto, in 1882. The following year he took a clerkship in the Post Office Department in Ottawa, where he worked the rest of his life. An idealist in every sense, Lampman was devoted to poetry, drawn to socialism, and concerned with fostering an indigenous culture. His letters and essays reveal one of the most attractive and humane personalities in Canadian literature. Although many of his poems appeared in leading periodicals of the 1880s and '90s, he struggled hard to have his first and second volumes published. A third, to be printed at his own expense, was in press when he died of pneumonia at the age of thirty-seven.

Lampman is the most problematic of nineteenth-century Canadian poets. He has been condemned as a circumscribed nature poet and ineffectual dreamer, and admired as a frustrated genius and a radical visionary. There is just enough truth in all of these judgements to make none of them appropriate. His early poetry is largely concerned with realizing the spiritual and aesthetic possibilities in nature, after the example of the English Romantics. Such poems as "Among the Timothy" and "Heat" reflect not only his rich feeling for landscape, but also a fruitful response to the works of Keats and Wordsworth. Typically, Lampman's landscape poems represent the speaker's relation to nature as a "dream" which evokes and contains the redemptive beauty and vitality of his surroundings. Implicitly, they also affirm the Romantic view that art can supplant a lapsed religious faith by transforming the conditions of life. Although he never abandoned nature poetry, Lampman gradually turned to a more direct involvement with questions of human relations. His transcendent vision gave way to a troubled sense of the temporal basis of human experience, and in this respect he approaches the issues which dominate Victorian literature. Quite apart from this general development in his work, Lampman lacked the powerful impulse toward unity which is characteristic of visionary poets, and his ideas are in some degree inconsistent. His finest individual poems, however, are splendidly resolved. He is significant both in his own right and as a harbinger of the Romantic voices in modern Canadian writing. His contribution is the more important for having preceded the sea-change of perspective, language, and technique in twentieth-century poetry. Lampman's best work in such traditional forms as the lyrical ballad, the sonnet, and the meditative landscape poem, constitutes an indispensable legacy in our literature.

Lampman's works include *Among the Millet and Other Poems* (1888); *Lyrics of Earth* (1895); *Alcyone* (1899); *The Poems of Archibald Lampman* (1900); *At the Long Sault and Other New Poems* (1943); *Archibald Lampman: Selected Prose* (1975); *Lampman's Kate: Late Love Poems of Archibald Lampman* (1975); *At the Mermaid Inn: Wilfred Campbell, Archibald Lampman, Duncan Campbell Scott in* The Globe *1892-3* (1979); and *An Annotated Edition of the Correspondence Between Archibald Lampman and Edward William Thomson 1890-1898* (1980).

Works on Lampman include Carl Y. Connor, *Archibald Lampman: Canadian Poet of Nature* (1929); Desmond Pacey, "Archibald Lampman," in *Ten Canadian Poets* (1958); Michael Gnarowski, ed., *Archibald Lampman* (1970); Lorraine McMullen, ed., *The Lampman Symposium* (1976); and George Wicken, "Archibald Lampman: An Annotated Bibliography," in *The Annotated Bibliography of Canada's Major Authors*, Vol. 2 (1980).

– L. R. EARLY

D. C. SCOTT

1862-1947

Duncan Campbell Scott's father was an itinerant Methodist minister and consequently moved his family from town to town throughout Ontario and Quebec. At age seventeen, Scott returned to Ottawa, his birthplace. He had been appointed to a clerkship, the beginning of a long career in the Department of Indian Affairs which culminated in his promotion in 1913 to Deputy Superintendent General. During the summers of 1905 and 1906, as one of the commissioners involved in negotiating Treaty No. 9, he travelled by canoe through Northern Ontario, an experience reflected in "The Height of Land." The home of this reserved and accomplished man was a gathering place for writers, musicians, and artists. A fine pianist (his first wife, Belle, was a violinist), Scott wrote poetry, short stories, a novel, contributed a column, "At the Mermaid Inn," along with Archibald Lampman and W. W. Campbell, to the Toronto *Globe* (1892-93), co-edited Archibald Lampman's poems, and was elected to the Royal Society of Canada in 1899. He founded the Ottawa Little Theatre and Drama League and actively participated in several literary societies. His only daughter died in 1907 and his wife in 1929. In 1931 he married Elise Aylen and after his retirement travelled extensively through Europe, Canada, and the United States, his travels inspiring many poems.

Scott's long life spanned several artistic movements from *fin de siècle* to Modernism and while he was unreceptive to the rebellious "New Movement in Poetry," he experimented with many forms — sonnets, quatrains, rhyming couplets, dramatic verse, narrative, musical structures, blank verse, odes, elegies. Quoting Coleridge, Scott asserted that in fine poetry it is "the blending of passion with order that constitutes perfection"—the order of form and the passion of belief. A recurring motif consistent with this idealism is the search for beauty, an elusive ideal, something that "comes by flashes / Deeper than peace—a spell / Golden and inappellable." Many of his poems are nature pieces—from the earlier imitative Pre-Raphaelite fantasies and descriptions of Canadian seasons and places to the later pensive journeys through the wilderness. The tones range from a romantic, melancholy yearning to the macabre and mystical. As Scott believed that man finds in "nature infinite correspondences with his spiritual states," his observations about nature reflected his more universal observations about man, art, the ideal of beauty and vice versa. Nature poems combine with meditations as in "The Height of Land" or "Night Hymns on Lake Nipigon" to muse over the condition of man, and his later poems more and more assumed a philosophical and inquiring note. In the longer narrative poems, the poet recounts a story, often relating to the Indian people, their tragic demise and assimilation into the white culture. Since Scott as Deputy Superintendent of Indian Affairs apparently contributed to their demise and assimilation through his policies, the pathos and beauty of his poems portraying the Indian torn between two worlds seem paradoxical. As many critics have noticed, one of the most striking characteristics of Scott's verse is paradox or "contrarieties" or a "dialectical pattern," the "blending of restraint and intensity." Contrasts between civilization and the wilderness, the north and south, the old world and new, Christian and pagan, dignified Indian and greedy white man, ascent and descent, storm and rest, terror and peace dominate theme and movement in many poems. How Scott attempts a resolution of these contrarieties—through nature, through inquiry, through mystical or divine apprehension—constitutes the art of his poetry. Sometimes, however, there can be no resolution; the "golden spell" remains "inappellable."

Scott's works include poetry: *The Magic House and Other Poems* (1893); *Labor and the Angel* (1898); *New World Lyrics and Ballads* (1905); *Lundy's Lane and Other Poems* (1916); *Beauty and Life* (1921); *The Poems of Duncan Campbell Scott* (1926); and *The Green Cloister, Later Poems* (1935); and fiction: *In the Village of Viger* (1896; 1945); *The*

Witching of Elspie, A Book of Stories (1923); *The Circle of Affection and Other Pieces in Prose and Verse* (1947); and *Untitled Novel; ca 1905* (1979).

Works on Scott include E. K. Brown, "A Memoir," *Selected Poems of Duncan Campbell Scott* (1951); D. G. Jones, *Butterfly on Rock* (1970); S. L. Dragland, ed., *Duncan Campbell Scott: A Book of Criticism* (1974); John Flood, "The Duplicity of D. C. Scott," *Black Moss*, No. 2 (1976), pp. 50-63; and K. P. Stich, ed., *The Duncan Campbell Scott Symposium* (1979).

—KATHY MEZEI

E. J. PRATT

1883-1964

Edwin John Pratt was born in Western Bay, Newfoundland, the son of a Methodist minister who had emigrated from Yorkshire. Upon graduation from St. John's Methodist College, he intended to follow in his father's footsteps and thus spent four years as a teacher and minister in the island's coastal villages. He entered Victoria College in the University of Toronto and took the degrees of B.A., B.D., and, in 1917, a Ph.D. in theology. In 1920 he was invited to join the English Department in Victoria College, and remained there until his retirement in 1953. Pratt was not only a distinguished scholar, but was also known and is remembered as a man of keen intelligence and wit, an enthusiastic teacher, and a dedicated humanist. His curiosity and exuberance for life were manifested in interests far beyond the purely literary: for example, physics, demonology, philosophy (especially Kant), psychology, and tales of the sea. For several years he was the editor of *Canadian Poetry Magazine*. On three occasions his books have won the Governor-General's Award for poetry.

Pratt currently holds a paradoxical position in the history of

Canadian literature. On the one hand, he is generally acknowledged as Canada's first major poet of the twentieth century, a poet whose inexhaustible curiosity about the interrelationship of man, nature, and God not only served to break with the tradition of landscape and sentimental poetry, but also resulted in poems which are at once original and classical. Northrop Frye is his staunchest defender. Earle Birney has written that Pratt is Canada's contribution to the tradition of poetic narrative handed down through Chaucer, Pope, and Milton. On the other hand, Pratt's achievement is often seen as having been important in its time, but as having little or no relevance to either the contemporary world or contemporary poetic theory. This paradox seems mainly due to the changing tides of Canadian poetry, to its enormous growth and advancement over the past three decades. Pratt's concern for metre, rhyme, heroism, complex narrative and symbolic patterns, morality, and the place of man in the universe — in short, all the elements of classical poetry — unfortunately limit contemporary appreciation of his work.

His Methodist upbringing and the intellectual influences under which he came during his first years at Victoria College combined to produce in him a lifelong interest in the relationship between religion and science. This is a field of investigation usually associated with the nineteenth century, and thus it is precisely Pratt's major interest which makes scholars defend him as an important poet, but succeeding generations of poets perceive him as representing a tradition against which they must rebel. A point that is often overlooked is Pratt's humour: a reader not only comes suddenly upon lines which are obviously comic, but also will discover threads of irony running through Pratt's narratives. Pratt's poetry is of a kind we are not likely to see written again. In terms of craft, thought, and ambition, his work stands almost alone in the Canadian poetic tradition.

Pratt's works include *Newfoundland Verse* (1923); *The Witches' Brew* (1926); *Titans* (1926); *The Titanic* (1935); *The Fable of the Goats and Other Poems* (1937); *Brébeuf and His Brethren* (1940); *Still Life and Other Poems* (1943); *Towards the Last Spike* (1952); and *The Collected Poems of E. J. Pratt* (1958; 1962).

Works on Pratt include John Sutherland, *The Poetry of E. J. Pratt* (1956); Earle Birney, "E. J. Pratt and His Critics" in *Our Living Tradition* (1959); Robert G. Collins, "E. J. Pratt: The Homeric Voice," *Review of National Literatures*, 7 (1976), 83-109; Glenn Clever, ed., *The E. J. Pratt Symposium* (1977); and Lila and Raymond Laakso with Moira Allen and Marjorie Linden, "E. J. Pratt: An Annotated Bibliography," in *The Annotated Bibliography of Canada's Major Authors*, Vol. 2 (1980).

– ROBERT BILLINGS

W. W. E. ROSS

1894-1966

William Wrightson Eustace Ross was born in Peterborough, Ontario, in 1894. He attended the University of Toronto and worked as a geophysicist with the Agincourt Magnetic Observatory. One of the early imagist poets in Canada, Ross published his first poem, "Soldiery," in the *Dial* in 1928. Four books of his poetry have been published, two in the thirties, one in 1956, and one in 1968. The dates of the books reflect the course of his career. Ross did his best writing in the twenties and thirties, for which he received only small recognition, then dropped out of sight to be re-discovered by younger poets—primarily Raymond Souster—who were influenced by the Imagists. He died in Toronto in 1966.

In his poetry Ross sought to capture Canadian scenes using Imagist form and concrete detail. His main subject was Canadian nature. He wrote to convey that "sharper tang of Canada" which "may mark us off / from older Europe." This attitude reflects the nationalistic mood of post-World War I Canada. He employed the Imagist form because "it is expressive now, / At other times other forms. / This form now. Expressive now." His style emphasizes visual and auditory experiences rather than highly developed themes. These sensory experiences are, he wrote, "our / Companions daily marching / Along with us." Most of his poems present nature scenes akin to those found in Group of Seven paintings:

The iron rocks
slope sharply down
into the gleaming
of northern water,
and there is a shining
to northern water
reflecting the sky
on a keen cool morning
("Rocky Bay")

Like Marianne Moore, with whom he shared a mutual admiration, Ross wrote syllabic verse. His most characteristic poems have three eight-line stanzas, usually with thirty-one to thirty-eight syllables per stanza and between 100 and 110 syllables per poem. This personally evoked structure combined flexibility with order. Ross worked within narrow limits of subject, form, and emotion. He wrote a few near-perfect examples of Imagism but the constraints he imposed on himself limited his achievement severely.

Ross's works include *Laconics* (1930); *Sonnets* (1932); *Experiment 1923-1929* (1956); and *Shapes and Sounds* (1968).

Works on Ross include Marianne Moore, "Experienced Simplicity," *Poetry* (Chicago), 38 (1931), 280-81; Raymond Souster "About the Author," in *Experiment 1923-1929* (1956); Barry Callaghan, "Memoir," in *Shapes and Sounds* (1968); Peter Stevens, "On W. W. E. Ross," *Canadian Literature*, No. 39 (1969), pp. 43-61; and Michael E. Darling, ed., "On Poetry and Poets: The Letters of W. W. E. Ross to A. J. M. Smith," *Essays on Canadian Writing*, No. 16 (1979-80), pp. 78-125.

– DON PRECOSKY

RAYMOND KNISTER

1899-1932

John Raymond Knister was born in Ruscomb, Essex County, Ontario. After studying at the University of Toronto, he worked on his father's farm, and in 1923 moved to Iowa City, as associate editor of *The Midland.* He lived in Chicago briefly before returning to Canada in 1924, and in 1926 started freelancing in Toronto. Knister married Myrtle Gamble in 1927, and in 1929 moved to the Port Dover area, where he wrote the novel *My Star Predominant*, which won the Graphic Publishers "Canadian Novel Contest" first prize of $2,500 in 1931. A daughter, Imogen, was born in 1930. From 1931-32 Knister lived in Quebec. Knister drowned while swimming off Stoney Point, Lake St. Clair.

Knister's poetry is usually discussed in terms of the depiction of nature and farm life, and the influence of Imagism. He has been associated with brief, powerful, and concise poems, such as "The Hawk." Yet Knister's range, technical and thematic, is greater than has been generally acknowledged. "Poisons" is a prose poem, "A Row of Horse Stalls" a series of poems, and "Corn Husking" an unpublished longer poem. The critical argument that the poetry is largely concerned with describing nature and man's relationship to it, and possibly the poetic process, overlooks the inclusion of such topics as love, war, ecology, and social climbing. "The Humourist" is an example of a poem that would not usually be considered to be in the Knister style, although it typifies the humour often found elsewhere in his writing.

Knister is recognized as one of Canada's first modern poets: David Arnason has described him as "perhaps the chief Canadian talent of the twenties." In his writing Knister called for a recognition rather than a denial of reality: "Birds and flowers and dreams are real as sweating men and swilling pigs." And he saw acceptance of the reality of "common things" as meaning that "In the end we in Canada here might have the courage of our experience and speak according to it only." Dorothy Livesay has identified as an expression of Knister's aesthetic sensibility the statement "Poetry is to make things real — those of the imagination, and those of the tangible world."

Works by Knister include *Collected Poems of Raymond Knister* (1949) and *Raymond Knister: Poems, Stories and Essays* (1975).

Works on Knister include Dorothy Livesay, "Raymond Knister: A Memoir," in *Collected Poems of Raymond Knister* (1949); Peter Stevens, "The Old Futility of Art: Knister's Poetry," *Canadian Literature*, No. 23 (1965), pp. 45-52; David Arnason, "Canadian Poetry: The Interregnum," *CV/II*, 1 (1975), 28-32; Bernhard Beutler, "'Herald of Imagism': Raymond Knister," in *Der Einfluss des Imagismus auf die moderne kanadische Lyrik englischer Sprache* (1978), pp. 41-53; and Don Precosky, "Ever With Discontent: Some Comments on Raymond Knister and His Poetry," *CV/II*, 4 (1980), 3-9.

– JOY KUROPATWA

F. R. SCOTT

1899-

The son of the poet Frederick George Scott, Francis Reginald Scott was born in Quebec City in 1899. He graduated from Bishop's College in 1919 and earned two degrees from Oxford while studying there as a Rhodes Scholar. McGill University became his professional home; he graduated from its Law School in 1927, joined its faculty, and became its Dean of Law in 1961, retiring from that position in 1964. In 1940 Scott was made a Guggenheim Fellow, and in 1952 he lived in Burma working with the United Nations. A strong sense of pity and justice and beauty runs throughout his writing, and he has lived a life of eloquent protest on both the literary and political levels. He was participant in the formation of the CCF and NDP and fought two court cases against censorship of D. H. Lawrence's *Lady Chatterley's Lover* in the 1950s. As an editor he is regarded for his work with *The McGill Fortnightly Review* (1925-27) and *Preview* (1942-45). As a poet, translator, social scientist, prose writer, and lawyer he has been awarded innumerable prizes and distinctions for his plural contribution to Canadian culture and society.

Along with his contemporaries A. J. M. Smith, Robert Finch, Leo Kennedy, A. M. Klein, and E. J. Pratt, Scott ushered modern Canadian poetry into the cosmopolitan tradition of Imagist rigour and Modernist insistence on the need to avoid poetic sentimentality, soft poetic diction, hackneyed themes, lyric self-absorption, and the reliance on redundant, traditional, very mechanical prosody. He was in his younger years aware of the critical tenets of T. S. Eliot and Ezra Pound, very awake to the new call for poetic tough mindedness, and yet not merely servile or derivative in his own poetic practice. Indeed, much of his poetry has as arguable an affinity with the Romantic passion of W. B. Yeats as it has with the urbanity of Pound and Eliot. Primarily because he wrote his first mature poetry in the 1930s and 1940s and was raised and educated in a Christian and Socialist tradition, his dominant poetic theme is very often socialist and satirical. Very like W. H. Auden, Stephen Spender, C. Day Lewis, and Louis MacNeice in Britain, and like e. e. cummings, Robert Frost, Carl Sandburg, and William Carlos Williams in America, Scott learned what he needed from the cosmopolitan poets of the early part of the century, but he turned that craft sophistication toward the framing of reality as he saw it in his own deprived society and his own natural locus. He blended it easefully into a highly individual response to his own time and place.

Scott is a very physical writer in the sense that fresh image and novelty of phrase are emphatic and alive in his verse, always surprising in the magic of their saying. His poems of social protest almost invariably end with an aphoristic and visual punchline, one that makes his insight gnomic and unforgettable. Analogously, as a poet attentive to the mystery of creation his verse moves continually toward epiphany, the suddenly discovered moment of beauty that transcends all of his previous lines. For all of the cleansing irony of his social poems and his identity as a demythologizer of history and politics, he remains an essentially warm poet who is highly romantic in his concern for common humanity, love, the legitimate claims of the heart, the pathos of poverty, his love of the land and the cosmos, and his imaginative hunger for social sanity and a beautific Beyond. In short, Scott's poetry embodies a lyrical, social, and existential vision that is toughened by his cosmopolitan awareness but is not simply intellectual and detached in its shape. Perhaps more than any other Canadian poet he has an empathetic sense of the lives of others and an intricate feeling for Canada's many landscapes in his art. Of all the poetic views of Canadian reality, his is the most Olympian and engaged at the same time, the most thorough.

Scott's works include *Overture* (1945); *Events and Signals* (1954); *The Eye of the Needle* (1957); *Signature* (1964); *The Dance Is One* (1973); and *The Collected Poems of F. R. Scott* (1981). His translations include *Poems of French Canada* (1977).

Works on Scott include Desmond Pacey, "F. R. Scott," in *Ten Canadian Poets: A Group of Biographical and Critical Essays* (1958); A. J. M. Smith, "F. R. Scott and Some of His Poems," in *Towards A View of Canadian Letters: Selected Critical Essays, 1928-1971* (1973); Michael Gnarowski, Introduction to *New Provinces: Poems of Several Authors,* (1976); and Sandra Djwa, "F. R. Scott," *Canadian Poetry: Studies, Documents, Reviews* (1979), pp. 1-16.

– TERRY WHALEN

ROBERT FINCH

1900-

Born in Freeport, Long Island, New York, 14 May 1900 to highly cultured English parents, Robert Duer Claydon Finch learned to read both French and English by the age of four. The family moved to Canada in 1906, returning briefly to the United States in 1908. Finch graduated from the University of Toronto (B.A. – Honour Moderns in French and German), winning the Governor-General's Proficiency Medal and after post-graduate studies at the Sorbonne, in 1928 joined the teaching staff of the French Department of his Alma Mater where he has had a distinguished career as a scholar. Concurrently cultivating his interests in music, drama, travel, and art, he has published eight books of poems and a masque, *A Century Has Roots.* Among many honours, he has won the Governor-General's Award twice, for *Poems* (1946) and *Dover Beach Revisited* (1961), been elected to the Royal Society of Canada, and been awarded the Lorne Pierce Gold Medal and Award. Though retired since 1968, he continues to work at Massey College, University of Toronto, on his scholarship and his poetry.

The thematic focus of the best of Robert Finch's work rests on the Arts (especially poetry, painting and sculpture, and music), nature (especially cultivated or relatively tamed nature), and human relationships. Additionally, he has written many poems about locales he has visited during his extensive travels. The voice of the satirist and social critic has always been heard in a Finch collection as has the voice of the Christian humanist. Never a very fashionable poet and apparently not an innovator in terms of prosody or form, Finch characteristically works within the demands of a closed form such as the sonnet and the exigencies of an iambic pentameter or tetrameter line, yet within those confines he experiments freely with rhyme patterns and stanza structures. His poems are basically neo-classical in spirit, reflecting the polish, erudition, and wit associated with that style and representing a view of the universe whose proportion, order, and design are often conveyed by presenting a picture within a frame such as that created by a window. The self-conscious artistry of much of his work is, however, frequently balanced by a wry sense of humour as the poet observes the foibles of humans in love, at work, and at play. There are few individualized characters within his poems, as Finch's affinity for the neo-classical style is also reflected in his preference for generic characters — the lover, the artist, the foreman — to represent the human condition. If his poems appear at times to lack vibrancy, the epigrammatic wit of the little poem "When" reminds the reader that Finch's ideal is to see passion tied to knowledge and reason dominating emotion.

Finch's works include *New Provinces: Poems of Several Authors* (1936); *Poems* (1946); *The Strength of the Hills* (1948); *A Century Has Roots* (1953); *Acis in Oxford and Other Poems* (1959); *Dover Beach Revisited and Other Poems* (1961); *Silverthorn Bush and Other Poems* (1966); *Variations and Theme* (1980); and *Has and Is* (1981).

Works on Finch include William Walsh, "The Poetry of Robert Finch," *Bulletin of Canadian Studies*, 2 (1978), 1-15; and Susan Gingell-Beckmann, "Against An Anabasis of Grace: A Retrospective Review of the Poems of Robert Finch," *Essays on Canadian Writing*, No. 23 (1982), pp. 157-62.

– SUSAN GINGELL

A. J. M. SMITH

1902-1980

Arthur James Marshall Smith was born 8 November 1902 in Westmount, Quebec. He attended McGill University, where he earned a B.Sc. and an M.A., and, with F. R. Scott, founded the *McGill Fortnightly Review.* After graduating from Edinburgh University with a Ph.D. in 1931, he taught at several American colleges before settling at Michigan State University. While still a young man, he published poems in some of the foremost literary magazines of his day, including *The Dial, Poetry*, and *New Verse.* As poet, critic, and anthologist, Smith championed the cause of modernism in Canadian literature, and his achievements were honoured with many awards, including the Governor-General's Award for poetry and the Medal of the Royal Society of Canada.

Few Canadian poets exhibit a wider range of styles and themes than does A. J. M. Smith, and this versatility has often proved a stumbling-block to critics seeking unity of tone or purpose in his canon. The earliest of Smith's poems to gain recognition were heavily indebted to W. B. Yeats and T. S. Eliot, but these have not endured as well as his imagist poems such as "The Lonely Land" and "Swift Current." Though never a favourite of his, "The Lonely Land" has been his most-anthologized work, widely admired for its precise evocation of the northern landscape. In the 1930s, Smith, along with most of his contemporaries, turned to poetry that dealt with social and political issues. "News of the Phoenix" is the best-known of his satirical poems, but its social criticism is less characteristic of his work as a whole than is its double-edged irony, which undercuts the speaker as well as his ostensible target. In two other poems of this period, "Far West" and "Noctambule," Smith is at his most complex, demanding the reader's ability to identify and appreciate a wide range of allusions that underlie an apparently surreal vision. These works especially give credence to the view of Smith as a metaphysical poet, not only in their juxtaposition of seemingly unrelated images, but also in their fusion of intellect and feeling, abstract ideas and human emotions. In his later poetry, he dwells increasingly on the theme of death. But his awareness of the inevitability of the grave produces not morbid fascination but defiant rejection of death's dominion. "Metamorphosis" and "The Wisdom of Old Jelly Roll," with their images of sensuality and regeneration, testify to Smith's unshakeable commitment to life, a theme which is most lovingly and dynamically explored in "The Archer," considered by many to be his finest poem.

Smith's works include five books of verse: *News of the Phoenix* (1943); *A Sort of Ecstasy* (1954); *Collected Poems* (1962); *Poems New and Collected* (1967); and *The Classic Shade* (1978); two collections of essays: *Towards a View of Canadian Letters* (1973) and *On Poetry and Poets* (1977); and numerous anthologies, of which the best-known are *The Book of Canadian Poetry* (1st edition, 1943) and *The Oxford Book of Canadian Verse* (1960).

Works on Smith include M. L. Rosenthal, "'Poor Innocent': The Poetry of A. J. M. Smith," *Modern Poetry Studies*, 8 (1977), 1-13 (reprinted as the introduction to *The Classic Shade*); Sandra A. Djwa, "A. J. M. Smith: Of Metaphysics and Dry Bones," *Studies in Canadian Literature*, 3 (1978), 17-34; Leon Edel, "The Worldly Muse of A. J. M. Smith," *University of Toronto Quarterly*, 47 (1978), 200-13; and John Ferns, *A. J. M. Smith* (1979).

– MICHAEL DARLING

EARLE BIRNEY

1904-

Born in Calgary (then part of the North-West Territories), Alfred Earle Birney grew up an only child in various farms and ranches in the mountains of Alberta and British Columbia. Having worked for two years after completing high school, Birney entered the University of British Columbia in 1922 to study science, but switched to literature under the tutelage of Professor Garnett Sedgwick. Most of Birney's adult life has been spent teaching English — at the University of Toronto from 1936-41, and at the University of British Columbia from

1946-63. After leaving Vancouver, Birney concentrated on writing while accepting various writer-in-residence positions in North America. A Trotskyist during the 1930s, a Major during World War II, a supporter of peace and nuclear disarmament since then, Birney has always been an ardent fighter for causes, and it is these commitments which frequently fuel his poetry.

Birney's early poetry (during the 1940s) reflects the conviction that writing can alter events. Poems about war and peace are intended to sway people's opinions, and in some way to lessen the carnage. Written in an allusive, heavily adjectival style, the poems compel diligent readers to sort out the meanings by referring to various myths and by looking up words in the dictionary. After the war, Birney allows more colloquial language to enter his poetry, and he loosens his reliance on external sources. In "Bushed," even though we still see the mythical elements from his earlier poetry, the narrative has been pared down and allowed to speak more directly. After a round-the-world trip in 1958-59, Birney enters his greatest and most productive poetic phase. His travel poems, such as "Bear on the Delhi Road," demonstrate a mastery of tone and a condensation of meaning achieved in a lyric format. During the 1960s he is attracted to the formal innovations of bpNichol and bill bissett, and at one point calls himself Canada's oldest hippie. Rejuvenated by the contact with younger poets, alarmed by what he sees around the globe, Birney concentrates more on man and his role as shaper/destroyer of the environment — a theme enunciated earlier in *Damnation of Vancouver.* Despite his anger and doom-saying, Birney now writes in a more relaxed, more confident, more accessible fashion. His recent love poems have been praised for their compassion and honesty, and for their unguarding of the poet's heart.

Works by Birney include *David and Other Poems* (1942); *Now Is Time* (1945); *Ice Cod Bell or Stone* (1962); *Near False Creek Mouth* (1964); *Selected Poems 1940-1966* (1966); *Pnomes Jukollages & Other Stunzas* (1969); *Rag & Bone Shop* (1971); *What's So Big about GREEN?* (1973); *The*

Collected Poems of Earle Birney (1975); *Ghost in the Wheels: Selected Poems* (1977); and *Fall by Fury & Other Makings* (1978).

Works on Birney include Frank Davey, *Earle Birney* (1971); Richard Robillard, *Earle Birney* (1971); Bruce Nesbitt, ed., *Earle Birney* (1974); Peter Aichinger, *Earle Birney* (1979); and *Perspectives on Earle Birney* (1981).

– JACK DAVID

LEO KENNEDY

1907-

Leo Kennedy was born in Liverpool, England; his family immigrated to Montreal when he was five. Kennedy first published poetry in the *McGill Fortnightly Review* (1926-27), where he was associated with A. J. M. Smith, F. R. Scott, and A. M. Klein. Later he was one of the founding editors of *The Canadian Mercury* (1928-29). Kennedy's single volume of poetry, *The Shrouding* (1933), was one of the first collections of verse published in Canada to reflect modern ideas about the writing of poetry. Kennedy also published a number of short stories in *The Canadian Forum*, and played an active role as editor, reviewer, and spokesman for modern writing in Canada (see "The Future of Canadian Literature," *The Canadian Mercury*, April-May 1929). In the late 1930s Kennedy moved to the United States, where he worked as an advertising copywriter and an editor at *The Reader's Digest*. In the late 1970s he returned to live in Montreal.

Leo Kennedy's poetic output can be divided into two phases, the period up to the publication of *The Shrouding* in 1933, and the period after 1934. In his article "Direction for Canadian Poets," Kennedy described *The Shrouding* as "reverting by way of (A. J. M.) Smith and (T. S.) Eliot to something of the matter of the metaphysicians" (the reference is to the English metaphysical poets, who were haunted by the interconnection between life and death, between bodily beauty and decay). A. J. M. Smith had previously published a poem titled "The Shrouding," and had written a critical appreciation of the metaphysical poets. In T. S. Eliot's *The Waste Land* (1922) Kennedy observed a poetic use of the myth of the death and resurrection of the god Adonis. This pattern of rebirth through death provides the main theme of Kennedy's volume. Although he was an outspoken advocate of modern poetry, Kennedy's own verse is highly traditional in form. There is very little free verse in *The Shrouding;* the cadences of Kennedy's line are regular and insistent; he frequently uses archaic diction and conventional poetic turns of phrase. From modern traditionalist poets like Elinor Wylie and Edna St. Vincent Millay, Kennedy learned the use of established metrical patterns such as the quatrain and the sonnet. Kennedy himself later repudiated his *Shrouding* manner, and turned to political and social themes in a number of poems written against the background of the Depression and the Spanish Civil War for the left-wing periodical *New Frontier* (1936-37). For the most part, the language of these poems is abstract and generalized, and the manner strident and imperative. Yet Kennedy's two poetic phases are of some historical significance, for they roughly parallel the development of poetry throughout the English-speaking world from the negativism of the 1920s to the positive, committed attitudes of the 1930s. In a poem like "Calling Eagles" Kennedy showed himself to be alert to the influences and requirements of the time.

Kennedy's *The Shrouding* was reprinted in 1975 with an introduction by Leon Edel.

Works on Kennedy include Peter Stevens, ed., *The McGill Movement* (1969); and Lorraine McMullen, "Leo Kennedy," *The Golden Dog/Le Chien d'Or,* 1 (1972), 46-62.

– FRANCIS ZICHY

RALPH GUSTAFSON

1909-

Born 16 August 1909, in Lime Ridge, Quebec, Ralph Gustafson grew up in Sherbrooke. After attending Bishop's University (B.A., M.A.) he moved to England in 1930. His first two volumes were published there. In 1939 he left London for New York, where he resided until 1963. During the 1940s he published *Flight into Darkness* (1944) and edited the *Anthology of Canadian Poetry (English)* for Penguin (1942). Gustafson returned to Canada and Bishop's in 1963. Appointed Poet-in-Residence in 1966, he remained there until his retirement in 1977. He has published thirteen volumes of poetry since 1960, winning the Governor-General's Award for *Fire on Stone* (1974). He has travelled extensively throughout the world and currently resides in North Hatley, Quebec.

A poet in the tradition of W. B. Yeats, T. S. Eliot, and Ezra Pound, Gustafson is one of our most thorough Modernists. He is also a profound humanist: a poet of celebration and praise in the midst of suffering, of wrath in the face of ignorance and complacency. This humanist core is expressed most cogently in his recent long poem *Gradations of Grandeur* (1979), where he writes: "Heaven or mud, / There's proof enough, grandeur is had." Poetry is proof: "But this alone, sure of: lacking / Art, a mess. Art's humanity, / And that, the way to waving heaven." The "mess" that man has made of himself and his world is Gustafson's starting-point. The early *Flight into Darkness* (1944) presents a highly cultivated sensibility wounded by the ubiquitous destruction of life and beauty. It is a highly allusive, difficult, and dense poetry: complex, even tortuous, in its syntax and rhythms. The poet seeks his way through hell with the ambiguous light of love. The power of love to endure its changes links the early with the later poetry. In 1960, *Rocky Mountain Poems* and *Rivers among Rocks* mark a renaissance in Gustafson's career. A fresh voice and renovated style, characterized by colloquial language and syntax, shorter and more varied lines, a more flexible (though still complex) music, carry the burden of knowledge more easily. Gustafson's modernism is evident in his view that "The very usefulness of a poem...is its intelligible architecture, its shaped resolution, its counterpointed harmony." The poet must craft his poem:

> The poet is artist, the maker of what is distinguished in itself, of what can stand alone without him; the golden bird on the golden bough that signs to drowsy emperors, as Yeats has it. A poem is not its content, not only; a poem is a verbal disposition that provides the inviolable meaning of the content. Poetry is crafty.

This craft is essentially moral; the poem must be true: "How to shape this heterogeneous world of experience so that, in its existence of harmony and order, the poem be praise though what it communicate is suffering." Gustafson's desire to be as sincere in affirmation as he is honest in doubt results in a continuous tension in his language and line. But he is committed to the traditional contract between poet and reader: the poem must mean something. "Poetry...to be itself carries a burden of logical meaning." Thus, while he always delights, Gustafson also dares to instruct—a posture that calls for a courage he shares with few other contemporary poets.

Gustafson's works include *Flight into Darkness* (1944); *River among Rocks* (1960); *Rocky Mountain Poems* (1960); *Sift in an Hourglass* (1966); *Ixion's Wheel* (1969); *Selected Poems* (1972); *Fire on Stone* (1974); *Sequences* (1979); *Landscape with Rain* (1980); and *Conflicts of Spring* (1981). *The Vivid Air* (1980) contains his collected short stories.

Works on Gustafson include Louis Dudek, "Two Canadian Poets: Ralph Gustafson and Eli Mandel," *Culture*, 22 (1961), 145-51; S. G. Mullins, "Ralph Gustafson's Poetry," *Culture*, 22 (1961), 417-22; Robin Skelton, "Ralph Gustafson: A Review and Retrospect," *Mosaic*, 8 (1975), 167-79; and Wendy Keitner, *Ralph Gustafson* (1979).

– DERMOT MCCARTHY

A. M. KLEIN

1909-1972

A. M. Klein was born in Ratno, in the Ukraine, in 1909, and was brought to Montreal the following year. He attended McGill University from 1926 to 1929, where he met A. J. M. Smith, F. R. Scott, Leon Edel, and Leo Kennedy, and the University of Montreal from 1930 to 1933, where he earned a degree in law. He married Bessie Kozlov in 1935. In 1938 he became editor of the *Canadian Jewish Chronicle* and in 1939 Samuel Bronfman hired him as a public relations adviser and speechwriter. In 1949 *The Rocking Chair and Other Poems* won the Governor-General's Award and in the same year Klein was badly defeated as the CCF candidate for parliament in Cartier. Soon after his defeat he was sent on a tour of Israel by the Canadian Jewish Congress, resulting in his novel, *The Second Scroll.* In the early fifties he began to suffer from depression, which led to suicide attempts, and to a gradual withdrawal from the world.

The central concern of A. M. Klein's work is the nature of community, of multiplicity as an expression of underlying unity. This concern is reflected in many aspects of the structure and texture of his poetry. Many of his poems consist of self-contained units which, through their kaleidoscopic interactions, suggest a common centre. A similar effect is created by Klein's frequent use of elaborate lists and complex, expansive metaphors as structural principles. On the level of texture this effect is enhanced by an abundant use of puns and assonance and by a diction which draws on archaisms and on vocabulary and constructions from several languages, especially Latin, French, Yiddish, and Hebrew. Klein's best early poetry was principally Jewish in theme and affirmative in tone, presenting a somewhat idealized portrait of the Jewish community through the ages. But this kind of poetry could not survive the effects of the Depression, the rise of Hitler, and Klein's own difficult personal circumstances. In the relatively little poetry Klein wrote in the late thirties he abandoned, for the most part, Jewish themes and turned to broader political ones, with not very satisfactory results. With the coming of the Second World War and the threat to the existence of the Jews, Klein found his public voice again as spokesman for his people. After the war, in poems mostly collected in *The Rocking Chair and Other Poems* (1948), he turned his attention to the Québécois community, which he could deal with more directly than with his own, constrained as he was by his role of public spokesman and advocate of his people. The Zionist novel *The Second Scroll* (1951) marked a return to Jewish themes in general, but not to the specific community of Jewish Montreal which he knew best. Sometime in the early forties Klein began to redefine his relationship with his community in dialectical terms, in an attempt to deal with his growing sense that he was not adequately appreciated; he came to see his experience of isolation as a necessary stage in a process of purification and self-exploration which would lead to greater achievement and eventual reintegration into a community which it was his ultimate task to redeem. This is the main thrust of his greatest poem, "Portrait of the Poet as Landscape," which is all the more moving for not being entirely convincing. Gradually Klein began to yield to feelings of persecution and self-contempt, feelings that were probably aggravated by his difficult relationship with Samuel Bronfman. In Klein's last major statement on the poet's relationship with his community, the essay "The Bible's Archetypical Poet" (1953), he develops themes latent in his earliest work, especially "Out the Pulver and the Polished Lens" (1931), but with a new and disturbing note of bitterness. By this time Klein had begun the collapse into silence and isolation from which he never recovered.

Klein's works include *Hath Not a Jew ...* (1940); *The Hitleriad* (1944); *Poems* (1944); *The Rocking Chair and Other Poems* (1948); *The Second Scroll* (1951); and *The Collected Poems of A. M. Klein* (1974).

Works on Klein include Tom Marshall, ed., *A. M. Klein* (1970); Miriam Waddington, *A. M. Klein* (1970); Seymour Mayne, ed., *The A. M. Klein Symposium* (1975); Gretl K. Fisher, *In Search of Jerusalem: Religion and Ethics in the Writings of A. M. Klein* (1975); and Usher Caplan, *Like One That Dreamed: A Portrait of A. M. Klein* (1982).

– ZAILIG POLLOCK

DOROTHY LIVESAY

1909-

Dorothy Livesay was born in Winnipeg, and educated in Modern Languages at the University of Toronto and the Sorbonne. She then became a social worker, and during the 1930s was actively involved in left-wing politics as a result of her observation of the social conditions of the Depression. After 1936 she lived in Vancouver, where she married, raised a family, and worked as a journalist and teacher. From 1960 to 1963 she taught English in Northern Rhodesia (now Zambia). Since returning to Canada she has taught at the Universities of New Brunswick, Alberta, Victoria, and Manitoba, among others. She now lives on Galiano Island, B.C.

The characteristic structural pattern of her poetry is the dialectic; a tension between contrary impulses—public and private life, social responsibility and imaginative freedom, youth and age, male and female—may be resolved or left unresolved. Her early poems were short personal lyrics strongly influenced by the Imagist movement. Her developing interest in revolutionary solutions to social ills led her to experiment with longer poetic forms in order to accommodate larger, more public subjects. The result was what she later called the "documentary" poem, one of the most successful of which is "Day and Night." It lacks the sustained narrative line which we normally expect from the traditional long poem; instead, various voices, scenes, and images are juxtaposed in a manner influenced by cinema, and are unified by thematic concerns— in this case, the alienation of the industrial worker from the products of his labour. In her later poems, she has made use of her "open" poetic forms, rather than the often stanzaic, rhymed forms of her earlier work. Here her political concerns are somewhat modulated. Some of them, such as "The Three Emily's," have a recognizably feminist tone. In "Artifacts: West Coast" she moves from the immediate present into a meditation on time and history that comprehends both the Indian culture and the Victorian colonial period in British Columbia. Because her gifts are essentially lyrical, and the lyric is best suited to the rendition of private experience, her attempts to move beyond that can sometimes seem merely topical, period curiosities. At her best, however, she renders the duality of experience with honesty, directness, and wit.

Dorothy Livesay's works of poetry include *Green Pitcher* (1928); *Signpost* (1932); *Day and Night* (1944); *Poems for People* (1947); *The Unquiet Bed* (1967); *The Documentaries* (1968); *Collected Poems: The Two Seasons* (1972); and *Ice Age* (1975). Prose works include *A Winnipeg Childhood* (1973) and *Right Hand Left Hand* (1977).

Works on Livesay include Jean Gibbs, "Dorothy Livesay and the Transcendentalist Tradition," *Humanities Association Bulletin*, 21 (1970), 24-39; Peter Stevens, "Dorothy Livesay: The Love Poetry," *Canadian Literature*, No. 47 (1971), pp. 26-43; Beverly Mitchell, S.S.A., "'How Silence Sings' in the Poetry of Dorothy Livesay," *Dalhousie Review*, 54 (1974-75), 510-28; and George Woodcock, "Sun, Wind, and Snow: The Poems of Dorothy Livesay," *Room of One's Own, Dorothy Livesay Issue*, 5, No. 12 (1979), 46-62.

– PAUL DENHAM

ANNE WILKINSON

1910-1961

Born in Toronto, Anne Wilkinson (nee Gibbons) spent much of her childhood in London, Ontario, and was educated in private schools in Canada and abroad. In an autobiographical prose sketch, "Four Corners of my World," she relates memories of her childhood. Although she wrote *Swann and Daphne*, a fable for children, and *Lions in the Way*, a history of the famous Osler family from which she descended, and was a founding editor of *The Tamarack Review*, she is best known as a poet. Wilkinson was the author of two books of poetry, *Counterpoint to Sleep* and *The Hangman Ties the Holly*, and she published a number of poems in periodicals during the last fifteen years of her life. *The Collected Poems of Anne Wilkinson and a Prose Memoir*, edited and introduced by A. J. M. Smith, was published in 1968 in recognition of her importance as a poet.

Anne Wilkinson's poems are highly stylized and her manipulation of riddles and puns demands careful attention on the reader's part if their full significance is to be understood. Ballads, carols, and nursery rhymes often provide a basis for sardonic irony, a distinguishing characteristic of her work. Northrop Frye suggests that her practise of altering a stock phrase is "a device that may owe something to Dylan Thomas." Like Thomas, Wilkinson wrote a number of poems that emerge as riddles, based on poetic conceits similar to those found in early Welsh poems.

If, as several critics maintain, Wilkinson is obsessed by death, she is equally preoccupied with life. Her poetry reveals an intimate and sensuous identification with nature and with the union of the four elements: earth, air, fire, and water. In "Lens," a poem dealing with the poet's unique way of perceiving and interpreting experience, Wilkinson presents an explicit poetic aesthetic: it is the duty of the poet to "keep and cherish my good lens."

Robert Lecker points out that her poetry and poetics are governed by a set of polar oppositions represented by the quick—"the actual lived moment of phenomenal experience"—and the dead—"the forces of time and tradition which limit experience and threaten the ecstasy of life-flux." The tension emerging in her poetry between these two extremes develops from the fact that the quick "arises from and is sustained by" a recognition of the dead. For Wilkinson, the world of the quick is the world of spring and childhood, full of vitality and growth, innocence and wonder. The contrasts between the quick and the dead appear in the symbols and images of Wilkinson's poetry. The quick is aligned with the jungle, the south, and with children, while the dead becomes associated with the city, the north, and with aging. The resolution of this central conflict comes through a recognition of life as a cyclical process of endless transformations in which death becomes not final but fluid.

Wilkinson's works include *Counterpoint to Sleep* (1951); *The Hangman Ties the Holly* (1955); *Lions in the Way; A Discursive History of the Oslers* (1956); *Swann and Daphne* (1960), and *The Collected Poems of Anne Wilkinson and a Prose Memoir* (1968).

Works on Wilkinson include A. J. M. Smith, "A Reading of Anne Wilkinson," *Canadian Literature*, No. 10 (1961), pp. 32-39; and Robert Lecker, "Better Quick Than Dead: Anne Wilkinson's Poetry," *Studies in Canadian Literature, 3* (1978), pp. 34-46.

– LINDA LEITCH

IRVING LAYTON

1912-

Irving Layton (Lazarovitch) was born in Rumania and immigrated with his family to Montreal at the age of one. He grew up in Montreal's small Jewish community and took a B.Sc. in Agriculture at Macdonald College and an M.A. in Economics and Political Science at McGill. Along with John Sutherland and Louis Dudek he edited the magazine *First Statement* and continued to do so after it evolved into the influential *Northern Review* which was instrumental in bringing to Canadian poetry the influence of modern American poets such as Charles Olson and Wallace Stevens. In 1952, Layton, Dudek, and Raymond Souster formed Contact Press, a small publishing house which catered to emerging poets. Many of Layton's early books were privately funded and printed. He has won the Governor-General's Award for poetry, been a teacher and writer-in-residence at several universities, and represented Canada at poetry festivals in many countries, including France, Italy, and Korea. In 1981, Italy and Korea combined to nominate him for the Nobel Prize for Literature.

In the history of Canadian poetry to date, Layton's work is unique in its broadness of vision, its versatility, effusiveness, and integrity. He has never hesitated — in poems, stories, articles, interviews, or letters to newspapers — to speak out against social and political injustice, dishonesty, repression of desire and curiosity, or anything else that threatens to limit or destroy the possibilities of life. He and his work are prisoners of and rebels against the often divisive, always rational and cynical forces which dominate Canadian culture. Early influences on his work were the American poets of the 1940s; subsequent influences include the work of Russian, European, and South American poets. Layton ignores the staples of Canadian poetry — harsh or lovely landscapes, wheat and snow, sentiment and vague neuroses, post-modern word games — in favour of the more universal concerns of what he has recently called a "voice made confident by rage." He is a traveller in both time and space: he cannot be identified with any one region; he is as much aware of the thought of ancient Classical and Jewish literature as he is of modern American and European. In his work he repeatedly adopts several roles or masks including victim, confessor, penitent, sensitive sensualist, boor, outraged human being, Jewish prophet, bon vivant, revolutionary, and Antichrist — usually in the same book. These facets of Layton are usually presented in a loose, conversational style which often includes allusions to history and mythology; but Layton can also work successfully in more traditional linguistic and structural forms, e.g., "Keine Lazarovitch." He is Canada's most prolific poet, a fact which results in an uneven quality in his work. Some critics are very harsh on him: sometimes they focus too much on Layton's public personality, and not enough on his poems; at other times they dismiss much of his work as rhetoric or lacking craft or subtlety. But generally, serious criticism recognizes that his range of subject and voice deserves no small or short fame. Throughout, it seems that he is a satirist in the best and widest sense of the term: he can either sling vituperation at the enemies of life or whisper a delicate admonition into a lover's ear. Except for poems about the Holocaust, the specifically Jewish content of Layton's work is often overlooked. He has been called an "immoral moralist," a label which comes very close to capturing the essence and intent of his work, but which is too reductive to encompass his range of voice, thought, vocabulary, feeling, and his vitally important contribution to the direction Canadian poetry has taken over the last forty years.

Layton's works include *Here and Now* (1945); *The Cold Green Element* (1955); *The Bull Calf and Other Poems* (1956); *A Red Carpet for the Sun* (1959); *The Collected Poems of Irving Layton* (1971); *Engagements: The Prose of Irving Layton* (1972); *The Darkening Fire: Selected Poems 1945-1968* (1975); *The Unwavering Eye: Selected Poems 1968-1975* (1975); *Taking Sides: The Collected Social and Political Writings* (1977); and *A Wild Peculiar Joy* (1982).

Works on Layton include Eli Mandel, *Irving Layton* (1969); Peter Hunt, "Irving Layton, Pseudo-Prophet — A Reappraisal," *Canadian Poetry: Studies, Documents, Reviews*, No. 1 (1977), pp. 1-26; Seymour Mayne, ed., *Irving Layton: The Poet and His Critics* (1978); and Kurt Van Wilt "Layton, Nietzsche and Overcoming," *Essays on Canadian Writing*, No. 10 (1978), pp. 19-42.

– ROBERT BILLINGS

P. K. PAGE

1916-

Born in Swanage, England, Patricia Kathleen Page came with her family to Red Deer, Alberta, in 1919. After attending schools in Winnipeg, Calgary, and England, she held a variety of jobs in St. John, New Brunswick, and Montreal. Alan Crawley encouraged her by publishing her poems in his *Contemporary Verse*, and in the later 1940s she became associated with the *Preview* group of poets in Montreal. John Sutherland published many of her poems and stories in *First Statement* and she became the British Columbia regional editor for *Northern Review.* After working as a script writer for The National Film Board, Page married W. Arthur Irwin who joined External Affairs and they lived in Australia, U.S.A., Brazil, and Mexico before moving to Victoria, British Columbia where they now live. She began drawing in Brazil and has had many shows under her married name.

Page's writing has consistently examined transformations in human experience. She finds images and symbols which concentrate the feelings and meaning of those stages in life when radical changes in perception, mood, and attitude take place. She often uses consistent images, for example, to describe the loss of childhood innocence (green foliage, water) because of puberty, or war, or entrapment in a social structure (metals, rocks, snow); the loss of romantic dreams (flowers) in marriage; the leaving of home and the discovery of strange landscapes (gardens, birds); and more recently, the loss of vitality in old age (shadows). Many of her poems are psychological portraits of characters who are working out strategies (often illusory ones) to regain, or compensate for, what has been lost. Images, symbols, and metaphors are chosen with such care that the poems and stories have a metaphysical quality to them, suggesting a yearning for wholeness and harmony. If nostalgia for past childhood innocence, or dreams of romance or power, is very often illusory, then looking forward by means of another kind of vision becomes a central concern for Page. The creative imagination can allow us a vision, if only by glimpses, of wholeness and harmony, and Page's poems often intimate the existence of a higher world through images of angels, birds, light, air, and the colours of gold and white. Page's central images and metaphors do not suggest a simple dualism, however, since they are often richly ambiguous, and since the source of her art is often in dream. She was initially influenced by such modern writers as T. S. Eliot, Stephen Spender, Patrick Anderson, W. H. Auden and particularly Garcia Lorca, Rainer Rilke, and Carl Jung; more recently she has been interested in such Middle Eastern mystical writers as Suhrawardi, Rumi, and Jami. She points out, however, that all of these writers have been only superficially influential on the development of her poetic style. Her more recent poems are not as densely packed with images as the earlier ones, and her tone of detachment has changed to one that is more personal and subjective. What has remained constant is Page's startling precision in her choice of words and sound patterns to express her vision clearly.

Page's works include the novel *The Sun and the Moon* (1944); part of the anthology *Unit of Five* (1944); *As Ten as Twenty* (1946); *The Metal and the Flower* (1954); *Cry Ararat! Poems New and Selected* (1967); *The Sun and the Moon and Other Fictions* (1973); *Poems Selected and New* (1974); and *Evening Dance of the Grey Flies* (1981).

Works on Page include A. J. M. Smith, "The Poetry of P. K. Page," *Canadian Literature*, No. 50 (1971), pp. 17-27; S. Namjoshi, "Double Landscape," *Canadian Literature*, No. 67 (1976), pp. 21-30; Constance Rooke, "P. K. Page: The Chameleon at the Centre," *The Malahat Review*, No. 45 (1978), pp. 169-95; Rosemary Sullivan, "A Size Larger Than Seeing: The Poetry of P. K. Page," *Canadian Literature*, No. 79 (1978), pp. 32-42; and Diane Schoemperlen, "Four Themes in The Poetry of P. K. Page," *The English Quarterly*, 12, Nos. 1-2 (1979), 1-12.

– JOHN ORANGE

MIRIAM WADDINGTON

1917-

Miriam Waddington, born in Winnipeg of Russian-Jewish parents, moved to Ottawa with her family in the early 1930s. She then studied English at the University of Toronto, graduating in 1939. In that same year she married journalist Patrick Waddington. After working for magazines doing some translations, she studied social work, eventually gaining a Master's degree from the University of Pennsylvania. She then lived in Montreal, teaching at McGill University until after her divorce in 1960 when she returned to Toronto to take up further studies in literature. She has remained in Toronto since then, becoming a professor of literature at York University.

While at the beginning of her career she felt not wholly committed to poetry, in the 1950s she became more fully conscious of her desire to write a strict and intellectual poetry, which derived in part from the conceits and argumentative teasing out with metaphorical exactitude found in the Metaphysical poets. At this time her poems depended on traditional form and regular metrical arrangements for the most part, even in the poems which arose from her deeply felt concern for the underprivileged, unemployed, and criminal elements she met in her life as a social worker. Even though she wrote a public and urban poetry, her strongest inclination was to write a more private, though not strictly confessional, poetry focussing on the commitments and estrangements of human love, together with a clear response to scenes within nature recorded in poems which expressed an involvement beyond the immediate to invoke a universal vision of nature. This more private and visionary world became the strongest thrust of her poetry as her writing took on a looser structuring. In the 1960s, while her poetry often retained stanzaic forms, the language turned to more colloquial patterns with a carefully controlled rhythmic flow, speechlike but with a rigorous hold on stress within lines. This ease of lining, diction, and rhythm worked within the dichotomies she felt about her principal themes: the search for roots and a place in the world with its continual flux set against the larger universal context of nature, the dissatisfactions and breakdowns of human relationships set against the urge to insist that human love is still possible, and the encroachments of barbarianism set against her belief in civilized and cultural anger at the passing of time and the inexorable process of ageing set against her acceptance of the mutability of human life.

Waddington's works include *Green World* (1945); *The Second Silence* (1955); *The Season's Lovers* (1958); *The Glass Trumpet* (1966); *Say Yes* (1969); *Driving Home: Poems New and Selected* (1972); *The Price of Gold* (1976); and *The Visitants* (1981).

Works on Waddington include Ian Sowton, "The Lyric Craft of Miriam Waddington," *Dalhousie Review*, 39 (1959), 237-42; D. G. Jones, "Voices in the Dark," *Canadian Literature*, No. 45 (1970), pp. 73-74; L. R. Ricou, "Into My Green World: The Poetry of Miriam Waddington," *Essays on Canadian Writing*, No. 12 (1978), pp. 144-61; Maria Jacobs, "The Personal Poetry of Miriam Waddington," *CV/II*, 5 (1980), pp. 26-33; and Albert Moritz, "From a Far Star," *Books in Canada*, May 1982, pp. 5-8.

– PETER STEVENS

MARGARET AVISON

1918-

Biographical details about Margaret Avison are not plentiful and can be summarized briefly. She was born 23 April 1918, in Galt (now Cambridge), Ontario, the daughter of Harold Wilson, a clergyman, and Mabel (Kirkland) Avison. Although she lived in Alberta for several years while a child, she was educated at the University of Toronto (1936-40) and returned there over twenty years later to do an M.A. in English literature (1964). She has worked at a wide variety of jobs, including librarian, research assistant, secretary, social worker, lecturer in English literature, and archivist. In the 1940s and 1950s she published poems and reviews in numerous magazines and journals (such as *The Canadian Forum*, *Poetry* (Chicago), and *Contemporary Verse*). She received a Guggenheim fellowship in 1956-57 and her first volume of poetry, *Winter Sun*, was awarded the Governor-General's Medal in 1960. She has also published translations of Hungarian poetry and written a history of Ontario for secondary students. She lives in Toronto. One of her most significant experiences was her conversion to Christianity which occurred (as the back cover of *sunblue* tells us) in 1963.

While reviewing several books of poetry in *The Tamarack Review* for Autumn, 1956, Avison remarked: "There is no alternative, really, to engaging in the creative process with the poets, old and new." Avison's often knotted and condensed style leaves her own reader, if he wishes to share the vision or "fancy" she commends ("The Apex Animal"), with "no alternative" but to accept her challenge and struggle with a poetry that is highly distinctive, yet seldom felt as mannered. Rapid shifts of syntax and perspective; the appearance of obscure diction and unusual combinations of words and images (e.g., "marbling / the surges"), neologisms, puns, and puzzling titles; the recourse either to successive independent clauses (to convey a sense of fragmentation) or to suspension (appositives, subordination, digression) in order to impede the reader from simply consuming the verse; and the compounding of epithets and the cataloguing of sense impressions; all these features compel intellectual and imaginative engagement and even, Avison would hope, foster revelation.

In Avison's view, fallen man is a prisoner of self and technology, passively persisting in an alien, urban wasteland. In *Winter Sun* one possible way to liberation, an unsealing of the "soul's gates," is through a Blakean cleansing of the "doors of perception." However, following the conversion recorded throughout *The Dumbfounding*, Jesus Christ emerges as man's only authentic liberator, the only "pivot for significance." Avison's conception of her poetic role correspondingly changes and so, instead of the explorer or wandering observer, we encounter the figure of the Christian devotional poet (most fully realized in *sunblue*). Christian imagery (implicit in such early poems as "Easter"), together with doctrinal assertions (e.g., "peace will brim up" in "Stone's Secret"), become explicit; nature is increasingly perceived emblematically and epiphanic experiences centre more specifically on Christ. Imaginative vision and the natural world continue to be stressed by Avison (faith is a matter of vision also), but the tone of laconic cynicism common to *Winter Sun* is gradually replaced by the more helpful stance grounded in Christian convictions. Although her metaphysical style also loosens and relaxes after her first volume, giving expanded range to colloquialism and description, Avison's elusiveness and difficulty remain. She knows that a reader's temptation is always to relax, to translate poetic image into rational abstraction (as "Strong Yellow" indirectly suggests). However, she will permit no easy salvation for her reader. She still makes no "concession / To limited imaginations."

Avison's works include *Winter Sun* (1960); *The Dumbfounding* (1966); and *sunblue* (1978).

Works on Avison include Ernest Redekop, *Margaret Avison* (1970), and "sun / Son light / Light: Avison's Elemental *Sunblue*," *Canadian Poetry: Studies, Documents, Reviews*, No. 7 (1980), pp. 21-37; Daniel W. Doerksen, "Search and Discovery: Margaret Avison's Poetry," *Canadian Literature*, No. 60 (1974), pp. 7-20; J. M. Zezulka, "Refusing the Sweet Surrender: Margaret Avison's 'Dispersed Titles,'" *Canadian Poetry: Studies, Documents, Reviews*, No. 1 (1977), pp. 44-53; and J. M. Kertzer, "Margaret Avison: Power, Knowledge and the Language of Poetry," *Canadian Poetry: Studies, Documents, Reviews*, No. 4 (1979), pp. 29-44.

– DAVID KENT

Jack David and Robert Lecker

Jack David teaches English at Centennial College in Toronto. He has written essays on bpNichol, Earle Birney, John Barth, and visual poetry. Robert Lecker teaches English at McGill University in Montreal. His book, *On the Line: Readings in the Short Fiction of Clark Blaise, John Metcalf, and Hugh Hood,* was published in 1982.

Together, David and Lecker edit the critical journal *Essays on Canadian Writing* as well as *The Annotated Bibliography of Canada's Major Authors* and (with Ellen Quigley) *Canadian Writers and Their Works.*

Lionel LeMoine FitzGerald

Born in Winnipeg, Manitoba in 1890, Lionel LeMoine FitzGerald's early work was much influenced by the French Impressionists. During the twenties he painted views of prairie landscapes in water color and oil, but towards the end of the decade he began to develop in the direction of reducing detail and tightening up composition. In 1933 he became a founding member of the Canadian Group of Painters. Yet he was never part of the Toronto artistic community and his relationships with artists in central Canada were not important. FitzGerald's lack of time to paint, coupled with his painstaking technique; resulted in a small production of works. In 1956 he died of a heart attack.

New Press Canadian Classics

Distinguished by the use of Canadian fine art on its covers, New Press Canadian Classics is an innovative, much-needed series of high-quality, reasonably priced editions of the very best Canadian fiction, nonfiction and poetry.

New Press Canadian Classics

Hubert Aquin *The Antiphonary*
Alan Brown (trans.)

Margaret Atwood *Surfacing*

Sandra Birdsell *Night Travellers*

Marie-Claire Blais *Nights in the Underground*
Ray Ellenwood (trans.)

Clark Blaise *A North American Education, Tribal Justice*

George Bowering *Burning Water*

Matt Cohen *The Expatriate*

Jack David & Robert Lecker (eds.) *Canadian Poetry, Volumes One and Two*

George Elliott *The Kissing Man*

Mavis Gallant *My Heart Is Broken*

Anne Hébert *Héloïse* Shelia Fischman (trans.), *In the Shadow of the Wind* Shelia Fischman (trans.), *Kamouraska* Norman Shapiro (trans.)

David Helwig *The Glass Knight, Jennifer, It Is Always Summer*

Hugh Hood *White Figure, White Ground, You Cant Get There From Here, The Swing in the Garden, A New Athens*

Robert Kroetsch *Alibi, Badlands, The Studhorse Man, What the Crow Said*

Félix Leclerc *The Madman, the Kite & the Island*
Philip Stratford (trans.)

Keith Maillard *Alex Driving South, Cutting Through, The Knife in My Hands, Two Strand River*

Antonine Maillet *Pélagie* Philip Stratford (trans.)

John Metcalf & Leon Rooke *The New Press Anthology: Best Canadian Short Fiction #1*

Brian Moore *An Answer From Limbo*

Michael Ondaatje *Coming Through Slaughter, Running in the Family*

H. R. Percy *Painted Ladies*

Leon Rooke *Fat Woman, Shakespeare's Dog*

George Ryga *The Ecstasy of Rita Joe and other plays*